Chop Suey

Chop Suey

A Cultural History of Chinese
Food in the United States

Andrew Coe

OXFORD
UNIVERSITY PRESS

2009

OXFORD
UNIVERSITY PRESS

Oxford University Press, Inc., publishes works that further
Oxford University's objective of excellence
in research, scholarship, and education.

Oxford   New York
Auckland   Cape Town   Dar es Salaam   Hong Kong   Karachi
Kuala Lumpur   Madrid   Melbourne   Mexico City   Nairobi
New Delhi   Shanghai   Taipei   Toronto

With offices in
Argentina   Austria   Brazil   Chile   Czech Republic   France   Greece
Guatemala   Hungary   Italy   Japan   Poland   Portugal   Singapore
South Korea   Switzerland   Thailand   Turkey   Ukraine   Vietnam

Published by Oxford University Press, Inc.
198 Madison Avenue, New York, NY 10016

www.oup.com

Oxford is a registered trademark of Oxford University Press

The Library of Congress Cataloging-in-Publication Data
Coe, Andrew.
Chop suey : a cultural history of Chinese food in the United States
/ Andrew Coe.
p.   cm.
Includes bibliographical references and index.
ISBN 978-0-19-533107-3
1. Cookery, Chinese.   2. Food habits—United States—History.   1. Title.
TX724.5.C5C64   2009
641.5951–dc22   2008054664

9 8 7 6 5 4 3 2 1

Printed in the United States of America
on acid-free paper

TO JANE ·

C O N T E N T S ·

ACKNOWLEDGMENTS · · · · · · · · · · · · · · · · ·

This journey into the less-charted realms of Chinese and United States history could not have been accomplished without the assistance of many individuals and institutions. During the seemingly endless research phase of this project, I depended on the collections, staff, and resources of the New York Public Library: the Humanities and Social Sciences Library, particularly its Asian and Middle Eastern Division, and the Chinese Heritage Collection at the Chatham Square Branch Library. I also consulted the Nixon Presidential Library, the National Archives at College Park, Maryland, and the magnificent Dr. Jacqueline M. Newman Chinese Cookbook Collection housed in the Special Collections and University Archives of the Frank Melville Jr. Memorial Library of the State University of New York, Stonybrook. I am indebted to a Linda D. Russo Grant from the Culinary Trust for allowing me to visit the Bancroft Library at the University of California, Berkeley, and the Chinese Historical Society of America. The exhibition "Have You Eaten Yet? The Chinese Restaurant in America" at the Museum of Chinese in the Americas was one of the inspirations for this book. During the writing phase of this project, I relied on the staff and workspaces of the New York Mercantile Library's Writers' Studio and the New York Society Library. For assistance during all phases of this project, I am grateful to Richard Snow, Magnus Bartlett, Andrew Smith, Anne

Mendelson, Harley Spiller, Jakob Klein, Anthony Chang, Charles Perry, H. Mark Lai, Madeline Y. Hsu, Harold Rolnick, Stella Dong, Paul Mooney, Eileen Mooney, Kenny of the Bronx's Golden Gate restaurant, Jacqueline Newman and *Flavor & Fortune*, Aaron and Marjorie Ziegelman, and, for technical support, my father, Michael D. Coe. Dwight Chapin, Charles Freeman, and Winston Lord generously granted me interviews on which I drew for the section on Nixon's China trip. Joanna Waley-Cohen and John Eng-Wong were indefatigable readers who gave me greatly needed perspective. At Oxford University Press, my editors Benjamin Keene and Grace Labatt were painstaking and patient. And thanks to my sons Buster and Smacky for loving Chinese food and usually letting me work.

LIST OF ILLUSTRATIONS ···········

Chop Suey

Stags' Pizzles and Birds' Nests

On a frigid morning in February 1784, the *Empress of China* set sail from New York harbor. It was embarking on the most ambitious expedition yet attempted by a United States vessel. At the helm stood Captain John Green, a pugnacious six-foot-four-inch veteran of the Continental navy, with many passages to Europe and the Caribbean under his belt. For this trip, he couldn't count on that experience. His only guide would be a British pilot's manual that listed what little was known about the reefs and shoals, ports and trade winds his ship would encounter on the journey. If she survived, Captain Green estimated the voyage would take over a year, perhaps as much as two. The *Empress of China* was setting out on the first American trip to China, the era's equivalent of the 1969 journey to the Moon.

As the ship emerged onto the open Atlantic, its timbers creaked and groaned under the weight of its cargo. Barrels in the hold carried almost $20,000 in Spanish silver and thirty tons of dried ginseng root from the mountains of

Pennsylvania and Virginia. The *Empress*'s owners, some of the young nation's most powerful businessmen, hoped to trade the silver and the ginseng for the tea, silks, and porcelain of China. To sustain the ship's forty-two-man crew, Captain Green had filled every remaining space both below and above deck with food and drink, enough provisions to last 14 months at sea. This included enough fresh water to last five months and 48 barrels' worth of alcoholic beverages, mainly white Tenerife wine, strong Madeira wine, brandy, and "old Jamaica spirits" (rum). The wine and brandy were reserved for the officers; the thirsty crew had to make do with the throat-scorching rum.

The Americans on board the *Empress of China* carried their culinary traditions with them. On their journey to the other side of the globe, they ate the food of the pan–North Atlantic tradition, from the United States to the British Isles, adapted for the ocean voyage. Their staples were salt beef, salt pork, potatoes, and bread. The food eaten by the officers and the food eaten by the crew were of distinctly different quality. Coops filled with chickens and pens of sheep, pigs, and goats were lashed onto the decks. While this supply of livestock lasted, they provided fresh meat for the officers' cabin. The bread for the officers was soft and baked fresh by the ship's cook; the crew had to gnaw on rock-hard, worm-infested ship's biscuit. Dinners at the officers' table could include butter, pea soup flavored with bacon, roast meat, meat pies, boiled potatoes and cabbage, cheese, apples, condiments, and cake or pudding for dessert. As they embarked in the dead of winter, fresh vegetables were almost totally absent. For the sailors, meals were a monotonous round of salt meat, potatoes and biscuit, interspersed with peas or beans. All of this was washed down with weak beer that was brewed on board. Three times a week, the crew enjoyed their rations of rum, and on Saturdays they were given the treat of a raisin and molasses-sweetened pudding. Both officers and crew were served a nautical specialty called lobscouse, a stew of salt beef, sea biscuit, and potatoes—though again, the sailors had to chew on the butt ends of the meat while the officers had the best cuts stewed with cabbage and carrots as well as potatoes. Everybody on board seasoned their food with vinegar to keep scurvy at bay.

A month into the voyage, the *Empress* landed at the Cape Verde Islands off the coast of Africa. Leaks in the side were caulked, and the crew loaded more water and fresh food for the officers: chickens and goats, two pigs, and some oranges. The next leg of the journey lasted three months and 18 days, during which the men hardly sighted land or other ships. It was "one dreary waste of Sky & water," the purser wrote. Toward the end, the men were so starved for fresh meat that they captured and threw in the pot some booby birds that appeared and flew around the ship. Samuel Shaw, an officer, noted that they "were lean, very fishy, and but indifferent food." The crew also attempted to snare an albatross, but it broke the line and escaped.

Shaw was the *Empress*'s periwigged supercargo: its business agent, and the second most important man on the ship. Aged twenty-nine, he was a native of Boston and from an early age had been "destined for commercial pursuits." In 1775, he had enlisted in the American army and risen to the post of aide-de-camp to one of George Washington's most important generals. At the war's end in 1783, Shaw had been recognized as a young man to watch. According to his biographer, "the judgement, fidelity, and capacity for business, which he had displayed in the American army, attracted attention and general interest; and an association of capitalists, who had united for the purpose of opening a commercial intercourse between the United States and China, offered to him the station of factor and commercial

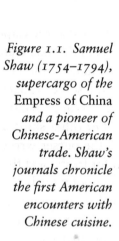

Figure 1.1. Samuel Shaw (1754–1794), supercargo of the Empress of China *and a pioneer of Chinese-American trade. Shaw's journals chronicle the first American encounters with Chinese cuisine.*

agent for the voyage."[1] Ambitious, and with barely a penny to his name, he had accepted immediately.

In mid-July, the men finally sighted Java Head, the tree-covered promontory on the Sunda Strait, the channel between the islands of Java and Sumatra. Their ship dropped anchor in Java's Mew Bay, where it was met by Muslim natives in two canoes proffering chickens, fish, turtles, vegetables, fruits, coconuts, and even live monkeys for sale as sailor's pets. Already at anchor in the bay were two French ships, including the *Triton*, which was also heading to China. The bonds of friendship between French and Americans were then particularly strong, thanks to the French backing of the Americans' side in their war for independence. Shaw and the other American officers were invited to dinner aboard the *Triton*—"as elegantly served as if we had been at an entertainment on shore."² The French captain offered to guide the *Empress* on the last leg of the journey, a proposal the Americans gratefully accepted because of the many islands and uncharted shoals between Java and China. Just before they set sail, the French and Americans spent a day planting Indian corn, oats, peas, beans, and potatoes on a nearby island. At the end of their work, they toasted the success of their garden, which they hoped to harvest on the return voyage, with bottles of Madeira wine and French champagne.

On August 23, 1784, after six months at sea, the Americans finally came within sight of the Chinese mainland. They had arrived at the coast of Guangdong Province, at the mouth of the Pearl River in southeast China. Here they encountered a Chinese fishing boat, crewed by the first Chinese they had ever seen, and for $10 hired its captain to guide them up the river. After maneuvering past some rocky coastal islands, the *Empress of China* and the *Triton* anchored off the city of Macau, on the river mouth's western banks. Administered by Portugal since the sixteenth century, this settlement had a distinctly southern European aspect, with large white-washed houses, narrow winding streets, and green trees and gardens. The *Empress* fired a salute of greeting, which was soon answered by a salute from the city's fort. Shaw had the honor of hoisting the red, white, and blue colors of what was then called the Continental flag, the first "ever seen or made use of in those seas." Early the next morning, a silk-robed Chinese customs inspector climbed aboard and took down the particulars of the boat and where it was from. He then impressed a piece of paper with the large seal that gave the *Empress* permission to travel further into China. After he left, the American ship was swarmed by little Chinese boats whose owners offered eggs, sugar, and breadfruit for sale. Two days later, the *Empress* raised anchor and set sail up the Pearl River for the city of Guangzhou, also known as Canton, sixty miles to the north.

The journey from Macau to the anchorage at Whampoa, twelve miles down the river from Guangzhou, was a favorite subject of the era's travel writers. This two-day passage gave European and American voyagers their first real encounter with the people and sights of one of the world's most fabled lands. As they sailed north, the river was increasingly crowded with all kinds of boats, including odd-shaped fishing boats, enormous flat-bottomed cargo boats, and the war junks of the Chinese navy. Some of the boats were evidently home to whole families and the flocks of ducks they tended. Others were piloted by fishermen who used tame cormorants to catch their fish, preventing the birds from swallowing their prey by fastening iron rings around their throats. The Western ships sailed past Chinese forts whose gun emplacements were painted with fearsome tigers and demons. As the land flattened out, the sailors saw bamboo and banana trees and then miles and miles of rice paddies as far as the eye could see. After two days, they arrived at Whampoa, the furthest upstream a deep-drafted ship could travel, where a line of tall masts was already waiting.

The *Empress of China* anchored at Whampoa on August 28, 1784, and fired a thirteen-gun salute to the other ships already riding there. French, Danish, Dutch, and English boats all returned the salute. Soon Shaw and Captain Green were visited by the officers of these ships, starting with the French, who assisted the Americans in getting moored and arranging their passage into Guangzhou. For anyone who hadn't yet heard of the American victory over the British, Captain Green carried copies of the articles of peace and the treaties between the United States and the various European powers. Two days later, the American officers took a Chinese "chop" boat into Guangzhou. As they approached the city, the sights and sounds and smells—the culture shock of being in China—would have overwhelmed them, as they passed pagodas nine stories high, temples, rice paddies, orange plantations, more forts, and hundreds or even thousands of boats painted with glaring colors. Every now and then they would have heard the crash of cymbals and gongs the Chinese boats used instead of cannons to greet each other.

From the river, the Americans could just barely glimpse the city itself. The view was blocked by a seemingly interminable line of one-story buildings, mostly warehouses that crammed the waterfront. Here and there between these buildings, the Americans would have glimpsed the crenellated city wall and behind it an occasional rooftop, a distant pagoda, and the roofs of some of the larger temples of the city, all topped with tile roofs. During their four months in Guangzhou, Green and Shaw were never allowed to enter the city proper. Instead, they landed on a wharf attached to a twelve-acre compound on the riverfront at the southwest corner of the city wall. Here the Chinese had built thirteen two- and three-story warehouses with white facades and columned verandas fronting the river. These buildings were called "factories" because they both housed and provided work spaces for the foreign "factors," the business agents of the European trading companies. According to imperial edict, this compound was the only place in China where Western nationals could come and go more or less freely.

After he returned to the United States, Shaw presented a report about his venture to John Jay, the U.S. secretary of foreign affairs (precursor to the secretary of state). Unlike many European travelers, Shaw did not feel that he could discuss Chinese life and culture:

> In a country where the jealousy of the government confines all intercourse between its subjects and the foreigners who visit it to very narrow limits, in the suburbs of a single city, the opportunities of gaining information respecting its constitution, or the manners and customs generally of its inhabitants, can neither be frequent nor extensive. Therefore, the few observations to be made at Canton cannot furnish us with sufficient data from which to form an accurate judgment upon either of these points.[3]

This statement was something of an evasion, particularly considering Shaw's status as leader of the first American expedition to China. Numerous writers with even less direct experience of China than Shaw penned extensive works both before and after his visit. It's more likely that he was actually not that interested in China itself. He was the first representative of the group that dominated American contacts with China for the next half century—the canny but narrow-minded New England traders. The vast, complicated, exotic, and ancient country of China lay just outside the door, but all they focused on was making a profit. Indeed, Shaw's description of his time in Guangzhou begins: "to begin with commerce,—which here appears to be as little embarrassed, and is, perhaps, as simple, as any in the known world."[4]

The Guangzhou factories were owned by a small group of wealthy Chinese merchants who had received imperial permission to trade with foreign trading firms. The most powerful of these, the British East India Company, also known as the "Honorable Company," occupied a sprawling factory in the heart of the compound, right on the central square; the Union Jack flew out front. British traders and Chinese authorities had a complicated relationship. Each side accused the other of arrogance. Backed by the mighty British navy from its base in Calcutta, the East India Company had established trading ventures throughout South and Southeast Asia. In China, however, the emperor limited their business to Guangzhou, cutting them off from the rest of the vast China market, and refused to meet with their representatives or even the English king's own emissaries. In Guangzhou, British traders occasionally vented their frustrations by beating any coolies who had the misfortune to bump into them on one of the compound's crowded streets. On the Chinese side, the main advantage of trading with the East India Company was the substantial revenues it brought to the emperor's personal coffers. The main disadvantage was, as the Chinese saw it, that the foreigners were crude and quarrelsome, pushy and utterly unwilling to adapt to Chinese customs. The emperor believed that letting them come any further into his empire would only upset the harmony of Chinese society. For now, the trade continued because it was profitable, although both sides could see the possibility of conflict further down the road.

Shaw's sympathies lay naturally on the European side of this relationship. However, as a newcomer to the region, and from such a young country, he wasn't exactly in a position to take a stand. His first concern was the business at hand: selling his ginseng. The Americans first stayed in the factory rented by the French but soon secured their own place of business. The first floor of their factory was divided between a warehouse, a counting room, and a treasury; the American living quarters were on the second floor. The landlords provided a phalanx of Chinese servants, from cooks to porters, to carry the Americans' goods and cater to all of their needs. In order to communicate with both these servants and the merchants, the Americans had to learn the crude local trade jargon known as pidgin Chinese.

The word "pidgin" probably derives from the word "business," and appropriately so, because it was primarily used for commercial transactions. Pidgin was a unique combination of Portuguese, English, and Cantonese, with a few words from India thrown in. The jargon had evolved from necessity; the disparate trading communities from the Bay of Bengal to the western Pacific needed a way to communicate with one another. "Go catchy chow-chow" meant "fix something to eat" in pidgin, which sounded very much like a parent talking to a recalcitrant and somewhat deaf child. Neither the Chinese nor the Europeans had bothered to learn their trading partners' native tongues, so pidgin was used in all interactions between them. (In a sense, both sides were talking down when they used pidgin. However, in contemporary English and American accounts of life in Guangzhou, we only hear the Chinese side of the conversation. To readers, this has the affect of infantilizing the speakers; it's hard to respect someone who talks in such an ungainly manner.)

For Shaw, his first problem was explaining to the Chinese exactly who the Americans were:

> Our being the first American ship that had ever visited China, it was some time before the Chinese could fully comprehend the distinction between the Englishmen and us. They styled us the *New People*, and when by the map, we conveyed to them an idea of the extent of the country, with its present and increasing population, they were not a little pleased at the prospect of so considerable a market for the productions of their own empire.[5]

Shaw was also insecure about how the European contingents in Guangzhou would treat the Americans. After all, the United States was barely eight years old, a toddler on the world stage, and had recently waged a bloody war with

Britain, the world's rising imperial power. He was gratified to find that "the attention paid us at all times by the
Europeans, both in a national and personal respect, [was]
highly flattering."[6] This was expected from their French
allies, but even the British went out of their way to shower
the Americans with attentions. During their first few
weeks in Guangzhou, each of the foreign factories invited
the American party to elaborate meals in their personal
quarters.

Shaw doesn't say it, but attending those dinners must
have caused him great anxiety. During the eighteenth and
nineteenth centuries, a man's character was very much tied
up with his manners. The more refined his social graces, the
more civilized he was thought to be. One's behavior in public was a matter of performance, constantly judged by those
present, and the most crucial of such performances was the
meal. As Dr. Johnson said, the hour of dinner was the most
important hour in civilized life. In the United States, Shaw
had dined at the tables of American generals, but he had
never before ventured abroad and had no experience of
foreign customs. All that was said about dinner-table etiquette in *Lord Chesterfield's Advice to his Son, on Men and
Manners,* the only etiquette book then published in post-
revolutionary America, was that every gentleman should
"study to acquire that fashionable kind of *small talk* or *chit
chat,* which prevails in all polite assemblies" and also learn
the art of carving: "a man who tells you gravely that he cannot carve, may as well tell you that he can't blow his *nose*;
it is both as easy and as necessary."[7]

In Guangzhou, Shaw would have been acutely aware
that his social status was, at best, unsettled. His hosts were
worldly Europeans, direct heirs to centuries of courtly tradition. Shaw and the American party were provincials, almost
frontiersmen, living in a land at the edge of the wilderness

and very, very far from the heart of European civilization. It was crucial for them to behave with grace and good manners, because a misstep would not only bring shame on them personally, potentially harming their China endeavor, but also dishonor their country.

The invitation that gave Shaw the most trepidation was probably his dinner in the sumptuous quarters of the East India Company. In accordance with their commercial dominance and their role as the de facto representatives of the world's rising imperial power, the British traders lived in regal luxury. On the second floor of their factory, they enjoyed a library, a billiards room, a chapel, and an enormous dining room called the Great Hall. When Shaw stepped into this room, it would have been decorated with crystal chandeliers, with portraits of the king and various directors of the Company on the walls. Doors opened onto a terrace overlooking the Pearl River. The long dinner table, set for thirty, glittered with silver candlesticks and cutlery and the finest porcelain. The guests were seated strictly according to rank, with the chief British trader acting as host and Shaw sitting next to him as the guest of honor. Although the meal was prepared by Chinese cooks, the food was strictly elite European cuisine. In the eighteenth century, this meant a strong French influence, the remnants of medieval spicing (including clove and nutmeg), and probably an Anglo-Indian curry or two. There would have been two courses of at least ten dishes each, from a cream-based soup to roast teal and blancmange, followed by a dessert of fresh and dried fruits and walnuts. Copious amounts of imported alcohol would have been poured throughout, including red, white, and Madeira wines. Frequent toasts, during which all the diners would stand, would have been made to the king, the U.S. president, the emperor of China, the success of the diners' business ventures, and so on. The richest men of Boston, New York, and Philadelphia could not have provided a more elaborate feast.

Apparently, the Americans' behavior at the dinner was a success, and they passed the social test. After the meal, the chief British trader pulled Shaw and Green aside for a little private talk. Over another bottle, he apologized for the Americans' reception in Guangzhou. He had meant for the British, not the French, to give the first reception for the newcomers: "For trust me, gentlemen, that *we* would not designedly have put you in such company."[8]

During his four months in Guangzhou, Shaw saw as much of the city as Europeans who had been trading there for a dozen years. In other words, he was mostly confined to the twelve-acre compound that held the factories and the three narrow thoroughfares that ran beside them—Old and New China streets and Hog Lane. These were lined with stores selling souvenirs, including silks and hand-painted porcelain, and grog shops dispensing rotgut liquor to the sailors. Beyond the compound, the streets into the city were blocked by gates that were manned twenty-four hours a day. The only way a foreigner could travel further was with official permission and in the company of a Chinese interpreter. Shaw made only a handful of trips outside the western compound. One of these was across the river to the island of Honam (also called Henan), where most of the Chinese merchants who traded with the foreigners kept sprawling homes and gardens. In the company of some French merchants, Shaw and Green were invited to dine at the house of Chouqua—the trade name of Chen Zuguan, a member of a prominent merchant family. Shaw was particularly impressed with Chouqua's gardens: "Much art and labor are used to give them a rural appearance, and in some instances nature is not badly imitated. Forests, artificial rocks, mountains, and cascades, are judiciously executed, and have a pleasing effect in diversifying the scene."[9] He tells us much less about what they ate. What struck him was that "on these occasions, the guests generally contribute largely to the bill of fare.... At Chouqua's...the French supplied the table furniture, wine, and a large portion of the victuals."[10] This was common practice during the eighteenth and nineteenth centuries, because most western merchants in Guangzhou were not culinary adventurers. The French brought the "table furniture" because they couldn't use Chinese spoons and chopsticks, the wine because they preferred that to hot Chinese rice wine, and the "victuals" because they couldn't stomach the dishes prepared by Chouqua's chef.

One of the exceptions to this rule was an English rake, William Hickey, who had been shipped east in 1769 to find his fortune—and to keep his hell-raising escapades from further blotting the family name. Unfortunately, he was more interested in fast living and sleeping with Chinese prostitutes than knuckling down to work. During his stay in Guangzhou, he and some other Englishmen were invited to a series of banquets at a Honam mansion. On the first night, the meal was served "*à la mode Anglaise*, the Chinamen on that occasion using, and awkwardly enough, knives and forks, and in every respect conforming to European fashion." On the second night, "everything was Chinese, all the European guests eating, or endeavouring to eat, with chop sticks, no knives or forks being at the table. The entertainment was splendid, the victuals supremely good, the Chinese loving high dishes and keeping the best of cooks."[11] By "high," Hickey probably meant that the dishes were rich and luxurious. (Another meaning of "high" is slightly rotten, as in the aged game dishes preferred at many English aristocratic tables. The Chinese, however, liked their meat absolutely fresh-killed.)

Figure 1.2. A western view of Chinese exotica: A toast at an aristocratic dinner party, with musicians and entertainers in the background.

After four months in China, Shaw finally sold his ginseng at a good price. It turned out that the quality of his product was better than anything his European competitors had brought. The Chinese merchant with whom Shaw sealed this transaction complimented him for not behaving like a rude, difficult Englishman: "But you speak English word, and when you first come, I no can tell difference; but now I understand very well." Nevertheless, he doubted that the American's polite behavior would last very long: "All men come first time China, very good gentlemen, all same you. I think two three time more you come Canton, you make all same Englishman too."[12]

By the end of December 1784, the *Empress of China*'s hold was packed with hundreds of chests of bohea and hyson tea, yellow nankeen cloth, silk, and porcelain. The customs authority issued its "Grand Chop," which gave the *Empress* permission to leave China, and on December 28, she raised anchor and set sail for the United States. Other American ships were already heading east across the Atlantic, around the Cape of Good Hope and then on to China. Shaw and the crew of the *Empress* had inaugurated the era of the China trade. For the next sixty years, traders from ports like Boston, New York, Philadelphia, and Salem, Massachusetts, would set sail for the other side of the world, lured by the chance to become rich by trading for the tea and finished products of one of world's largest and oldest nations. These traders' adventures led to one of the most remarkable—and unlikely—culinary exchanges of the last few centuries.

In 1784, the United States and China were, respectively, the youngest and oldest countries on Earth. The Americans were then still working out the most basic principles of government (the Constitutional Convention would take place three years later) and just beginning the process of deciding what made their culture distinct from England and the rest of the Old World. The Chinese, in contrast, had become one country over two millennia earlier and could trace their lineage as a culture back to the dawn of history. Unlike the new nations of Europe who could not ignore the achievements of Mesopotamia, Egypt, Greece, and Rome, China had almost always been the dominant culture in its region, East Asia. As a consequence, many Chinese thought of their country as the "Middle Kingdom," the center of human civilization. It was thanks to some of their legendary rulers that humankind had first learned to use fire, to hunt and to fish, to sow crops and build houses, to treat illness with medicine, to write, and to mark time with calendars. The Chinese had also developed a highly complex system of government, at whose apex stood the emperor, ruling under what they called the Mandate of Heaven: as long as the emperor remained virtuous, Shangdi, the supreme ruler of Heaven, would give him command over all humanity. In 1784, China was governed by the great Qianlong Emperor of the Manchu-dominated Qing Dynasty. He wielded power from his throne in the Hall of Supreme Harmony in Beijing's Forbidden City, which was off-limits to all except his closest retainers.

Expanding outward from this point, the Chinese traditionally divided the world into a series of five concentric circles, based on an ancient plan ascribed to the legendary Yü Emperor. First came the royal domains, meaning all the lands within the borders of China directly ruled by the emperor. All Chinese were, by definition, civilized. The core of these domains was what Westerners called China Proper: the eighteen provinces extending from what is now Hebei in the northeast to Hainan Island (then part of Guangzhou Province) in the south and to Sichuan in the west. Just beyond China's borders lay the lands of the tributary royal princes: the kingdoms of Korea, Laos, Vietnam, Tibet, Mongolia, and others. Made humble by the presence of the Chinese behemoth next door, their rulers had decided that it was usually far better to accept Chinese supremacy in East Asia than fight it. They learned Mandarin Chinese, converted to the Chinese calendar system, and at regular intervals donned Chinese costume and traveled to the court at Beijing to give costly tribute to the emperor. In return, he would invite them to an imperial Manchu banquet, sixth grade. Beyond these tributary kingdoms lay the zone of pacification, where the people were in the process of adopting Chinese civilization. For some, this process was remarkably rewarding. The ancestors of the Qing Dynasty's Manchu emperors were Jurchen tribesmen, seminomadic farmers and hunter-gatherers in northeastern China. Over the centuries, the Jurchen chiefs carefully studied the Chinese imperial system. When the Ming Dynasty fell apart in the early seventeenth century, the Jurchen roared down from the north and occupied Beijing. They renamed themselves the Manchu and founded the Qing Dynasty, on a basis of strict obedience to the Chinese imperial system, in effect becoming more Chinese than the Chinese.

Beyond the tribal lands and tributary kingdoms, the rest of the world was encompassed by the outer two circles of the Yü Emperor's map, called the zone of "allied barbarians" and the zone of "cultureless savagery." The allied barbarians were the peoples who had regular contact with Chinese civilization but did not have the wisdom to adopt it. This title encompassed many of the tribes on the empire's northwest frontier whose regular raids across the border had led to the construction of the Great Wall. The rest of the world's peoples lived in the zone of "cultureless savagery," of which the ancient Chinese had no direct experience. Instead, their knowledge was based on tomes like the *Shanhaijing*, "Guideways through Mountains and Seas" (fourth century BCE–first century CE), a kind of guidebook to Heaven and Earth that blends geography, cosmography, mythology, and natural history. Much the way Greek, Roman, and medieval European works describe unseen lands, the *Shanhaijing* describes those who live in the far corners of the Earth as looking not like, well, people. Beyond China's borders lie the Land of Hairy People, the Land of Feathered People, the Land of People with Perforated Chests, the Land of Three-Headed People, the Land of Giants, the Land of Midgets, and so on. The book tells readers nothing about how these weird inhabitants actually live. For that, the Chinese would apply what they had learned from their interactions with tribes on the margins of the empire, as in this passage from the *Li Chi*, a book of ritual form that Confucian scholars drafted (fifth century–221 BCE):

The tribes on the east were called I. They had their hair unbound, and tattooed their bodies. Some of them ate their food without its being cooked. Those on the south were called Man. They tattooed their foreheads, and had their feet turned in towards each other. Some of them [also] ate their food without its being cooked. Those on the west were called Zung. They had their hair unbound and wore skins. Some of them did not eat grain-food. Those on the north were called Tî. They wore skins of animals and birds, and dwelt in caves. Some of them also did not eat grain-food.[13]

Qing Dynasty accounts also often speak of alien peoples— including Europeans and Americans—and their customs in similarly belittling terms, describing their primitive taste in food, almost animal-like physical appearance, and so on.

Over the millennia, this streak of antiforeign bias in Chinese culture was balanced by intense curiosity about the outside world. From the Han Dynasty (206 BCE–222 CE) on, the Chinese did have regular contact with the rest of Asia. Chinese ambassador Zhang Qian roamed across Central Asia and even as far south as India, documenting the regional cultures and economies for his Han emperor. Regular trade between China, India, and the West began with the opening of the Silk Road by 100 BCE (and likely earlier). Traffic in goods and ideas also traveled by sea, on oceangoing junks sailing to Japan, to many ports in Southeast Asia, and across the Indian Ocean to East Africa. Perhaps the most lasting result of those contacts was the dissemination between the second and seventh centuries CE of Buddhism, which originated in India. Over the centuries, the tribute network the Middle Kingdom established with its various vassal states became the official channel by which the finest products of foreign lands, from gems to foodstuffs, directly reached the emperor for his pleasure and enjoyment. Between 1405 and 1433, the Yongle Emperor of the Ming Dynasty sent Admiral Zhen He's fleet of three hundred ships on expeditions extending from Southeast Asia to Africa to assert Chinese power and expand the tribute system. In 1601, another Ming emperor hired the Italian Jesuit priest Matteo Ricci to serve as his court mathematician and cartographer. Ricci introduced western geometry and trigonometry and drafted accurate maps of the world showing latitude and longitude and the main continents. He could speak, read, and write Chinese, saw no contradiction between Catholic and Confucian beliefs, and converted many scholars and officials to Christianity. Even today, the Chinese admire Ricci for his deep knowledge of and respect for their culture.

Figure 1.3. Large flags proclaim the western presence in the "factory" compound on the outskirts of Guangzhou. Until 1842, this was the only part of China where Europeans and Americans were allowed to live and trade.

By the time Ricci died, in 1610, Europeans were a constant presence at the edges of the Chinese empire. This incursion had begun in 1517 with the arrival of Portuguese traders, who soon acquired the rights to anchor at and then settle in Macau. They were followed by the Dutch and then, in the seventeenth century, the Spanish, French, English, and other European powers. The imperial government saw their presence as decidedly a mixed blessing. The European trade became highly profitable to the emperors, who took most of the profits directly into their coffers, restricting contacts with the European traders to the port of Guangzhou in order to protect their imperial monopoly, and for fear of foreign contagion. Imperial China was a highly organized yet delicately balanced machine—who knew what kind of cultural, economic, or political instability these strangers would bring? Official knowledge about Europe and its various peoples was designedly inadequate, because it was considered dangerous to learn more. Aside from the storerooms of the Forbidden City, the only place where Chinese could have seen European maps was Guangzhou. In the mid–eighteenth century, imperial courtiers drafted a massive, ten-volume encyclopedia, the *Illustrations of the Tribute-Bearing People of the Qing* (1761), that gave the official view of the outside world—one heavily influenced by the view of ancient texts like the *Shanhaijing*. All foreign peoples are defined by their level of allegiance, imaginary or not, toward civilization, that is, the Middle Kingdom. The authors do not bother to correctly locate England, France, Italy, Holland, Russia, or even the Atlantic Ocean. The inhabitants of the European countries are described as having "dazzling white" skin, "lofty" noses, and red hair. They favor tight clothes; their disposition is warlike; they esteem women more than men; and all they care about is trade. (In traditional China, since at least the days of Confucius, merchants were relegated to the lowest rung of social status.) To imperial officials, the behavior of the Europeans resembled more that of dogs or sheep than that of civilized human beings. When the *Empress of China*—a European style of ship, with a crew who spoke the same language as the English—arrived in Guangzhou, local businessmen like Chouqua may have been curious about these people's native land and glad to have new trading partners. To imperial officials, however, they were just more red-haired, white-skinned foreigners from the far-off zone of "cultureless savagery."

At the end of the American War of Independence, Americans knew slightly more about China than the Chinese did about the United States. For about a half century, the American beverage of choice had been Chinese tea, which was shipped from Britain in crates marked with the stamp of the British East India Company. In 1773, dozens of citizens of Boston dressed as Mohawk Indians dumped crates of "Company" tea into Boston Harbor to protest unjust British duties on their favorite drink. Those Americans who could afford it drank their tea from delicate white cups of imported Chinese porcelain. Their image of China closely resembled the charming little scenes painted on the cups' sides: stylized little blue willow trees, a river, and a bridge with one or two white-faced figures on it. George Washington was supposedly surprised to hear that the skin of Chinese was not bone-china white.

During the eighteenth century, the British East India Company enjoyed a monopoly on all trade with Asia. Merchants in the American colonies were forbidden to travel to China or deal directly with Chinese merchants. What little the colonists could learn about China was gleaned almost entirely from books and other accounts written by European travelers. Probably the most famous was the encyclopedic

General History of China, by the French Jesuit priest Jean-Baptiste Du Halde. Both Benjamin Franklin and Thomas Jefferson owned copies, as did Franklin's Library Company of Philadelphia (in 1770) and the New York Society Library (in 1789). Du Halde never visited China, but he gathered his material directly from many Jesuit priests who had spent years there. His *General History* held up China's government, law, and philosophy as models for emulation—Voltaire became a Sinophile after reading it. Those Americans lucky enough to peruse the tome could learn of the Great Wall and the emperor's palace in Beijing, read the sayings of a sage named Confucius, and marvel at the rituals of a Chinese banquet where the most delicious dishes were "Stags Pizzles and Birds-Nests carefully prepared."[14]

Also widely disseminated was the anonymous work *The Chinese Traveller* (1772), supposedly based on the experiences of Jesuits and "other modern travellers." A collection of stories of exotic customs and wide-eyed adventures in foreign lands, it reads more like *Gulliver's Travels* than Du Halde's measured account. Some of the information provided appears to have been picked up down at the London docks, including tips on where to find pleasure girls and warnings about trade: "the Chinese excel the Europeans in nothing more than the art of cheating."[15] About Chinese food, the *Chinese Traveller* notes many oddities, including the use of chopsticks, the prevalence of rice, and the practice of chopping the food into little bits before bringing it to the table. What particularly interests the author is the wide variety of animals the Chinese ate: "they not only use the same kind of flesh, fish and fowl, that we do, but even horse flesh is esteemed proper food. Nor do they reckon dogs, cats, snakes, frogs, or indeed any kind of vermin, unwholesome diet."[16] This description of the meats sold in Guangzhou delves deeper into that custom:

I was very much surprised at first, to see dogs, cats, rats, frogs, &c. in their market-places for sale. But I soon found that they made no scruple of eating any sort of meat, and have as good an appetite for that which died in a ditch, as that which was killed by a butcher. The dogs and cats were brought commonly alive in baskets, were mostly young and fat, and kept very clean. The rats, some of which are of a monstrous size, were very fat, and generally hung up with the skin upon them, upon nails at the posts of the market-place.[17]

In nearly every western description of Chinese food from the late eighteenth and early nineteenth centuries, this information is repeated: the Chinese dine on dogs, cats, and rats. Some of it comes from doubtful texts, like the *Chinese Traveller*, but in other texts the information has enough detail to give it the ring of truth. (And anyone who has visited modern Guangzhou's markets can see that they still sell an incredible variety of live animals for food, including dogs and cats.) If readers of the time remembered anything about Chinese culinary habits, it was that they extended their eating habits to include beloved pets and filthy vermin.

Books like Du Halde's *General History* and the *Chinese Traveller* were also popular because they contained large amounts of information about the country's economic life: the principal products of China, the goods it most commonly imported, and the workings of its commerce. Americans did not read these sections idly, because the major source of their revenue was foreign trade. Merchants needed all the information they could find on the world outside their borders. After the War of Independence, Britain was still the dominant sea power, and its blockades kept American ships from much of Europe and the Caribbean. However, British power did not yet control the Pacific or

Figure 1.4. An engraving from The Chinese Traveller *depicts men catching water fowl. According to the* Traveller, *ducks were trained to weed the rice fields and eat such pests as insects and frogs.*

the sea lanes leading to the world's most populous nation. In the 1780s, the ports up and down the East Coast of the United States hummed with plans for voyages to China. The main promoter of these ventures was John Ledyard, an adventurer who had sailed with Captain Cook on his last voyage around the world. Ledyard proposed an enterprise to collect sea otter skins in the Pacific Northwest and sell them in Guangzhou for huge profits. When his backers realized that the scheme was too costly, they turned to what they knew from Du Halde's *General History.* The Chinese were said to pay enormous prices for ginseng, which they used in their traditional medicine. Within months, the hold of the *Empress of China* was packed with ginseng root and heading east to China.

From 1784 to 1844, the yearly ritual of the China trade was nearly always the same. The American ships anchored at Whampoa at any time from August to October and unloaded their goods. The merchants took up residence in the American factory, with its "flowery flag" flying out front, and began the process of selling their wares to their Chinese counterparts. In the evenings, they retired to their quarters to eat sumptuous Western meals, washing the food down with copious amounts of imported alcohol, or traded social visits with the other foreign merchants. For recreation, they could promenade along the factory compound's waterfront, compete in rowing races on the river, or stroll in the nearby Chinese gardens in the company of an interpreter. We know that life in the factories was claustrophobic but little else about what the Americans thought about China, because they were businessmen first and foremost. They left few records of their experiences there, particularly during the first decades of the trade. After their wares were sold, they purchased Chinese goods to sell back in the United States: tea, silk, porcelain, nankeen cloth, and sundry knickknacks with which they decorated their stateside homes. The Western ships usually sailed out of Whampoa in January. American merchants could then either sail home or spend the months until the next trading season in nearby Macau. With its picturesque setting, warm sea breezes, and large European colony, Macau was always considered a more pleasant place to stay than Guangzhou.

From the beginning, American merchants faced a perennial quandary of what to bring to China for trade. The Guangzhou merchants accepted Spanish silver dollars, then the principal trade currency, but the Americans only had a limited supply of them. When the ginseng trade soon began to play out, traders remembered Ledyard's tales of huge sea otter colonies in the Pacific Northwest. They also discovered that the forests of the Sandwich (Hawaiian) Islands were filled with aromatic sandalwood trees whose wood the Chinese favored. For a few decades, American traders in Guangzhou made fortunes with ships filled with fur and sandalwood, until they killed nearly all the sea otters and chopped down all the sandalwood forests. The Americans next fixed on a commodity they first saw in Guangzhou's markets: piles of what looked like lumpy brown, gray, and black cigars, with a distinctive rank, fishy odor, sold from big straw market baskets. These were dried sea cucumbers, also known as trepang or *bêche-de-mer* ("worm of the sea"): soft-bodied invertebrates, related to sea stars and sea urchins, that live in shallow tropical seas. For centuries, the Chinese have considered sea cucumbers one of the great delicacies of their cuisine, because of both their culinary properties and the boost to strength and virility they supposedly imparts. Chefs soften the dried animals in water and then cook them in delicately flavored stews, where they absorb the flavors of the sauce and add their slightly fishy taste and spongy, glutinous texture.

All the American merchants knew was that the sea cucumbers would find "a ready sale in the Chinese market." On their journey across the Pacific, they stopped at islands like Tonga, Samoa, and the Fijis and hired troops of islanders through the local chief, whom they paid in trade goods like guns, gunpowder, and hatchets. (These weapons greatly increased the death tolls of the frequent battles between tribal factions on the islands.) The natives collected as many sea cucumbers as they could find in the nearby waters, while the Americans set up drying sheds on the beach. The animals were boiled in great iron kettles, gutted, and then smoked. Once thoroughly dried, they were packed in straw baskets and loaded on the American ships. The most valuable variety could fetch 115 Spanish silver dollars for a 125-pound box in the Guangzhou market. A French traveler who tasted freshly cleaned sea cucumber on the coast of Malaya remarked that it "had some resemblance to lobster."

Another odd product Americans noticed in the Guangzhou market was the edible bird's nest. It appeared to be nothing more than a fragile, yellowish shell, but the prices for it were nothing short of astronomical—136 pounds of the finest bird's nest would sell for 3,500 silver dollars! The richest sources of birds' nests were caves lying along the tropical coasts from India to Southeast Asia that were home to two species of swiftlet, a bird that resembles a swallow. It attaches its cup-like nest, which it makes almost entirely from its own saliva, high up on these caves' walls. Holding sputtering torches, the natives had to climb up towering, rickety ladders in the caves to find and harvest the nests. The most precious variety was almost white and free of any sticks or other detritus; the darker "black" nests had to be carefully cleaned before cooking. In the hands of Chinese chefs, these nests had almost no taste themselves; they were used to absorb the flavors of soups and stews and add a special glutinous texture. Du Halde wrote: "they mix them with other meats, which give them a good relish."[18] Like sea cucumbers, birds' nests were also considered useful for enhancing strength and potency. As soon as American merchants figured out the best sources of supply in Southeast Asia, they began to add birds' nests to their cargoes bound for China.

During this first era of the China trade, the few hundreds of Americans and Europeans working in Guangzhou constructed a kind of cocoon of western culture around themselves. While their every need from waking to going to bed was met by an army of Chinese servants, they continued to wear western dress, largely refused to learn the local languages (in fairness, imperial edict forbade the teaching of Mandarin or Cantonese to these barbarians, though a few still received tutoring on the sly), worshipped in Catholic or Protestant chapels, socialized almost exclusively with other westerners, and gathered at the table for three meals a day of western food and drink. This was an incredible act of communal will, because the Chinese city was never more than a stone's throw away and sometimes just outside their windows. They must have smelled the aromas from Chinese kitchens wafting over from Chinese houses. They could not have missed the "long line of victualing stands, furnished with fruits, cakes, sweetmeats, soups, and such like" in the narrow streets that formed the border between the factory compound and the greater city.[19]

Nevertheless, the first account we have of Americans eating Chinese food does not appear until 1819, thirty-five years after Shaw's visit. It was written by Bryant Parrott Tilden, a young trader from Salem who acted as supercargo on a number of Asia voyages. In Guangzhou, he was befriended by Paunkeiqua, a leading merchant who cultivated good relations with many American firms. Just before Tilden's ship was set to sail home, Paunkeiqua invited the American merchants to spend the day at his mansion on Honam island. Tilden's account of that visit, which was capped by a magnificent feast, is not unlike the descriptions Shaw or even William Hickey wrote a half century earlier. First, he tours Paunkeiqua's traditional Chinese garden and encounters some of the merchant's children yelling "Fankwae! Fankwae!" ("Foreign devil! Foreign devil!"). Then Paunkeiqua shows him his library, including "some curious looking *old Chinese maps of the world* as these 'celestials' suppose it to be, with their Empire occupying three quarters of it, surrounded by nameless islands & seas bounded only by the edges of the maps." Finally, his host tells him: "Now my flinde Tillen, you must go long my for catche chow chow tiffin." In other words, dinner was served in a spacious dining hall, where the guests were seated at small tables.

"Soon after," Tilden writes, "a train of servants came in bringing a most splendid service of fancy colored, painted and gilt large tureens & bowls, containing soups, among them the celebrated *bird nest soup*, as also a variety of stewed messes, and plenty of boiled rice, & same style of smaller bowls, but alas! no plates and knives and forks." (By "messes," Tilden probably meant prepared dishes, not unsavory jumbles.)

The Americans attempted to eat with chopsticks, with very poor results: "Monkies [sic] with knitting needles would not have looked more ludicrous than some of us did." Finally, their host put an end to their discomfort by ordering western-style plates, knives, forks, and spoons. Then the main portion of the meal began:

> Twenty separate courses were placed on the table during three hours in as many different services of elegant china ware, the messes consisting of soups, gelatinous food, a variety of stewed hashes, made up of all sorts of chopped meats, small birds cock's-combs, a favorite dish, some fish & all sorts of vegetables, rice, and pickles, of which the Chinese are very fond. Ginger and pepper are used plentifully in most of their cookery. Not a joint of meat or a whole fowl or bird were placed on the table. Between the changing of the courses, we freely conversed and partook of Madeira & other European wines—and costly teas.[20]

After fruits, pastries, and more wine, the dinner finally came to an end. Tilden and his friends left glowing with happiness (and alcohol) at the honor Paunkeiqua had shown them with this lavish meal. Nowhere, however, does

Tilden tell us whether the Americans actually enjoyed these "messes" and "hashes."

In 1830, American missionaries joined the traders in Guangzhou and Macau. The United States was then decades into a religious awakening that had spread from New England west to the frontier. A key tenet of this evangelical Christian movement was the solemn duty to spread the Protestant gospel to every corner of the nation and the globe. One of those who caught the fervor was a Massachusetts farmer's son named Elijah Coleman Bridgman. After devoting his life to God at a local revival meeting, he was eventually ordained as a "minister to Christ, and as a missionary to the heathen." When he learned that more heathens lived in China than any other country on Earth, Bridgman took a berth on the next boat to Asia. Soon after he landed in Guangzhou, he took a tour of a Chinese temple and was invited by the priest to share some food. With the help of a translator, he quizzed the priest about his beliefs over Chinese tea and "sweetmeats," probably candied fruits. At the end of this repast, Bridgman "thanked and rewarded him for his hospitality, and left him as we found him, a miserable idolater."[21]

Bridgman soon concluded that the Middle Kingdom was the most morally debased land on Earth: "Idolatry, superstition, fraud, falsehood, cruelty, and oppression everywhere predominate, and iniquity, like a mighty flood, is extending far and wide its desolation."[22] To make matters worse, the Chinese were deaf to his gospel-spreading efforts. Guangzhou authorities refused to allow missionaries to proselytize in the Chinese city, and the local Chinese in Macau showed little interest in his message of salvation. After twenty years of preaching, Bridgman and his fellow American missionaries could count literally no Chinese converts; the few who had embraced the Christian faith had all reverted to their heathen ways!

With his dour and implacable faith, Bridgman was adept at conveying his vision of China to anyone who would listen. In 1832, he became the Guangzhou tour guide of Edmund Roberts, an American diplomat on a round-the-world journey to improve trade ties. Roberts published a long account of his voyage that is filled with virulent xenophobia. Of the Chinese he writes:

> In their habits they are most depraved and vicious; gambling is universal and is carried to a most ruinous and criminal extent; they use the most pernicious drugs as well as the most intoxicating liquors to produce intoxication; they are also gross gluttons; every thing that runs, walks, creeps, flies, or swims, in fact, every thing that will supply the place of food, whether of the sea, or the land, and articles most disgusting to other people, are by them greedily devoured.[23]

His outrage about Chinese culinary habits may have been particularly spurred by the fact that his window in the American factory overlooked the afternoon dog and cat market in Old China Street.

Other missionaries who joined Bridgman in Guangzhou included Peter Parker and Samuel Wells Williams. Parker, another Massachusetts farmer's son, had been educated at Amherst and Yale at a time when these schools produced more lawyers and ministers than anything else. A classmate described him as short, fat, and sluggish, but "quick as a toad" when he wanted to be. After Parker decided that he, too, wanted to save the Chinese heathens, his advisors suggested that he study medicine as a backup. Stymied in his missionary efforts in Guangzhou, Parker opened a clinic to treat the Chinese for eye disorders. Samuel Wells Williams, the only one of this group who wasn't ordained as a minister, was the son of a devout printer in Utica, New York. Williams considered becoming a botanist before his father secured him the job of running the missionary printing press in Guangzhou. Shortly after landing, he wrote to his father:

> I have been here a week, and in that short time have seen enough idolatries to call forth all the energies that I have.... To take a circuit thro' one of these streets about eventide, and see the abominations practiced against the honor of Him who has commanded, "Thou shalt have no other gods before me," and not be affected with a deep sense of the depth to which this intellectual people has sunk, is impossible to a warm Christian man.[24]

Williams joined Bridgman in writing and printing a monthly journal, the *Chinese Repository*. During its lifespan, the *Repository* became an encyclopedic compilation of Western knowledge about China, including its culinary customs.

Four months after arriving in Guangzhou, Williams was invited to his first Chinese meal—"it should be more properly termed a gratification of curiosity than any pleasure"—the obligatory banquet at a merchant's house:

> At 7 p.m. the dinner began with a soup of birds' nests which we ate with chop sticks; these we used somewhat clownishly at first, as it required a little practice to eat a soup with two ivory sticks. Then followed dishes whose names and contents were unknown, but which tasted pretty much all alike. They were all in cups about the size of tea-cups, and when given to each guest always eaten with these same chop-sticks. In eating liquid dishes, as soups, the mouth is put down to the edge of the dish and the contents shoveled in. They will eat rice as fast again in this way as I could ever manage with a spoon. Some of the dishes we had were birds' nests, lily roots, pigs' tongues, fishes'

stomachs, sharks' fins, biche-de-mer, fishes' heads—
and others to the number of fourteen. After this a
European dinner was served, but rather inferior.[25]

The main difference between these American missionaries and the traders in Guangzhou was that Bridgman and
his compatriots were actually interested in the lives of the
Chinese. This curiosity was driven by their mission work,
because they realized they couldn't convert their audiences
unless they knew something about their history, beliefs, and
customs. Bridgman and Williams researched a wide variety
of aspects of Chinese life, from weights and measures to
grammar to the practices of the imperial court, and published all their findings in the *Chinese Repository*. These
articles were reprinted in many United States periodicals
and avidly read by merchants looking for information they
could use in the China trade.

In 1835, Williams wrote a long essay for the *Repository*,
on the "Diet of the Chinese." His scientific background shows
itself in his thorough investigation of every aspect of his subject.
He admits that due to the restrictions on foreign travel within
China, his article gives only a fragmentary look at the country's
cuisine: "in endeavoring to ascertain the sources from whence
food for so great a population is derived, and the various modes
which are employed to fit it for use, we shall resort to all means
of information within our reach. Our inquiries, however, must
be confined chiefly to those persons who have come more or less
in contact with foreigners." Using travelers' accounts as well
as his own observations in and around Guangzhou, Williams
first gives a long description of the grains, vegetables, fruits,
oil plants, fish, domesticated animals, birds, insects, beverages,
and liquors the Chinese consume. He then turns to Chinese
kitchens, cooking methods, and meal customs and mentions
the huge numbers of "taverns, eating-houses, and cook-stalls"

in the cities. Of the larger restaurants, he remarks that "we should suppose that they were much patronized, but by what particular class, or whether by all classes, we do not know." The edict forbidding foreign entry into the city still held, so no foreigner had ever dined in a Guangzhou restaurant. About halfway through this article, Williams lets slip his unvarnished opinion about Chinese food. Here we finally learn what all the traders really thought about the weird dishes served at the banquets across the river at Honam:

> The cooking and mode of eating among the Chinese are peculiar.... The universal use of oil, not always the sweetest or purest, and of onions, in their dishes, together with the habitual neglect of their persons, causes an odor, almost insufferable to a European, and which is well characterized by Ellis, as the "repose of putrefied garlic on a much used blanket." The dishes, when brought on the table, are almost destitute of seasoning, taste, flavor, or anything else by which one can be distinguished from another; all are alike insipid and greasy to the palate of the foreigner.[26]

It's unclear how the Chinese dishes could be both insipid and stinking of garlic, onion, and rancid oil. In fact, Westerners smelled that aroma everywhere. Even outside the dining room, this was what many Americans and Europeans apparently thought the Chinese smelled like—garlic, onions, and body odor.

By the late 1830s, relations between the Chinese and the barbarians had grown strained. The westerners were tired of being cooped up in Guangzhou and Macau; they ached to sell their goods in the whole of China. Americans and Europeans had also grown weary of Chinese arrogance, of what Bridgman saw as China's "absurd claim of universal supremacy." To them, any nation that rejected Christianity could not claim to be the center of human civilization. On the Chinese side, the Daoguang Emperor and his top officials believed that the barbarians must be reined in, if not kicked out of the Middle Kingdom altogether. They had good cause. For decades now, the British had been smuggling opium into China from India. This was against Chinese law (and western morality), but the profits were too great for the Crown to stop: income from opium helped Britain maintain its status as the dominant seagoing power. Tired of trading in sea cucumbers and birds' nests, American merchants began shipping in their own opium from Turkey. By the early nineteenth century, hundreds of thousands of Chinese had become opium addicts, a situation that ruined lives and weakened local economies. Half the officials along the South China coast had become corrupted by bribery. Finally, in 1839 Daoguang Emperor ordered the blockade of Guangzhou and the arrest of the principal traffickers. This action precipitated the disastrous Opium War of 1840–42.

The emperor thought it enough to strengthen the Guangzhou harbor blockade and set up cannons along the Guangdong coast. The British fleet bypassed Guangzhou and sailed up the east coast of China bombarding cities. They then doubled back to Guangzhou and encircled the city, forcing its officials to capitulate and hand over a large ransom. In 1842, when the rest of the British Asia fleet arrived from India, the combined force included dozens of fully armed warships and ten thousand soldiers. They sailed up the China coast again, capturing the major port cities and even threatening Beijing. Chinese resistance was fiercest along the Yangzi Valley, but the British weapons and soldiers proved unstoppable. The western army marched up the Yangzi, one of China's richest districts, destroying any opposition it met. As his military evaporated, the emperor vacillated, unable to decide whether to surrender or fight on. Finally, he summoned his trusted aide Qiying, who like himself was a Manchu and a direct descendant of the Qing Dynasty's founder. Qiying had seen the awesome power of the British military machine up close and advised the emperor that a policy of appeasement was the only option. Realizing that the war threatened the survival of his dynasty, the emperor agreed to sue for peace. In August 1842, Qiying signed the Treaty of Nanking aboard a British battleship. The Chinese agreed to have full diplomatic relations with Britain, to cede Hong Kong to the Queen, to open four more ports to trade, and to pay a massive indemnity. It was China's most humiliating defeat at the hands of barbarians since the Mongol invasion of the thirteenth century.

Putrified Garlic on a Much-used Blanket

*T*he white sails of the U.S.S. *Brandywine*, a frigate carrying forty-four guns, appeared off the coast of South China in February 1844. Its most important cargo was the first United States ambassador to China: Caleb Cushing, bearing a letter from President John Tyler to China's emperor. A large party assembled at Macau's docks to welcome him ashore, while a marine band played and cannons roared a salute from the Portuguese fort. As the boat carrying Cushing, rowed by a dozen American sailors, hove into view, his costume appeared first: he wore a white ostrich feather atop a large, navy blue hat, a blue coat covered in gold buttons, white pantaloons with a gold stripe down the side, tall boots, and spurs—the uniform of a major general. Some of the women tittered behind their fans; the European merchants whispered wry comments to each other. When Commissioner Cushing alighted and the crowd caught sight of his face, the snickering stopped. He looked the model of the nineteenth-century authority figure—tall, with a strong chin, a

stern mouth line, and a flowing moustache. His deep baritone voice could fill the largest meeting halls. In fact, the
only thing that had kept him out of the highest political
posts was his aloof and uncompromising disposition—he
lacked the common touch. As Cushing shook the hands
of the dignitaries at the dock, the people could sense the
seriousness with which he took his mission. After sailing
halfway around the world at some risk to his life (one of
his boats had been destroyed by fire), Cushing was determined to do whatever it took to formalize a treaty estab-
lishing diplomatic relations between the United States and
China—even if it meant eating at a Chinese table.

In the aftermath of the 1840–42 Opium War, the United
States was intent on increasing its influence in East Asia.
President Tyler and Secretary of State Daniel Webster
knew the terms of the Treaty of Nanking and had heard
that British merchants were at the forefront of opening up
new markets in China. The letter to the Chinese emperor
that Cushing carried (which introduced its bearer as
"Count Caleb Cushing, one of the wise and learned men
on this country") proposed opening a new era of "peace
and friendship" between China and the United States.
Tyler's terms for this friendship included full diplomatic
relations, trading privileges for American merchants that
were at least as favorable as the Treaty of Nanking's, and
permission for American missionaries to live and proselytize among the Chinese. Over the next few decades,
American diplomats, merchants, and missionaries would
indeed have much greater access to Chinese officials and
to China's 300 million customers and souls. However, the
post–Opium War years did not necessarily usher in a new
era of friendship between the two peoples—with direct
consequences for the American experience of Chinese
food.

In the decades before the Opium War, the relations between the two countries had been purely commercial. The American merchants in Guangzhou had actively rejected the idea of a U.S. treaty with China, not wanting to upset their lucrative status quo. This attitude had changed during the blockade of Guangzhou, when American traders had asked for the intervention of American warships to protect their lives. The war started before the ships could be sent out. As a result, in 1841 Parker had traveled to Washington to make the case to Tyler and Webster for a formal U.S.-China agreement. Parker was deeply afraid that the conflict would cause China to close its doors to the West. Not only would American business suffer; the heathens might lose the "moral benefits" of the missionary enterprise. Parker's choice to lead the first U.S. diplomatic mission to China was ex-president John Quincy Adams, who had already given a rabble-rousing speech on the Opium War. The war's real cause, Adams had said, was not the opium trade but "the pretension on the part of the Chinese, that in all their intercourse with other nations, political or commercial, their superiority must be implicitly acknowledged, and manifested in humiliating forms."[1] He went on: "it is time that this enormous outrage upon the rights of human nature, and upon the first principles of the rights of nations, should cease."[2] If negotiations with the Chinese didn't work, Adams, like Parker, was quite prepared to enforce American claims to trading rights with a fleet of warships.

Webster wasn't quite so fast on the trigger, but he had his own reasons for pushing for a treaty with China. The term "manifest destiny" hadn't been coined yet, but the concept behind it was already widespread in the early 1840s. Many American politicians believed their country had a divinely given right to possess the land running all the way to the Pacific Ocean. That meant Texas, California, the Oregon

Territory, and maybe even the British colony of Canada. Webster had already declared that the Sandwich Islands, known to its natives as Hawai'i, lay within the American "sphere of influence." The next step was to check the British Empire's growing power on the other side of the Pacific. As soon as Webster had received word of the Treaty of Nanking, he had begun to plan for America's first high-level diplomatic mission to China. Its goals were to open full diplomatic relations with the imperial government, achieve favorable trading terms for American merchants, and make clear that the United States, unlike Britain, had no belligerent intentions toward China. To lead this effort, Webster had turned to Caleb Cushing, who shared his faith in an aggressive, expansionist foreign policy. Cushing told a crowd in Boston: "I go to China, sir, if I may so express myself, in behalf of civilization and that, if possible, the doors of three hundred million Asiatic laborers may be opened to America."[3]

In Macau, Cushing was not exactly welcomed by the local American population. They were afraid that his inexperience in dealing with imperial officials (and his ludicrous uniform!) would only worsen their relations with the Chinese government. Their fears were confirmed when the emperor categorically denied Cushing's request to come to Beijing. The arrival of a rude and awkward foreigner would only upset the ritual of the imperial court. Cushing was not fazed. He quickly hired Parker and Bridgman to act as his translators and resident experts on Chinese affairs. While he continued to pester the emperor with demands to travel to Beijing, Cushing learned all he could about local customs from Parker and Bridgman. He wanted to be able to face any eventuality, both at the negotiating table and at the dinner table. Finally, the emperor decided to send his relative Qiying, by now an imperial commissioner and China's de facto foreign minister, to negotiate with the barbarian

Figure 2.1. Caleb Cushing, the U.S. Commissioner to China from 1843 to 1845, arrived in China after eight years in Congress, including two as chairman of the House Committee on Foreign Affairs.

emissary. Qiying took his time; he arrived in Macau in the middle of June 1844. With his retinue, including aides, dozens of servants, and a troop of soldiers, he made his headquarters the Wang Xia Temple (now known as the Kun Iam Temple) just outside Macau's city walls. He immediately sent word to Macau that he would visit the American legation there the next day.

The following morning, Qiying undertook the mile-and-a-half trip into Macau with all the pomp and solemnity of his exalted position. First a messenger ran ahead bearing an edict that announced the coming of the high official. Then the procession set off from the Wang Xia Temple under the steamy subtropical sun. At its head marched two fearsome military officers, one brandishing a long-handled axe, the other a whip to clear pedestrians from the path. A troop of regular soldiers followed and then a military band banging gongs and blowing horns to signal that the envoy was in transit. Next came three aides on sedan chairs carried by servants, and then Qiying himself, idly fanning himself in the heat. He was short, stocky, and obviously well fed, with an elegant little goatee and moustache and a glint of humor and intelligence in his eyes. His light silk robe, cool in the summertime, was tied with the yellow sash that signaled that he and the emperor were kinsmen. The red ball and peacock's feather on top of his hat denoted his exalted rank. Like all Chinese men, he showed his fealty to the Manchu-ruled Qing Dynasty with his hairstyle: shaved in front, with the long braid called a queue hanging in back. It had been many decades since this corner of China had seen so powerful an imperial official.

The parade entered Macau and wound its way down the Praya Grande, the main waterfront avenue, to the mansion housing the American legation. Three American warships bristling with cannons stood at anchor in the harbor. As Qiying descended from his sedan chair, an honor guard of U.S. Marines fired three salutes. The Americans stood ready to greet him, sweating copiously in their heavy wool uniforms. From this point on, things didn't go so well. Parker and Bridgman had briefed Cushing on Chinese etiquette, but the behavior of Qiying and his aides still unnerved the Americans. Rather than shaking the Americans' hands, the Chinese gave the traditional Chinese greeting of bowing and clasping their own hands. They then entered the legation building without removing their hats. The language barrier compounded the awkwardness. Qiying spoke Mandarin, while Parker and Bridgman only understood Cantonese, and that poorly. Luckily, one of Qiying's aides was fluent in Cantonese. Next Qiying embarrassed the Americans by asking all of them their ages. Then came a rustle of skirts, and an American woman appeared: Mrs. Peter Parker. A stunned silence fell over the Chinese party. In China, wives and daughters were kept at home, locked behind closed doors as Confucian ideals demanded. Qiying later told the emperor that the barbarian habit of parading their women before strange men was one of the many signs of their "stupid ignorance." Nevertheless, when the meal was announced, Qiying bravely extended his arm for Mrs. Parker to take as they entered the dining room.

At the table, the Americans did their best to show respect for the Chinese party. The places had been set with chopsticks, and the honored guests were seated to the left rather than the right of the host. Otherwise, the meal followed the strict etiquette of a western-style banquet. The precise menu has been lost, but we can get a pretty good idea of it from other descriptions of western food served in mid-nineteenth-century China. Bread and butter were provided at all the places. After the first course, a soup, came an over-cooked fish in a cream-based sauce, perhaps a curried meat on a mound of overcooked rice, side dishes of boiled potatoes and some pallid greens, and then the meal's high point: a roast leg of meat, most likely mutton. As host, Cushing ceremoniously carved the joint with a large knife; the blood-streaked juice flowed from the meat. Dessert probably included fruit, nuts, and perhaps a large Stilton cheese just off the boat from London.

We don't have any eyewitness accounts from the Chinese side of how they responded to this meal. In fact, most early Chinese writings about interactions with foreign traders remain politely mute about western food. In his 1855 memoir *Bits of Old China*, the American "China hand" William C. Hunter includes a letter he says was written by a young Chinese who had been invited to dine in the American factory. To pass the idle hours in their compound, westerners occasionally liked to write satirical poems and prose burlesques, so his claim must be taken with a grain of salt. Still, there is probably a layer of authenticity behind this text:

> Judge now what tastes people possess who sit at table and swallow bowls of a fluid, in their outlandish tongue called *Soo-pe*, and next devour flesh of fish, served in a manner as near as may be to resemble the living fish itself. Dishes of half-raw meat are then placed at various angles of the table; these float in gravy, while from them pieces are cut with swordlike instruments and placed before the guests. Really it was not until I beheld this sight that I became convinced of what I had often heard that the ferocious disposition of these demons arises from their indulgence in such gross food.... Thick pieces of meat being devoured, and the scraps thrown to a multitude of snappish dogs that are allowed to twist about amongst one's legs or lie under the table, while keeping up an incessant growling and fighting, there followed a dish that set fire to our throats, called in a barbarous language of one by my side *Ka-Le* [curry], accompanied with rice which of itself was alone grateful to my taste. Then a green and white substance, the smell of which was overpowering. This I was informed was a compound of sour buffalo milk, baked in the sun, under whose influence it is allowed to remain until it becomes filled with insects, yet, the greener and more lively it is, with the more relish it is eaten. This is called *Che-Sze*, and is accompanied by the drinking of a muddy red fluid which foams up over the tops of the drinking cups,

soils one's clothes, and is named *Pe-Urh*—think of that![4]

Actually, Manchus like Qiying were among the few imperial subjects known to have a taste for milk products, including a mild kind of cream cheese. However, an aged, blue-veined Stilton would likely have nauseated the Chinese party.

An abbreviated description of the meal was later given by Fletcher Webster, the American mission's secretary and the son of Daniel Webster. The Chinese "showed little inclination to eat, but a decided taste for the barbarian liquors, champagne and cherry bounce." The last was a mixture of cherry juice, whiskey, and sugar, a popular western drink that Parker knew was liked by Chinese merchants in Guangzhou. The Chinese party's heavy imbibing did not reflect any sort of alcoholism; they were simply showing their good breeding by practicing typical Chinese banquet etiquette. After repeated toasts around the table, some of Qiying's aides were quite drunk. Even though the Chinese hardly tasted the food, they still showed regard for their hosts by feeding the Americans with their own chopsticks. Cushing and the others tried to hide their disgust at eating from utensils that had touched Chinese mouths. "They are not particularly nice in their eating," said Webster, "and their teeth are by no means pearls." The Americans retaliated by stuffing food back into their guests' mouths.

Finally, the meal ended, and the diners moved out to the cool of the veranda. Here Qiying and his aides further discomfited the Americans by examining every piece of their clothing, from their sword belts down to their sweat-stained shirts. "Fortunately," said Webster, "our good genius, Dr. Parker, told us this was the very acme of politeness, and to be imitated without delay." So the Americans began to scrutinize the Chinese dress ornaments, from the peacock feathers on their caps down to the agate rings at the end of their thumbs. After two hours, it was time for the Chinese to retire: "The procession re-formed, gongs beat and pipes squealed, the executioners yelled, the little ponies were pulled between their riders' legs, and we were left to reflect upon Chinese men and manners."[5]

The awkwardness of this encounter did not impede the negotiations that followed over the next two weeks. Both sides wanted a treaty too much. By July 3, 1844, the final copies of the agreement were ready for signing. The ceremony took place in a windowless room at the back of the Wang Xia Temple. The Chinese were cool and comfortable in their summer silk robes. Dressed in their usual tight wool uniforms, the Americans nearly passed out from the hot, airless atmosphere. After Cushing fixed his seals to the papers, the Chinese brought out the great seal of the emperor himself to mark the document with imperial approval. To celebrate, Qiying invited the Americans to enjoy a "repast of fruits and tea." This turned out to be the most elaborate Chinese meal any American had tasted up to that day—a "Manchu-Chinese" banquet. To China's gourmets, this was the cutting-edge cuisine of the time, a blend of Manchu and Chinese regional dishes emulating the food served at the imperial court in Beijing. Even Parker and Bridgman probably never realized what an honor they were being given.

The meal took place in a larger room of the temple where a rectangular table with 20 places had been set. Platters filled with bananas, mangoes, oranges, figs, and other fruit already covered the table. On entering, Qiying insisted that the Americans remove their wool coats. Here was another Chinese custom: that one's guests be comfortable and relaxed during banquets. Of course, this went against the Americans' standards of proper dinner etiquette and only made them more uncomfortable. After the diners nibbled on the fruit, the meal proper began with a "pudding" Qiying himself had supposedly invented just for the occasion. Webster remarked that it was "excellent and spoke volumes for the gastronomic talents of the high Commissioner." Then the servants began to bring in the dishes one after the other: meats, pastries, soups, stews, and so on until a hundred silver vessels "filled the table from one end to the other."

The high points were sea cucumbers, roofs of hogs' mouths, and birds' nests. It is unclear whether the last were in a soup or some other kind of dish. Webster called them "by no means disagreeable, being somewhat between vermicelli and tapioca, stringy like the one, transparent like the other, and quite tasteless." The other dishes were deemed "no great addition to our festive boards." All of this was washed down with copious toasts of a potent hot rice wine called "samchou." Once again, the Chinese honored their guests by feeding them with their own chopsticks. All the Americans could do was "gape, simper, and swallow!"

A few hours into the feast, there was a pause in the service, after which the food changed from Chinese to Manchu. Six cooks entered the room, each bearing a large piece of roast meat—pig, ham, "turkey," and so on—on a silver platter. These weren't the singed and bloody roasts that came out of western kitchens but edible works of art resembling polished Chinese lacquerware. The cooks placed the roasts on special chopping blocks and carved off thin slices of well-cooked meat that were distributed to the guests. These were the only dishes during the banquet that resembled any kind of American food. Finally, after four hours of eating and drinking, came the last course, a large bowl of "very nice" soup. Qiying "took it up with both hands, drank out of it, and then passed it to the Minister; and then it went the round of the whole table." To the Americans, it seemed as if they had just eaten a western meal in reverse, beginning with fruit and ending with soup. As they returned to Macau, they felt no happy glow. Instead, they exclaimed, like Macbeth, that they had "supped full of horrors."[6]

In signing the Treaty of Wang Xia, Qiying believed he had achieved his goal of appeasing the barbarian power. It was now unlikely that the Americans would force their way into China as the British had. He also had successfully beaten back all of Cushing's demands—the most important being his insistence on traveling to Beijing for an audience before the Heavenly Throne. Qiying wrote to his emperor: "The envoy was rewarded with a banquet to show our bounty and confidence, and was greatly pleased. He is presently residing at Macau, entirely peaceable, thus providing some solace to the Imperial Breast."[7]

It remained doubtful, however, that the Americans would ever join the ranks of the civilized, like the tribute-bearing kings of Korea and Siam. For instance, Qiying saw no sign that the Americans had advanced in appreciation of Chinese cuisine. The foreigners had attended magnificent banquets where they had been served the most delicate and costly dishes. They had smiled in appreciation of the bird's nest soup or roast Manchu pig. But then, after all they had been exposed to, the Americans always went back to their stinking, half-raw food! Qiying found their meals so crude that he felt he had to apologize to his emperor for sharing them:

> At…Macau on several occasions Your slave gave dinners for the barbarians and anywhere from ten-odd to twenty or thirty of their chiefs and leaders came. When he, on infrequent occasions, met them in a barbarian house or on a barbarian ship they also formed a circle and sat in attendance and outdid themselves to present food and drink. He could not but eat and drink with them in order to bind their hearts.[8]

Cushing was also proud of his achievement. He had proved his detractors in the local American colony wrong. The terms of the treaty allowed American merchants to do business in the same five coastal cities as British merchants but arguably on better terms. Americans could now own property in China, proof that their rights were fully recognized. Cushing had built a solid foundation for American relations with China, and without a huge fleet of battleships and ten thousand troops. The United States now had a political presence in East Asia, and the door had been opened for a flood of merchants and missionaries looking to convert China to the economic and spiritual glories of western civilization.

Cushing's return to the United States stimulated a modest China craze among the American public. Thousands of visitors flocked to the "Chinese Museum," an exhibition of China trade artifacts that opened in Boston's Marlboro Chapel. (Eight years earlier, a Mr. Dunn had opened a similar but smaller museum of things Chinese in Philadelphia.) The building's doorway was decorated to look like the ornate entrance to a Chinese temple; characters above the door purported to say "Extensive View of the Central Flowery Nation." For a mere 25 cents, visitors saw hundreds of paintings and other objects from China, including dozens of lanterns hanging from the roof and a full-size "Tanka boat." Their tour of the display cases began with figures depicting the emperor and his court and then continued through exhibits devoted to religion, the Lantern Festival, women, farming, printing, and even opium smoking, with a real live "John Chinaman" lying in a stupor on a Chinese bed. At the very end, they finally came to a small collection of Chinese foodstuffs, including dried noodles, birds' nests, and sea cucumbers. The museum catalogue asserted that "a Chinese dinner would be nothing without stews made of birds' nests, sharks' fins, deers' sinews, bircho-de-mer [*sic*], or sea slugs, and many other such dishes, used and appreciated only by the Chinese, and all of which to the uneducated and barbarous taste of a native of the western world, possess a similarly insipid or repulsive flavor."[9]

Both Cushing and Fletcher Webster took advantage of this enthusiasm by embarking on lecture tours of the major East Coast cities. Webster, the more entertaining of the two, told of the diplomats' many adventures, including the "horrors" of their Chinese banquets. He may have realized he went too far in these descriptions, because one reporter in the lecture hall wrote: "Mr. Webster went on to say that he did not mean to ridicule the customs of the Chinese, but that on seeing them for the first time, they of course would strike any one as singular."[10] In his drier and more didactic lectures, Cushing particularly dwelled on the oddness of Chinese customs: "To an American or European, cast for the first time into the midst of Chinese society, everything seems contrary to his own established usages. Not only does he find himself at the antipodes, geographically speaking, but equally so with respect to manners, customs, and morals." Everything Chinese was spectacularly strange: the costumes, music, and mourning customs; the practice of reading from top to bottom and right to left; and so on. And of course, among those customs was their manner of eating: "Food is eaten with two sticks, and it requires some skill to dexterously pick it up and convey it by their means; every thing is served cut up, in small bowls; and it is considered a compliment to hand a morsel to your neighbor with your sticks, he taking it on his own."[11] In an era before the notion of men from Mars had popular currency, in a sense Cushing's Chinese filled the role of our era's space aliens—the perfect opposite of everything Americans considered right and proper.

It's impossible to know what picture of Chinese food stuck in the minds of the American audience of 1845. The culinary descriptions passed on by Guangzhou merchants, missionaries, and diplomats were based on firsthand experiences, but they may not have been what Americans remembered. A few months after Cushing returned, at least a dozen newspapers printed this little tale:

> It is said that Caleb Cushing, on being asked to dine with Mandarin Lin, discovered on the table something of which he ate exorbitantly, thinking it to be duck. Not speaking Chinese, and wishing to know what it was, he pointed to it, after he had finished, saying to his host interrogatively, "Quack, quack, quack?" The Mandarin, with equal brevity, replied, with a shake of the head, "Bow, wow, wow." Mr. Cushing's feelings may be imagined.[12]

Actually, this joke was at least a half century old, with the British ambassador filling the role of Cushing. That didn't matter to the newspapers, which told their readers that this little yarn was "too good" not to repeat. If the average American knew anything about the food of China, it boiled down to the idea that the Chinese people's preferred food was dogs.

The Treaty of Wang Xia was unanimously ratified by the U.S. Senate on January 16, 1845, and signed by President Tyler the next day. For diplomats, it formalized ties to the Chinese government; for merchants and missionaries, it gave them far greater access to Chinese markets and Chinese souls along the Chinese coast. It did not, however, lead to a golden age of understanding between the peoples of the two nations. After a brief era of goodwill, American diplomats soon became frustrated at what they saw as the "arrogance and conservatism" of Chinese authorities. They still were unable to trade and travel through *all* of China, and they chafed at continued implications that Western culture was inferior to the Chinese. To them, the West's victory in the recent Opium War confirmed not only its superior military technology but the rightness of its morality—the hand of divine providence had guided the cannon fire against the pagans. On the Chinese side, resentment also increased—over the valuable tracts of Chinese territory foreigners now controlled and the unabated traffic in opium, which was slowly poisoning the populace. The most positive thing the Chinese authorities could say about the Americans was that they weren't the British, who were at the forefront of the opium trade and would use any excuse to demand, often at gunpoint, further trading privileges in China. Instead, the U.S. diplomats played a kind of double game: they wouldn't pick a fight with the Chinese, but they wouldn't hold back the British either. For American merchants and missionaries in the latter half of the nineteenth century, the Qing empire's gradual descent into chaos meant unparalleled opportunity.

The speedy opium clippers were western traders' vessels of choice. As soon as each new treaty port opened up—first in Amoy, Fuzhou, Ningpo, and Shanghai, later in a host of smaller coastal and river cities—the traders built their docks, warehouses, offices, and residences. Back in Guangzhou, they had railed against their confinement to the factory quarter and their isolation from the Chinese city. Now, strangely, they replicated that isolation, although on a more spacious scale, in gated communities well separated from the Chinese cities. The British, the dominant faction among the merchants, set the social tone here. There was to be no mingling with "inferior" races beyond what was necessary for trade. The westerners considered life inside the Chinese walls dirty, smelly, noisy, crowded, overwhelming, and best avoided. The only time they ventured there was when they had business with the local authorities or for the obligatory banquet with a Chinese merchant. As they strode through the crowded city streets, many Europeans would use their canes as clubs, beating a path through the Chinese men, women, and children so they could walk unmolested. The Chinese authorities could do nothing, because they had little authority over the foreigners in the treaty ports.

The Americans and Europeans preferred to spend time among their own kind, dividing their leisure hours between walks along the waterfront, rowboat excursions, sports like cricket and rackets, riding, drinks at the club, and elaborate meals. Here's the menu of a typical dinner for western traders in Shanghai:

> rich soup, and a glass of sherry; *then* one or two side dishes with champagne; *then* some beef, mutton, or fowls and bacon, with *more* champagne, or beer; *then* rice and curry and ham; *afterwards* game; *then* pudding, pastry, jelly, custard, or butter and a glass of port wine; *then* in many cases, oranges, figs, raisins, and walnuts...*with* two or three glasses of claret or some other wine.[13]

All of these dishes would have been carried in by armies of Chinese servants, who were hired so cheaply that even the lowliest clerk could expect to be waited on hand and foot. Not until well after 1900 did western merchants admit to actually liking Chinese food or eating in a Chinese restaurant.

A British trader later summarized the dominant attitude of traders in China: "Commerce was the beginning, the middle, and the end of our life in China...if there were no trade, not a single man, except missionaries, would have come there at all."[14] In the twentieth century, this attitude morphed into something called the "Shanghai mind," which one observer said resembled "a comfortable but hermetically sealed and isolated glass case."[15] Inside that case, western merchants devoted themselves to business and the observance of an elaborate and highly stratified social code, which boiled down to "us," the westerners, versus "them," the Chinese. For any European or American to show interest in China or Chinese life beyond trade was social and professional suicide. Unlike the original generation of merchants who lived in the Guangzhou factories, the American businessmen working in late nineteenth-century China rarely thought it worthwhile to write about their experiences.

Missionaries made up the other main group of American China hands in the decades after the Treaty of Wang Xia. Unlike the merchants, missionaries had to live in the Chinese cities, learn the local dialects, and study local customs to further their goal of saving souls. In order to inspire more Americans to come to China to continue their holy work, many of them wrote books about the country, its people, and their experiences. Perhaps the most influential of these was written by Samuel Wells Williams, the editor and printer of the *Chinese Repository*. In 1845, Williams had returned to the United States on furlough. He wished to see his father, who was terminally ill, and he hoped to raise money for his China work. Specifically, he wanted the funds to purchase a complete set of Chinese type, so he could publish Bibles, tracts, and other works in Chinese. His backers on the missionary board were dubious—they actually wanted to cut back on the printing work—but Williams managed to raise $600 from his home church in Utica. Then, like Cushing and Fletcher Webster, he set out to lecture on China in any church or public hall that would invite him. The tour lasted over a year, covering a dozen states. During this time, Williams met, courted, and married his wife Sarah, and decided to turn his lecture notes into a book. He had noticed that many in his audiences thought the Chinese ridiculous—"as if they were apes of Europeans, and their social state, arts, and government, the burlesques of the same things in Christendom." China hands like himself, he said, were expected to tell tales of

> Mandarins with yellow buttons, handing you
>   conserves of snails;
> Smart young men about Canton in nankeen tights
>   and peacocks' tails.
> With many rare and dreadful dainties, kitten cutlets,
>   puppy pies;
> Birdsnest soup which (so convenient!) every bush
>   around supplies.[16]

This quatrain by Lady Dufferin, a popular British poet, was apparently all the rage at the moment. Williams feared that if all that Americans remembered about China were cartoonish images like these—or stories about dishes that went "Bow, wow, wow"—they wouldn't take seriously the great task of converting China. By the end of 1847, he had compiled *The Middle Kingdom*, a two-volume, 1,250-page tome that remained the principal American reference work on China into the twentieth century. (Its frontispiece features a perhaps inadvertently insulting portrait of the imperial emissary Qiying that shows him bareheaded and in a costume stripped of all sign of rank.)

Williams wrote *The Middle Kingdom* to show that "the introduction of China into the family of Christian nations, her elevation from her present state of moral, intellectual, and civil debasement, to that standing which she should take, and the free intercourse of her people and rulers with their fellowmen or other climes and tongues, is a great work, and a glorious one." Furthermore, he says, the holy work of converting the Chinese "is far more important than the form of their government, the extent of their empire, or the existence of their present institutions." He then contradicts

Figure 2.2. Rice sellers at a military station, c. 1843. In The Middle Kingdom, *Williams describes the grain as "emphatically the staff of life.... Its long use is indicated in the number of terms employed to describe it."*

this claim by spending most of the two volumes discussing China's government, empire, culture, religion, and so on with the utmost scholarly rigor. In fact, there's a strange dichotomy throughout the book between learned investigation and reductive moralizing. For instance, he begins the first volume with a thoughtful discussion of the name "China" itself, which is used in many foreign languages but not by the Chinese themselves. The word may derive from "Qin," or "Ch'in," the name of the dynasty that unified China and ruled it from 221 to 206 BCE. During the first millennium of the Common Era, "China," whose location was uncertain, was the fabled source of the costly fabric, worn by emperors and kings, that came from the East on camel-back along the Silk Road. In the minds of the Christian West, "China" only became firmly fixed as the great empire at the opposite end of the Eurasian continent with the writings of Marco Polo and the other travelers who followed him into Asia. Williams says that over the centuries, the Chinese themselves have called their land "Beneath the Sky," "All Within the Four Seas," and the "Middle Kingdom." (Today, the nation's formal name is Zhonghua Renmin Gongheguo, "People's Republic of China," literally "People's Republic of the Middle Prosperous State.") But then the missionary in him comes forward to render judgment on these presumptions: "All these names indicate the vanity and the ignorance of the people respecting their geographical position and their rank among the nations."[17]

Williams based the information in *The Middle Kingdom* on Chinese sources, his own observations, and most of all, the first dozen years of the *Chinese Repository*. He essentially sought to condense that publication into a more palatable form for readers who were not experts on China. We see this in the book's discussion of Chinese food, in which he mostly follows the outline of his *Repository* article "Diet of the Chinese," covering rice and other grains, vegetables, fruits, oils and fats, beverages, meats, poultry, fish, and the three delicacies birds' nests, sea cucumbers, and sharks' fins. He notes with care the Chinese revulsion toward western dairy products like butter and cheese. Predictably, he attacks the idea that cats, dogs, and rats commonly appear in the Chinese diet:

> Few articles of food have ... been so identified with the tastes of a people as kittens and puppies, rats and snails, have with the Chinese. The school geographies in the United States usually contain pictures of a market-man carrying baskets holding these unfortunate victims of a perverse taste (as we think), or else a string of rats and mice hanging by their tails to a stick across his shoulders, which almost necessarily convey the idea

that such things form the usual food of the people.... However commonly kittens and puppies may be exposed for sale, the writer never saw rats or mice in the market during a residence of twelve years there.... He once asked a native if he or his countrymen ever served up *lau-shang tang*, or rat-soup, on their tables; who replied that he had never seen or eaten it, and added, "Those who do use it should mix cheese with it, that the mess might serve for us both."[18]

Though Williams tones down the harshness of his *Repository* article's judgments, he still cannot bring himself to enjoy the food of China. The "repose of putrefied garlic on a much-used blanket" is gone. Now, the food is admired as "sufficient in variety, wholesome, and well cooked," but it remains "unpalatable to a European from the vegetable oil used in their preparation, and the alliaceous plants introduced to savor them." He treats only minimally the question of how the Chinese prepare their dishes, commenting that they like to cut up their food into small pieces before stewing or frying. In sum, he reported: "the art of cooking has not reached any high degree of perfection among the Chinese, consisting chiefly of stews of various kinds, in which garlic and grease are more abundant than pepper and salt."[19] One of the world's great cuisines was reduced to a couple of oily stewpots. Judgments like these would dominate American opinion of Chinese food for many decades.

Unfortunately, when Williams returned to Guangzhou in 1848, he discovered that the community of Western China hands was no longer interested in that country's history and culture, except as they furthered their own narrow interests. He wrote home: "the class of merchants here now take very much less interest in China than they used to, and the publication is carried on at a loss."[20] In fact, he soon had to stop publishing the *Chinese Repository* because subscriptions dropped dramatically. (He spent the next few decades of his life in the U.S. consular service and then retired to teach at Yale University.) He also found that the missionaries who were then arriving in China—those who had answered his call—were a different breed than the earlier generation. The missionary boards back in the United States had grown tired of supporting men like Williams, Parker, and Bridgman, with their printing presses, schools, hospitals, and scholarly work. Now they wanted young, energetic, devout, and single-minded men and women who could concentrate on the task of saving Chinese souls. These turned out to be far more interested in Williams's examination of China's moral "debasement," especially the three pages he devotes to female infanticide, than his scholarship about Chinese life and customs.

When the new crop of missionaries landed in the treaty ports (usually, to their embarrassment, aboard opium schooners), they settled in Chinese neighborhoods and quickly began the tasks of preaching to anyone who would listen, distributing Chinese-language tracts, and building Christian chapels. This description of the Presbyterian preacher John B. French in his home near Guangzhou clearly shows how these new missionaries viewed the world outside their doors:

> The sides and rear of his little two story dwelling...was [sic] closely packed in by small Chinese houses swarming with heathen life—blocked off by narrow, dark, and filthy foot-paths as the only streets; presented but a dismal home for a man in the freshness of youth and refinement of feeling. Still here he lived alone, with a Chinese boy to bring him water and cook his rice, and a Chinese teacher to aid him in the study of the language. And he was happy and cheerful. He had daily communings with the pure above though

surrounded by pagans below—and while every
thing around him was dark and filthy, and deafening
discord—within his heart all was peace, and within
his house all was neatness and order. [21]

The author of that paragraph was William Dean, a Baptist
from upstate New York. When he was first recruited for the
mission field, he was "tall, broad-shouldered, with muscles
hardened on his father's farm, with dark brown eyes that
could sparkle with fun or glow with the fire of determined
purpose." But after preaching to the "heathens" for fifteen
years, six of those in China, he was tired out, weakened by
tropical disease, old wounds from Malaysian pirates' spears,
and the deaths of two wives in the Far East. Even in convalescence, he retained his faith in his holy work. In 1859, he
published *The China Mission*, a kind of instruction manual for young evangelists. Its four hundred pages include
every point he thought relevant about the Middle Kingdom,
from geography to religion, as well as inspirational stories
about the triumphs of Protestant missionaries—and about
their not infrequent martyrdoms. (Many observers noticed
that missionary wives seemed to die with particular rapidity in Asia.) He dispatches the cuisine of China in one short
paragraph:

If you ask what they eat—we answer, they do not eat
beef nor bread, mutton nor milk, butter nor cheese;
but they do eat fowls and fishes, pigs and puppies, rats
and rice, maize and millet, wheat and barley, pumpkins
and potatoes, turnips and tomatoes, ground-nuts and
garlics, pears and peaches, plantains and pumeloes,
grapes and guavas, pineapples and pomegranates,
olives and oranges, sharks' fins and birds' nests. But
why so much curiosity to learn what they eat, while
so little concern for the fact that they are hastening by

millions to a world of everlasting starvation, while we hold in our hands the bread which came down from heaven, of which a man eat he shall live forever—and we refuse to give it to them, at the peril of our salvation and theirs.[22]

Cursory and sprinkled with errors (Dean knew from sources like *The Middle Kingdom* that beef and mutton were at least occasionally eaten), this description is typical of missionary writings of the era. There was no reason to dwell on the old, pagan, depraved habits of the Chinese because all of that would soon be swept away by the clean, pure, "civilizing" influence of western Christianity.

There were a few exceptions to this attitude, at least regarding food. Charles Taylor, a medical missionary sent to Shanghai in the early 1850s by the Methodist church,

Figure 2.3. An American missionary with her Chinese converts in Fuzhou, c. 1902. After the signing of the Treaty of Wang Xia, most Americans in China were either missionaries or traders.

whose 1860 book *Five Years in China* is liberally larded with Christian condemnation, also reveals a scientist's knack for direct observation. He was curious about every aspect of Chinese life, from housing to criminal punishment, and his section on foodstuffs shows clearly that he actually tasted, and enjoyed, bamboo shoots, frogs' legs, and ripe persimmons. He is not put off when his Chinese host ladles soup into his bowl with a spoon that has touched his own lips or cleans his guest's chopsticks with his fingers—"after having sucked them clean." And he is one of the rare Americans of the nineteenth century who admits to having enjoyed the occasional formal Chinese banquet:

> The variety of preparations is certainly very great, and many of them are as delicate and well-flavored as any one could desire. Such at least is my own opinion, founded on actual experience; for just in order to inform myself, I have done what, perhaps, few foreigners who visit China venture upon—imagining the presence of some canine or feline ingredient—have tasted most of the dishes at a fashionable Chinese dinner, even when the appearance and odor suggested something disagreeable, and have found them exceedingly palatable.[23]

The Americans who lived and worked in China during that time were mainly interested not in what it was but in what they thought it should be—an economically and technologically modern Christian nation. To them, imperial China was an antiquated monolith akin to ancient Egypt or Rome and best relegated to the dustbin of history. Even by the 1890s, few Americans had seen much more of the country than the coast and a few inland cities, and only a small minority had mastered Chinese. Their culturally limited viewpoint profoundly influenced the reception on American soil of Chinese immigrants and Chinese food.

Coarse Rice and Water

In 1795, when the Americans were still marveling at Chinese food from the confines of Guangzhou, the Middle Kingdom's most famous poet, Yuan Mei, wrote of the deterioration caused by advancing age:

> When I was young and had no money to spend
> I had a passionate longing for expensive things.
> I was always envying people for their fur coats,
> For the wonderful things they got to eat and drink.
> I dreamt of these things, but none of them came my
>   way,
> And in the end I became very depressed.
> Nowadays, I have got quite smart clothes,
> But am old and ugly, and they do not suit me at all.
> All the choicest foods are on my table;
> But I only manage to eat a few scraps.
> I feel inclined to say to my Creator
> "Let me live my days on earth again,
> But this time be rich when I am young;
> To be poor when one is old does not matter at all."[1]

Yuan Mei was born poor in 1716 in the city of Hangzhou. His teachers realized the power of his intellect very early; after he passed the official examinations, he became a district magistrate in the city of Nanjing on the lower Yangzi River. Passionate, irreverent, and disrespectful of authority, he soon realized that he was unfit for official life. Already famous for his poetry, he decided to take up the writing life full time. In 1748, he resigned his posts and retired to a sprawling estate— the Sui Gardens—he had built in the outskirts of Nanjing. His gardens included twenty-four decorative pavilions, a scholar's library and studio, arched bridges over a pond, and a kitchen. There, for the rest of his life, he devoted himself to poetry and friends, sexual indulgences, and refining the gastronomic arts.

Like many with sensitive stomachs (probably caused by too much early indulgence), Yuan Mei was obsessed with food. He hired a chef, Wang Xiaoyu, who shared his culinary passion and aesthetic. Wang told him:

> To find an employer who appreciates one is not easy. But to find one who understands anything about cookery, is harder still. So much imagination and hard thinking go into the making of every dish that one may say I serve up along with it my whole mind and heart. The ordinary hard-drinking revelers at a fashionable dinner-party would be equally happy to gulp down any stinking mess. They say what a wonderful cook I am, but in the service of such people my art can only decline.... You, on the contrary, continually criticize me, fly into a rage with me, but on every such occasion make me aware of some real defect; so that I would a thousand times rather listen to your bitter admonitions than to the sweetest praise.[2]

Wang brought to the poet's kitchen his ability to cook the simplest ingredients in a way that preserved and enhanced their natural characteristics. "If one has art," he said, "then a piece of celery or salted cabbage can be made into a marvelous delicacy."[3] Yuan also expanded his kitchen's repertoire by eating widely, both at the houses of friends and on his extensive travels throughout China. When he encountered a dish he liked, he took notes, barged into the kitchen to interrogate the chefs, even brought them home to demonstrate its preparation. His tastes ran to simple meals, due both to his stomach problems and because he thought a cook could only make four or five successful dishes at a time. After a banquet where more than forty different kinds of food had been served, he wrote, "when I got home I was so hungry that I ordered a bowl of plain rice-gruel [congee]."[4]

At age eighty, when the choicest morsels had lost their savor, Yuan Mei decided to sum up a lifetime of eating in his book *Suiyan Shidan*, "Recipes from the Sui Gardens." It contains more than three hundred recipes for fish, shellfish, meat, poultry, vegetables, bean curd, noodles, breads, and rice dishes. More important, he prefaces the book with a dozen pages of culinary rules and taboos that give readers a grounding in the general principles of how food should be cooked and served. Like Chef Wang, Yuan holds that foods should exhibit their own characteristics when cooked, and each dish should have one dominant flavor. "Then the palate of the gourmand will respond without fail, and the flowers of the soul blossom forth."[5] Comparing cookery to matrimony, he writes that ingredients should complement one another and criticizes cooks who pile too many incompatible meats into one pot. In the kitchen, the chef should keep his workspace and knives clean to avoid contamination of flavors. Guests at the table should not "eat with their eyes" or be overwhelmed by a profusion of elaborate, poorly prepared dishes. And they should not "eat with their ears" or be impressed by hearing of the cost of rare dishes like birds' nests and sea cucumbers. Yuan preferred well-prepared bean curd and bamboo shoots and declared chicken, pork, fish, and duck "the four heroes of table."[6] Above all, the host should never allow the standards of his kitchen to slip: "into no department of life should indifference be allowed to creep; into none less than into the domain of cookery."[7]

Yuan's recipes embody the food preferences of a cultivated scholar-gourmet. They are neither street food nor the pricey, pretentious dishes the wealthiest merchants favored but fall somewhere in between. These recipes also represent the apogee of the regional cuisine of eastern China during the late eighteenth century, particularly of the cities along the lower Yangzi River. Yuan's cookbook has been so influential that dishes like drunken prawns (live shrimp that are flash-cooked at the table in flaming rice wine) are staples of Chinese restaurants today. That Yuan Mei, a highly educated member of China's elite, a poet and a government official, would have thought it worth his time to write a cookbook is not surprising. (Of American statesmen, only Thomas Jefferson displayed a similar interest in cuisine.) Since nearly the dawn of Chinese culture over three millennia ago, the Chinese have considered cookery an essential art, one of the defining elements of their culture.

Although Chinese cuisine has changed greatly over the centuries and has continually been open to outside influences, it has always been composed of the same basic building blocks. Like all cuisines, it is based on the combinations of specific raw ingredients, flavorings, preparations, and manners of serving and eating dishes. It is also intimately entwined with the country's vast and varied landscape, its climate, and many millennia of human history. In fact, you cannot explain China's cuisine without also describing its geography and the way agriculture came to assume a particularly central role in its culture and history. In the mid–nineteenth century, the emperor of China held sway over more of the Earth's surface than any ruler except the queen of England and the czar of Russia. Beyond the eighteen provinces of China Proper, the Daoguang emperor also ruled over Manchuria, which was the Manchu tribal homeland to the northeast, and an enormous swath of colonial possessions. These included the vast "western Regions": Tibet, Mongolia, and the arid steppes of Central Asia, all the way to present-day Kazakhstan and Kirghizia. (With the exception of Mongolia and parts of Xinjiang, the People's Republic of China now encompasses nearly the same territory.) In its size and complexity, China in many ways resembled western Europe, with its provinces corresponding in size and cultural variation to Europe's nations.

The emperor thus ruled over a wide range of landscapes and climate zones, ranging from rocky high-altitude desert to frozen steppe to tropical rain forest. Surprisingly, very little of China's land is arable. More than a third of it consists of mountains and steep, untillable hills, and most of its northwestern quarter is an arid zone with only isolated areas fit for growing crops. These mountains and deserts form a natural barrier that for centuries protected China from outside invaders. But this terrain also forced the people very early to develop intensive agricultural practices that made the best of what land they had, mostly along its great rivers. Many of the largest waterways rise in the Tibet Plateau, which is capped by Qomologma, or Mount Everest, the "Mother Goddess of the Earth." To the north of this region of snow-capped peaks and arid basins lie deserts and rocky steppes—the route of the Silk Road linking China with the Middle East. To the east, where the Tibet Plateau slopes down toward the Pacific Ocean, the great rivers of East and Southeast Asia begin, including the Huanghe, or Yellow River. From its source in the mountains, the Huanghe follows a long, looping course, carrying with it enormous amounts of yellowish loess— sedimentary deposits that have been spread for millennia on the North China Plain, a sprawling area of flat lowlands. Three thousand or more years ago, this fertile area became the birthplace of Chinese civilization, and it remains one of the most humanized landscapes on Earth. The Huanghe's legacy has not always been benevolent; periodic floods with devastating effects on the human population have earned the river the name "China's Sorrow."

The Tibet Plateau is also the source of China's Yangzi, the third longest river in the world. After leaving the mountains and traveling along the southern border of Sichuan's fertile "Red Basin," the Yangzi enters a region of steep valleys, at the eastern end of which the Chinese government has erected the controversial Three Gorges Dam. Downstream, the river flows through a series of wide valleys and plains before finally disgorging into the China Sea. The cities and agricultural regions along this stretch are among the oldest and most important in China. Traditionally, the lower Yangzi has marked the boundary between the northern and southern halves of China Proper, with their differences of climate, agriculture, and culture. (Northerners have long looked down on the South, calling it a zone of heat, humidity, and insects.) Lying between the Yangzi and the border with Vietnam, the South is a region dominated by low mountains and hills that has much less arable land than the North. The most populous districts are located right along the hilly coastline, in pockets of flat land formed by bays or river valleys. The largest of these is the valley of the Xi ("West") River, which begins in Guangxi Province and connects with two other river systems to form the Zhu, also known as the Pearl River. Along its banks lie the cities of Guangdong, Macau, and Hong Kong and the wide expanse of the Pearl

River Delta. For many reasons—proximity to Southeast Asia, distance from Beijing, lack of natural resources, and so on—the people of South China's coast have always been far more oriented toward the outside world than those in other parts of the Middle Kingdom.

China's climate has always been both its curse, with frequent floods and droughts, and its blessing, helping to feed a vast population. Some writers have pointed out the similarities between the weather conditions of China and North America, which has an analogous latitudinal position on the globe. In truth, however, China is generally colder, hotter, wetter, and more arid than North America. Two great seasonal weather patterns cause this climate of extremes: the waves of cold, dry air that push into China from Siberia and the warm, moist air associated with the Asian monsoon coming from the south. The interplay between these two systems leads to the baking heat of China's summers and the bitter cold of its winters. From Central Asia all the way to the Pacific, the climate of North China is generally dry. The failure of the rains to arrive has meant drought, crop failure, and starvation for millions of people. If too much rain falls, the rivers can overflow their banks and submerge wide swathes of the countryside. In 1888, two million people perished when the Huanghe flooded the North China Plain. South China is generally warmer and its rainfall heavier and more reliable. The floods that do occur are usually less destructive because they are constrained by the hilly landscape. Farmers there do have to contend with typhoons, the western Pacific Ocean's counterpart to hurricanes, which can cause landslides, floods, and widespread crop destruction.

China's diverse climate and geography have allowed a vast array of plant and animal life to thrive. In terms of sheer number of species, China is one of the richest geographical regions on Earth. Since at least the era of Peking Man, five hundred thousand years ago, the human population has seen all of this natural bounty as potential foodstuffs. This is true even today, as one can see from the displays of wild water and land animals for sale in tanks and cages in Guangzhou's sprawling marketplace. (Unfortunately, many of these species are now in danger because of the persistence of the same practices of hunting and gathering.) And the Chinese people learned very early to support themselves by domesticating plants and animals. The inhabitants of prehistoric China may have been one of the earliest groups to learn this skill. According to a 2002 joint Sino-Swedish DNA study, the first domesticated animals were dogs, which diverged genetically from wolves around 13,000 BCE in East Asia. From China all the way to Europe, they became important to humans both as an aid to hunters and as a source of food. East Asia's first domesticated plant was probably rice, in South China (not, as was long believed, millet in North China). Archaeological excavations at sites along the lower and middle Yangzi River have revealed that wild rice was first domesticated around 8500 BCE. Some grains of this rice have been found amid the shards of crudely decorated ceramic urns and bowls that are among the earliest pottery found on the Eurasian landmass.

During approximately 6000–3000 BCE, a series of regional cultures rose and flourished across China. We don't know much about their culinary habits except that they were omnivorous, with a gradually increasing reliance on grain as a staple. In the North, particularly in the dry plains along the inland Yellow River, relatively drought-resistant millet became the principal crop, along with persimmons, peaches, other fruits, and various nuts. Chinese cabbage, an important vegetable, was eventually joined by leeks, onions, and mallow, whose mucilaginous leaves were probably used as a thickener. The most common animals were dogs and pigs, which had been domesticated in China by 7000 BCE. From the Yangzi River all the way through Southeast Asia, rice was clearly the dominant grain. Pigs and dogs were, again, the main domestic animals in South China; water buffaloes arrived somewhat later. Southerners also consumed large amounts of fish and shellfish and foraged for an abundant number of edible wild plants. During this era, life wasn't completely consumed by the struggle for sustenance. At the Jiahu village site in Henan Province, archaeologists have found the earliest musical instruments, as well as pots containing the residue of an aromatic liquor made from rice and honey and flavored with fruits.

Scholars date the birth of a recognizably "Chinese" culture to the centuries between 3000 and 1554 BCE and to the area stretching from the Pearl River Delta in the South to the Great Wall in the North. This was the era of the legendary Xia Dynasty, when villages grew into large towns, with hundreds of houses and clear evidence of stratified social life (particularly elite tombs filled with offerings and decorated with murals) and regular trade between communities. Most of these population centers have been found in North China from Shandong to the west (archaeological work has lagged in South China). Some of this region's rulers may have been the original models for the legendary god-kings of early Chinese history. These included Sui Ren, who first tamed fire; Fu Xi, who taught people to hunt and fish; and Po Yi, who domesticated the first birds and beasts. According to a story from the third century, Shen Nong, the Farmer God, taught his people the rudiments of agriculture:

> In ancient times the people ate plants and drank from rivers, and they picked fruit from trees and ate the flesh of crickets. At that time there was much suffering due

to illness and injury from poisoning. So the Farmer God taught the people for the first time how to sow the five grains and about the quality of soil.... He tasted the flavor of every single plant and determined which rivers and springs were sweet or brackish and he let the people know how to avoid certain things. At that time he himself suffered from poisoning seventy times in one day.[8]

Even at this early stage, it was clear that cooking was considered one of the most important arts. The most famous of the mythological kings, Huang Di, the "Yellow Emperor," was credited with teaching dozens of essential skills, from leadership to medicine to cooking, including steaming grain and boiling grain to produce gruel or congee, called *zhou* or *mi fan* in Mandarin or *jook* in Cantonese. In fact, mastery of the art of cooking was considered one of the dividing lines between barbarism and civilization. The Book of Rites, attributed to Confucius (551–479 BCE), discusses this crucial difference:

Formerly the ancient kings had no houses. In winter they lived in caves which they had excavated, and in summer in nests which they had framed. They knew not yet the transforming power of fire, but ate the fruits of plants and trees, and the flesh of birds and beasts, drinking their blood, and swallowing (also) the hair and feathers.... The later sages then arose, and men (learned) to take advantage of the benefits of fire. They moulded metals and fashioned clay, so as to rear towers with structures on them, and houses with windows and doors. They toasted, grilled, boiled, and roasted.[9]

In 1554 BCE, a ruler named King T'ang overthrew the Xia Dynasty and founded the Shang Dynasty, which lasted over five hundred years. The Shang were masters of bronze casting; the most impressive artifacts from that era are hundreds of elaborate bronze vessels that were used as receptacles for food—mainly cooked millet and stews—and various kinds of liquor. As the Shang rulers were considered earthly representatives of the celestials, these comestibles were used both as ritual offerings and as food for the aristocratic courts. Later court annals even record the history of Yi Yin, a Shang Dynasty cook who rose to become a regional governor under King T'ang. Yi Yin is most famous for his discourse on the culinary arts in which he says that the cook's principle role is to overcome the offensive odor of raw meats. This is done by properly blending the five flavors—salty, bitter, sour, hot, and sweet—and using fire and water:

> The transformations in the cauldron are so utterly marvelous and of such subtle delicacy, the mouth cannot put them into words, and the mind cannot comprehend them. They are like the subtlety of archery and charioteering, the transformations of the *yin* and the *yang*, and the cycle of the four seasons. Thus, the food is cooked for a long time but is not ruined, well-done but not over-done, sweet but not sugary, sour but not bitter, salty but not briny, hot but not biting, bland but not insipid, fat but not lardy.[10]

The raw materials that go into Yi Yin's massive bronze cooking vessels were far more diverse than such Shang staples as millet, pork, and dog meat. He lists all the delicacies found both within the realm of Shang and outside its borders, including orangutan lips and yak tails, and such fantastic foods as phoenix eggs and the six-legged vermilion turtle with pearls on its feet. The moral of his discourse is that the art of cooking is similar to the art of governing. In fact, the bronze cauldron, or *ting*, is the main symbol of state power. If King T'ang applies the different powers of a ruler as a chef blends flavors, and he follows the way of Heaven, he will then enjoy all those rare and wondrous foods. This list of food shows that the Chinese from the earliest era had a fascination for the broadest range of possible foods—everything edible that could be grown, traded for, or gathered from the wild.

During the Zhou Dynasty, from 1100 to 256 BCE, the food of China began to take on a form we would recognize today. The first Zhou rulers condemned their Shang predecessors for their decadence and overindulgence in fermented beverages. This asceticism eventually gave way to more hedonistic habits as the central government weakened under a succession of ineffectual emperors. In the Zhou court, it is estimated, 2,300 people worked in cooking and food preparation. During the latter half of Zhou rule, the troubled times known as the Spring and Autumn Period and the Warring States Period were eras of cultural ferment and creativity. Confucius and Laozi, the founder of Daoism, lived during

Figure 3.1. Bronze cooking vessel from the Shang Dynasty, c. 1600–1046 BCE. Used for both rituals and banquets, these vessels symbolized state power.

these centuries, and the first great annals and compendia of ritual behavior were written. A theme in many of these writings is food—its proper preparation, consumption, and ritual use. Confucius wrote: "with coarse rice to eat, with water to drink, and with a bent arm for a pillow, there is still joy. Wealth and honor achieved through unrighteousness are but floating clouds to me."[11]

Both ancient literature and archaeological excavations tell us that in North China the five staple grains were panicum millet, setaria millet, wheat (originally from the Near East), soybean (actually a legume), and rice. Rice alone clearly dominated south of the Yangzi River. After the hulls (or soybean pods) were removed, these staples probably were boiled or steamed until soft and fluffy or until they turned into runny porridge like modern-day congee. These grains were also mixed with water and flavorings and fermented to produce a wide variety of beer-like alcoholic drinks that commoners and rulers alike enjoyed. The technology of milling flour was in its infancy, so noodles, breads, and dumplings were almost unknown. In the Zhou Dynasty ritual literature, the high-status grain is clearly millet, nutty in flavor and rich in protein and vitamins, as is indicated by the name of the dynasty's founder, Hou Ji, or "Lord Millet," who brought this crop to his people:

> He sent down cereals truly blessed,
> Both black millet and double-kernel millet;
> Pink-sprouting millet and white;
> Black and double-kernel millet spread all over,
> And he reaped many an acre.
> Pink-sprouting and white millet spread all over,
> Carried on his back, carried over his shoulder.
> He brought them home and inaugurated the
>   sacrifice.[12]

From the dawn of Chinese civilization, it was a primary task of kings and emperors to make sacrifices to ensure the continued harmony of the universe. The invisible forces of the universe—gods, spirits, and ancestors—needed to be fed. These rites continued through the nineteenth century, when the Qing emperors annually made the Grand Sacrifice at the Altar of Heaven. Spotless oxen, sheep, and deer were ritually slaughtered, while the palace chefs prepared the rarest rice and millet, crystalline soups, cooked meats, tempting pickled vegetables, and fragrant grain wines to be placed on the altar in the hope that the God of Heaven would accept the offering. If he did, then the emperor's divine mandate was renewed, and the universe would continue on its correct course for another year. People also offered prepared foods, fruit, wines, and liquor at their household altars, at temples on festival days, and at rituals marking major life events like weddings and funerals, to ensure luck, longevity, wealth, and progeny. After some ceremonies, the people ate the food—the spirits' sustenance was the sights and smells of the offering; after others, the food was ritually burned or simply discarded. Just before Chinese New Year, it was (and still is) customary to place sweet offerings before the image of the Kitchen God, one of the main household deities, and smear his lips with honey so he won't tell Heaven of any sins the family has committed. In the nineteenth century in California, Chinese people covered the graves of the dead with treats like roast pig, fruit, and bread; after local (non-Chinese) drunkards and urchins began to raid cemeteries for a free meal, the Chinese buried the spirit food with the dead. Today, most Chinese Americans who perform these funerary rituals bring the food home afterward for consumption.

The Chinese also treated food as medicine. Meals were structured so as to maximize the health benefits (beyond simple nutrition) to all parts of the human body. The Chinese saw the universe as a series of microcosms and macrocosms, each reflecting and responding to the others. As the legendary Yellow Emperor wrote, "Heaven is covered with constellations, earth with waterways, man with channels."[13] Illness was understood to be the result of one's being out of balance with the basic forces of the universe. Food therapy was one of the ways of returning the body to harmony with these forces. The Yellow Emperor again: "The five grains act as nourishment; the five fruits from the trees serve to augment; the five domestic animals provide the benefit; the five vegetables serve to complete the nourishment. Their flavors, tastes and smells unite and conform to each other in order to supply the beneficial essence of (life)."[14] After the doctor made his diagnosis—usually by taking the patient's pulse—he prescribed a specific culinary regimen. Each food and flavor was classified according to how it affected the organs, which depended on the balance of yin and yang and a complicated system of energy flows. Today, the highly refined system of Chinese food therapy is often used in conjunction with Western medicine. This therapy also forms the basis of the Chinese meal's primary organizing principle: the careful balance of flavors and ingredients.

In imperial mythology, South Chinese rice was long considered a second-class grain. The rice-growing regions from the Yangzi watershed south to Guangdong were subjugated during a series of military campaigns by the Qin and Han Dynasty emperors beginning in 221 BCE. The imperial officials who took control of this area did their best to erase all southern religious cults centered on rice; southerners were instructed to make offerings not to Lord Rice but Lord Millet when observing fertility rites. Southern rice farmers supported a huge population using much less land than did millet and other northern crops. These farmers had developed a highly sophisticated growing system based on advanced irrigation networks (complete with water pumps), diked fields, and crop rotation, planting rice in summer and wheat in winter. With the introduction of quick-growing Champa rice from Vietnam in 1012 CE, this system became even more productive; farmers could then produce two rice crops a year. When the Jurchen tribesmen captured most of North China in 1126 CE, these rice fields also fed millions of fleeing northerners. The imperial capital was relocated to Hangzhou, well south of the Yangzi, where officials realized how much they owed to rice. The trade in rice became one of China's most important; from then on, rice was inextricably connected with the qualities of what might be called "Chinese-ness." With official approval, artists and poets created works praising the virtues of rice farming that were widely circulated.

Confucius didn't restrict himself to cooked grains, or *fan*. All but the poorest Chinese supplemented their *fan* with *cai*—a word that encompasses any meat, vegetables, or aquatic creatures that are eaten with grain. In fact, the *fan-cai* combination became the most basic building block of Chinese cuisine—without both grain and a little protein or vegetable for a topping, one did not have a meal. In Shanghai, *fan-cai* could mean a bowl of rice topped with pickled mustard greens and mixed pork; in Beijing, it could include spicy wheat noodles cooked with Chinese cabbage. The most common *cai*, especially for rural peasants, was (and still is) a vast array of vegetables. The highly nutritious plants of the *Brassica* genus—that is, hundreds of types of Chinese cabbage, radish, turnip, and mustard, are still found in nearly every kitchen across China, where cooks find a use for nearly every part, from root to flower. Americans who visited the Middle Kingdom in the nineteenth century noticed the preponderance of *Allium*, the onion genus, which also includes leeks, scallions, and garlic, and its "pervasive" smell in Chinese cooking. The most common native root or tuber plants were lotus (whose seed was also used), water chestnuts, and taro (generally deemed a famine food). The tender shoots of various varieties of bamboo have been considered delicacies fit for the most aristocratic tables going back millennia. Soybeans, on the other hand, were most often cooked for peasant gruels until the technology to produce tofu was developed—probably during the Han Dynasty (206 BCE–220 CE). The other important bean—the red bean (known as the azuki in the United States)—was used as a fermented seasoning and in sweet desserts. Varieties of the muskmelon (*Cucumis melo*), with their sweet meat and their seeds, were treated more as a fruit. Winter melons (*Benincasa hispida*), also known as wax gourds, were used to make the savory soups and stews that frequently appear at Chinese banquets. While not strictly speaking vegetables, an immense variety of mushrooms and other fungi were put to similar use in Chinese kitchens. Finally, edible seaweeds were often used to season soup, particularly along the South China coast. Today, the typical fare in South China is a bowl of rice topped with some kind of cooked *Brassica* and tofu.

Although a meal with meat as the primary food, as in an American steak dinner, is unthinkable in traditional Chinese cuisine, the Chinese do season their grain foods with cooked meat when circumstances permit. In Zhang and Zhou Dynasty China, the six principal livestock were chickens, cattle, sheep, pigs, dogs, and, less frequently, horses. Cattle and oxen were used as draft animals and were eaten by humans and gods alike; as these were the most important sacrificial animals in ancient imperial rites, beef was likely the high-status meat at this time and certainly during the Han Dynasty that followed. Sheep, first domesticated in the Near East, were the other main pasture animal in North China, where mutton and lamb remain popular meats today. Domestic pigs, which need far less land to survive and were typically housed in the farmstead's garbage pit, were probably the principal meat source across China since early Neolithic times. From nose to tail, pork remains the most popular meat by far. The other early domesticated animal, the dog, was eaten by both emperor and commoner in ancient times, and special breeds of dog are still raised for their meat today, but the dishes are expensive and now mostly reserved for gourmets. The only fowl on this list, chicken, may have been first domesticated in China around 5500 BCE; by the Zhou era, even the poorest farms across China had them. Beyond the farmyard, anything that flies, creeps, or walks has been cooked on Chinese stoves, from ducks and geese to insect larvae, from snakes and lizards to the rarest of wild game, including monkeys, bears, and the elusive (and now nearly extinct) South China tiger.

The omnivorous Chinese also turned to their rivers, lakes, and seashores for the *cai* that supplemented their grain food. Remains of fishing nets made from twisted fibers and bone fish hooks have been found at sites tens of thousands of years old. Carp, the most important freshwater protein source, came to symbolize good fortune and abundance; the colorful varieties known as koi and goldfish were often also kept for ornamental display. For the emperor, the choice fish was the sturgeon, which was reared at the imperial fish farms. Indeed, the Chinese were probably pioneers of aquaculture; they developed sophisticated techniques to trap, breed, and harvest many types of freshwater fish. Along the coast, particularly in the South, the variety of saltwater fish was staggering; in the nineteenth century, Europeans said that in Macau you could eat a different fish every day of the year. The most popular amphibians were frogs, and among the aquatic reptiles, softshell turtles (another symbol of longevity), which were often served in elegant soups at imperial banquets. Archaeological evidence also shows that from a very early date, the Chinese considered many types of crustacean and mollusk, and probably jellyfish, suitable for their tables.

Native fruits have always had an important place in Chinese culinary culture. The Chinese people long associated succulent peaches with longevity, believing that they were the main sustenance of the Celestial Immortals, including the supreme Jade Emperor himself. While the Japanese often add pickled and salted fruits to their rice bowls, the Chinese are more likely to eat fruit as a snack, as dessert, or at the beginning or end of a formal banquet. Peaches have been part of the East Asian diet for at least seven thousand years, and peach trees, fruits, and blossoms are common subjects in Chinese painting. Their close relations plums, Chinese apricots (*Prunus mume*), and apricots (*Prunus armeniaca*) also have an ancient history in China. During the Zhou Dynasty, Chinese apricots were added to soups and stews to provide both thickening and tartness. Apricots were also the source for pickles, plum wine, and the plum sauce that was used as a condiment. Jujubes (Chinese dates), a sweet native fruit grown widely in the North, were eaten as snacks, made into tea, and cooked in a number of sweet dishes, including the Eight Treasure Rice served at Chinese New Year. The crisp, juicy Asian pear (*Pyrus pyrifolia*) and the Chinese persimmon (*Diospyros kaki*) have long been popular. Today, the most common fruit offering is probably the mandarin orange, often served in South China because its Cantonese pronunciation sounds like *gum*, the Cantonese word for "gold." Many other kinds of citrus are native to South China, including kumquats, pomelos, perhaps even both sweet and sour oranges. This area is also home to such succulent tropical and subtropical fruit as longans, loquats, and lychees, which the imperial concubine Yang Guifei

(719–756 CE) loved so much that she had them shipped by speedy messengers to her palace in North China.

Although the Chinese did have contacts with the outside world before the Han Dynasty, their cooking ingredients and tastes were almost all native-grown. The expansion of the Silk Road and the initiation of trade with the kingdoms of Central Asia, India, and Persia stimulated culinary exchange. The caravans that carried silk and other precious goods west brought back cucumbers, pomegranates, carrots, walnuts, pistachios, coriander, green peas, spinach, and dates. The trade routes across the seas and over the mountains of Sichuan led to the introduction of South Asian spices; most important were black pepper, cardamom, and nutmeg. Portuguese merchants carried new ingredients from the New World to India and Southeast Asia, and these were brought by boat or caravan to China. Maize (corn) and sweet potatoes became known as peasant foods and livestock feed (sweet potatoes are also now a popular street snack); peanuts, tomatoes, and particularly chili peppers gained more widespread acceptance. Today, the regions that lie along the main mountain trade route—Sichuan and Hunan provinces—have the highest chili pepper consumption of China.

In ancient China, the proper preparation of grains, vegetables, meats, and fruits was a topic that concerned emperors and poets as well as cooks. Confucius held very firm ideas about how his meals should be prepared:

His rice is not excessively refined, and his sliced meat is not cut excessively fine. Rice that has become putrid and sour, fish that has spoiled, and meat that has gone bad, he does not eat. Food that is discolored he does not eat, and food with a bad odor he does not eat. Undercooked foods he does not eat, and foods served at improper times he does not eat. Meat that is improperly carved, he does not eat, and if he does not obtain the proper sauce, he will not eat.... He never dispenses with ginger when he eats. He does not eat to excess.[15]

Rice, millet, and other grains were most often cooked by steaming. Archaeologists have found ceramic steamers—three-legged cooking pots into which fit pots with perforations in the bottom—dating back seven thousand years. In the millennia before stoves were invented, the pot's legs allowed it to be put directly over the open fire. Bamboo steamers, today found in nearly every Chinese kitchen, appeared around the time of the Song Dynasty (960–1279 CE). For millennia, Chinese chefs likely used steaming and boiling most commonly as their methods of cooking vegetables.

Many of the important texts of the Zhou and Han dynasties address the proper preparation of meat, poultry, fish, and other seafood. Large animals had to be butchered before they were fit for the stove; this task could be elevated to an art form:

> Ting, the butcher of King Hui, was cutting up a bullock. Every blow of his hand, every heave of his shoulder, every tread of his food, every thrust of his knee, every sound of the rending flesh, and every note of the movement of the chopper, were in perfect harmony—rhythmical like the *Mulberry Grove* dance, harmonious like the chords of the *Ching Shou* music.[16]

Next the meat had to be cut, a step so important that food preparation was sometimes called "cutting and cooking." We can guess that it was already the rule that meats be brought to the table chopped or sliced—the emperor would never have to wield a knife to eat his food. Steaming, boiling, and poaching were used to cook some kinds of animal flesh, particularly young chicken and fish. Chefs used the slow boil, or simmer, to prepare soups and particularly the rich, complex stews that had been favorite dishes since Shang times. Meats also were braised, grilled, or shallow-fried in a pan using a little animal fat. Beef tallow and lard, as well as lamb and dog fat, were all thought to contribute distinctive flavors to a dish. The ancient Chinese did not use deep-frying and stir-frying; there simply wasn't enough animal fat available to make these possible. The technology of pressing oil from seeds—sesame, hemp, perilla, and others—was developed during the Tang Dynasty (618–907 CE); by the Song Dynasty, vegetable oil had become one of the necessities of Chinese life. Meat or poultry also could be parched (heat-dried), roasted, broiled, baked in clay, or skewered and cooked over open flames.

The Shang Dynasty chef Yi Yin, in addition to discussing raw ingredients and cooking methods, describes the third component of the best cooking as the focus on the relationship between flavors and textures. In a properly prepared dish, all five of the basic flavors—bitter, sour, sweet, pungent, and salty—should be present, to greater or lesser degrees, often depending on the season, but always in harmony with each other. According to Yi Yin, the bitter flavor comes from various herbs, the sour from fruit or vinegar, the sweet from malt sugar and honey, and the salty from salt. The pungent was, and is, a little more complex: it refers to the group of flavors that is sharp, stinging, or biting to the tongue and olfactory receptors. Chili peppers were unknown in ancient China; the prime sources of pungency were leeks, scallions, shallots, ginger, garlic, Chinese cinnamon (cassia), and dried Sichuan pepper (also called *fagara* in the West)—not actually a pepper but a tiny citrus fruit that produces a pleasant (and addictive) spicy yet numbing sensation in the mouth. Yi Yin also recognizes that fat adds both a taste and a texture to a dish that must be balanced. If a stew contains too much grease, it won't feel right in the mouth. Today, Chinese cuisine is one of the few that recognize the importance of texture at the table. Besides an array of ingredients and flavorings, the dishes must contain a variety of textures, from slippery to crunchy to gummy.

Although the ancient Chinese limited their flavor pantheon to five, they clearly recognized the importance of a sixth taste, savoriness, also known by the Japanese term *umami*. This flavor comes from naturally occurring glutamates and other compounds found in meats, mushrooms, aged cheese, and some fermented products. From the Shang Dynasty on, Chinese chefs added to their dishes a wide variety of preserved condiments, including pickles, marinades, and sauces, to heighten their savory qualities. These concoctions were essential components of meals from the imperial level on down. Simple pickles, made from vegetables, salt, and water, were probably the earliest of these preserves, but these only added saltiness. By the time of the Zhou Dynasty, the Chinese had become masters at fermenting foods, a process which not only preserves the foods but intensifies their savory qualities. The active agent of this fermentation was a moldy grain that was added to jars of cooked meat, fish, vegetables, and various kind of seafood and sometimes mixed with wine; the whole was aged until it became a savory compound that could range in texture from chunks in sauce to a thin liquid. Clear evidence for the production of soy sauce, or *jiang you*, doesn't appear until at least the late Song Dynasty a millennium later, but jars of fermented beans and bean paste discovered in Han Dynasty tombs point to earlier tastes for fermented soybeans. By the eighteenth century, fermented meats and vegetables (though not pickles) had largely disappeared from Chinese tables and were replaced by fermented soybeans, soy paste, and soy sauce, now the ubiquitous seasoning of Chinese cuisine. Nonetheless, the descendants of the ancient fermented compounds live on in the many kinds of fermented fish sauce found across Southeast Asia.

The kitchens where the ancient art of Chinese cuisine was practiced could range from the vast culinary complex that served the emperor to the corner of the peasant's hut. By the time of the Han Dynasty, the *zao* (cooking stove) had replaced the open fireplace. A large rectangular box usually made from various types of brick, the *zao* is about three feet high and four feet wide, with a chimney rising from the back. In the top are two large holes into which fit the large, round-bottomed pottery (and later iron) cooking pots, today called *guo* (Mandarin) or *wok* (Cantonese). The rounded base of the wok allows cooks to use the absolute minimum of precious oil and firewood for stir-frying—an important feature for the Chinese peasant—but these pots can also be used for frying, boiling, steaming, cooking rice, and preparing soup. The pots' bottoms are suspended over an open, wood-burning fire that is contained inside the stove and is regulated by a hole in front. Efficient and perfectly suited to the high heat needed for Chinese cooking (particularly stir-frying), the *zao* is still used across China. You may see updated, gas-fired versions of it, with holes for the woks replacing the familiar burners, in many Chinese restaurants in the United States.

By the end of the Han Dynasty, many of the fundamental tenets of Chinese cuisine had been established; but it is important to remember that none of this was set in stone. The story of Chinese food, like any great cuisine, has always been one of constant change and evolution—with an occasional revolution. One revolution occurred during the Han period, when rotary mills for grinding grain became widespread in the North. For millennia, the Chinese had milled their grains using saddle querns, slightly convex stones on which grain is crushed by hand with a cylindrical stone. A quern was probably used to prepare the millet flour that was used to make the four-thousand-year-old noodles, the world's oldest, recently discovered in a pot at the Lajia site on the Huanghe River in northwestern China. Millstones were unknown across southern and central China, because rice is soft enough not to need grinding; it is merely husked and then steamed or boiled.

Another revolution happened as the Han era concluded. In the North, farmers had long grown small amounts of wheat and ground it into flour to extract its nutrients. The revolution began with the kneading of wheat flour with water and encompassed a world of new dishes made from this preparation, known as *bing*: steamed breads, grilled flatbreads, noodles, and probably some kinds of dumpling. These dishes were so delectable that they inspired Shu Xi (c. 264–304 CE), a court poet, to compose his famous "Ode to *Bing*," including these lines:

Flour sifted twice,
Flying snow of white powder,
In a stretchy, sticky dough
Kneaded with water or broth, it becomes shiny.
For the stuffing, pork ribs or shoulder of mutton,
Fat and meat in proper proportion,
Cut into small bits,
Like gravel or the pearls of a necklace.
Ginger roots and onion bulb
Are cut into a fine julienne,
Sprinkled with wild ginger and cinnamon ground
    fine,
Boneset and Szechuan pepper,
All mixed with salt and seasonings,
Blended into a single ball....

To dip them into a black sauce,
We grip them with ivory chopsticks;
Back stretched tight like a tiger waiting in ambush,
We sit close, knee against knee, flank against flank.[17]

From rural villagers to emperors, the taste for *bing* was apparently universal in early medieval China. *Bing* makers sold their products from boats, and vendors hawked steamed breads and noodle soups on the streets. Among the offerings were *mantou*—now, simple steamed breads; then, stuffed with chopped, seasoned meat. According to legend, they were invented by a general who had been told that in order to assure victory he must offer the head of a sacrificial victim to the gods. He fooled them by concocting a head-shaped loaf of steamed bread stuffed with meat and painted with a human face. Today, similar meat-stuffed dumplings are found from Turkey (*manti*) to Korea (*mandoo*). In China, large steamed stuffed breads are now known as *baozi*. Another popular *bing* was wonton, a meat or vegetable dumpling enclosed in a thin wrapping. In Cantonese, the word *wantan* is written as "cloud-swallowing," while the Mandarin term *huntun* means "chaos," referring to the primordial state before the separation of Heaven and Earth. Both terms aptly invoke the sight of airy, white dumpling wrappings billowing in a bowl of soup. In 1959, archaeologists unearthed dehydrated wontons from a Tang Dynasty tomb in the Sinkiang desert; they also found ancient versions of *jiaozi*, dumplings with slightly thicker wrappings that are still a favorite snack across northern China. As the Chinese became more adept at working with wheat flour, they discovered that they could separate its starch from its gluten by washing. Tender, white, and flavorful, cooked gluten became a favorite delicacy with many culinary uses. Buddhists mixed gluten with mashed roots and flavorings to give it a texture remarkably like meat; wheat gluten "beef," "duck," "chicken," and "fish" became mainstays of Buddhist vegetarian meals.

During the Tang Dynasty, the world of *bing* underwent a lexicological division. Fried, baked, or steamed breads and boiled dumplings remained *bing*, but noodles became *mian*. Lacking the hard durum wheat of western Asia, the Chinese concentrated on making fresh noodles for eating immediately rather than dried noodles for storage. These included *mian* made from rolling dough into ropes, cutting sheets of it into strips, or pushing very soft dough through the holes of a sieve into boiling water. Over the century or two that followed, *mian* grew in importance from a beloved snack into the full-fledged basis of northern Chinese meals. Bowls of noodles, either dry

Figure 3.2. Two kinds of steamed dumplings, with either meat or vegetable fillings. Dumplings have been part of the Chinese menu for well over a millennium.

or in broth, were topped with all kinds of meat, seafood, and vegetables and slurped down with chopsticks. When invaders from the north and west overran northern China, beginning in the twelfth century, noodle-making technology was carried down to the Yangzi basin and then all across the South. (Marco Polo did not carry this knowledge back to Italy, where they had already been making fine noodles and lasagna for centuries.) Unfortunately, wheat didn't flourish in the warm, moist South, so the region's *mian* makers experimented with making noodles from rice and various kinds of roots and legumes, most notably mung beans, the basis of *fen si*, or cellophane noodles. To improve the flavor, eggs were added to wheat noodle dough around 1500 CE—perhaps the last great innovation in Chinese dough cookery before a Taiwanese businessman in Japan invented instant noodles in 1958.

Another great revolution began with the invention of the first fermented drinks. Although Confucius extolled the virtues of water, it's clear that the favorite beverage of the ancient Chinese was wine fermented from grains. They mastered the fermentation of sauces and pickles early on; likewise the complicated art of brewing this wine. Mixing boiled millet, rice, or wheat with sprouted grain (to add sugar from the malt), water, and a special "ferment" made from moldy grain that added the necessary yeast to turn the sugar into alcohol. They aged and filtered the resulting liquid to produce a fairly strong, flat drink—more like wine than beer—that was usually drunk warm in small cups. It was by no means the only beverage—people drank parched grain tea (like barley tea), fruit drinks, water in which grain had been boiled, a kind of sour milk, and perhaps even distilled liquors—but wine was certainly the most celebrated. Today, the Chinese still enjoy their rice wine, particularly at banquets, but the primary mealtime drink is now quite different.

During the Han Dynasty, a new thirst-quencher appeared, originating in the Sichuan basin: tea or *cha*, brewed by boiling in water the fresh leaves of the tropical and subtropical bush *Camellia sinensis*. Tea's flavor was first appreciated along the Yangzi basin and south of it; in the North, Buddhist monks, who noticed that drinking tea helped keep them awake during long periods of meditation, spread its use. The virtues and rituals of tea drinking were promoted by Lu Yu's eighth-century work *The Classic of Tea*, which gave the elite precise instructions on how to enjoy the brew (an art that lives on in the Japanese tea ceremony). By the time of the Yuan Dynasty (1271–1368 CE), tea drinking had spread to the lower classes, becoming one of the "seven necessities" of everyday Chinese life. (The others were fuel, rice, oil, salt, soy sauce, and vinegar.) This is not the place to enumerate the many varieties of tea or the new means for processing the leaf that were developed from the Yuan Dynasty on. Suffice it to say that by the seventeenth century, when tea first appeared in western Europe, tea had become the universal drink of China and one of the defining characteristics of its civilization. Tea was also one of China's most important exports, as the taste for it brought first the Dutch, then the English, and finally the Americans to trade at Canton.

The chief arena for the display of all the main building blocks of Chinese cuisine, from foodstuffs to theories of health, was the banquet table. Indeed, from the Zhou Dynasty on, the feast was seen as a kind of stage where the participants reaffirmed the correctness and value of Chinese civilization, from the structure of its political and religious life to family relations. In the palace kitchens, chefs followed an encyclopedic rulebook that determined not only the appropriate type of banquet for each occasion but precisely how much food and wine guests of different rank were to be served, the table settings, even the musical entertainment. The Qing emperors preferred Manchu food (boiled pork, wild game, sweet breads, milk products) for their court banquets, offering the top three grades to the gods and deified ancestors as sacrifices. Fourth-grade banquets were served to the imperial family, while envoys from tributary states like Korea were given the honor of fifth- and sixth-grade banquets. Women never mingled with men at these functions; cloistered by traditional Chinese morality, they ate in separate rooms, hidden from anyone who wasn't family. Outside the palace walls, government officials and scholars who passed their examinations could enjoy six grades of more familiar Han Chinese banquets. The food served marked each diner's place in the elaborate hierarchy of Chinese life (a system that was disrupted by the arrival of the tall, pale-skinned foreigners who disdained, among other things, Chinese food).

Private banquets also reflected and enhanced social status, but the rules were far looser. Pleasure, in fact, was often the guiding principle—in one's choice of food, grain wine, drinking games, and guests. Menus could include as few as eight or well over one hundred dishes in multiple courses. At lesser events, a group of Chinese merchants staying in nineteenth-century Nagasaki, for example, would order eight-course banquets, for second-class occasions ten courses, and for really important events sixteen courses, featuring fish belly, dried mussels, crab sauce, steamed fish, goose, duck, two kinds of chicken, pigs' feet, fried lamb, sea cucumbers, birds' nests, sharks' fins, deer's tails, and bears' paws.[18] Although Yuan Mei scorned them, these rare delicacies were included to display the host's wealth and sophistication. After all, the ancient Chinese philosopher Mencius had said: "I love fish, so do I bear's paw; but if I cannot get both, I give up fish and take bear's paw."[19] Birds' nests, sharks' fins, and sea cucumbers commonly came from Southeast Asia and in fact comprised the bulk of Chinese trade with that region. All three are notable more for their texture than their flavor (as well as for how much they add to the banquet's cost).

Intimate, shared, low-key, and generally nonalcoholic, the Chinese family meal was the daily counterpoint to the occasional banquet. Depending on the region, this main meal was consumed at midday, in the late afternoon, or at night. Until the twentieth century, men and women usually ate separately, and the men often enjoyed the tastiest, richest morsels. Places were set with cups for tea and bowls for soup and *fan*, along with chopsticks and spoons. In the middle of the table were placed—at the same time, in one large course—the *cai* dishes, including soup, a vegetable, and, if the family could afford it, a meat dish and a fish dish. Everybody shared, using chopsticks to pluck morsels from the serving dishes and place them on their *fan*. Greediness was frowned on; children knew that if they did not clean their bowls, they risked marriage to "a wife (or a husband if you are a girl) with pockmarks on her face, and the more grains you waste, the more pockmarks she will have."[20] These family-style meals were also consumed in many workplaces, including at Chinese restaurants. Today, if you visit a Chinese eatery nearly anywhere in the United States between the end of lunch and the beginning of dinner, you will likely see chefs and wait staff sitting down to a tasty, nutritious, highly traditional Chinese meal.

Restaurants have a very long history in China. At a time when fine food in western Europe was confined to a handful of great monasteries, the Song Dynasty capital, Kaifeng, supported hundreds of commercial food businesses and a rich gourmet culture:

The men of Kaifeng were extravagant and indulgent. They would shout their orders by the hundreds: some wanted items cooked and some chilled, some heated and some prepared, some iced or delicate or fat; each person ordered differently. The waiter then went to get the orders, which he repeated and carried in his head, so that when he got into the kitchen he repeated them. These men were called "gong heads" or "callers." In an instant, the waiter would be back carrying three dishes forked in his left hand, while on his right arm from hand to shoulder he carried about twenty bowls doubled up, and he distributed them precisely as everyone had ordered without an omission or mistake.[21]

Some of the city's restaurants were so renowned that the emperor himself ordered out for their specialties; they could also cater the most elaborate banquets, in their own halls or at the homes of the wealthy. Kaifeng's many eateries also included teahouses where men could sip tea, gossip, and order snacks or full meals, as well as wineshops, which were more popular at night. There, music and singing accompanied wine and food; brothels were often attached to these establishments. Further down the social ladder, workers and poor families could buy their daily food from a huge variety of simple cookshops and street vendors. The offerings included noodles, congees, offal soups, fried and steamed breads, mantou, and many types of sweet and savory snacks. To the poorest, vendors sold boiling water in which they could cook their meager rations.

China's vibrant restaurant culture continued unabated through the end of the Qing Dynasty. The English clergyman John Henry Gray, one of the few Europeans with a serious interest in Chinese food, summed up the typical nineteenth-century urban eatery thus:

The restaurants are generally very large establishments, consisting of a public dining-room and several private rooms. Unlike most other buildings, they consist of two or three stories. The kitchen alone occupies the ground floor; the public hall, which is the resort of persons in the humbler walks of life, is on the first floor, and the more select apartments are on the second and third floors. These are, of course, resorted to by the wealthier citizens, but they are open to persons in all classes of society, and it is not unusual to see in them persons of limited means. At the entrance-door there is a table or counter at which the proprietor sits, and where each customer pays for his repast. The public room is immediately at the head of the first staircase, and is resorted to by all who require a cheap meal. It is furnished, like a *café*, with tables and chairs, a private room having only one table and a few chairs in it.[22]

The upper rooms, generally reserved for the elite, were used for dinner parties and banquets of all sizes. Downstairs, customers could order simpler, less expensive fare, noodle soups and roast meats, for a quick lunch or dinner. All guests, rich and poor, entered the restaurant through the ground-floor kitchen, where they could judge for themselves the skill of the chefs, the quality of the roasted ducks, chickens, and pigs hanging from the ceiling (right above the chopping block), and the facility's cleanliness. When the Chinese immigrated to the United States, they carried this style of restaurant intact to their new homeland.

For more casual dining, the Chinese could choose from a variety of establishments. Teahouses were particularly ubiquitous after the spread of tea drinking to every rank of Chinese society. All of them were important social centers where men, in particular, liked to gather to relax, sip tea, crunch on salted melon seeds, gossip, smoke their pipes, listen to singers or storytellers, and perhaps have a more substantial bite to eat.

In some teahouses, patrons could order and savor rare and delicious teas; in others, mainly in the South and especially in Guangdong Province, the food predominated. Gray wrote of the "tea-saloons" of the type he knew in Guangzhou:

> Each consists of two large saloons furnished with several small tables and stools. Upon each table is placed a tray, containing a large assortment of cakes, preserved fruits, and cups of tea. A cashier seated behind a counter at the door of the saloon receives the money from the guests as they are leaving the establishment. There is a large kitchen attached to all of them, where cooks remarkable for their cleanliness are daily engaged in making all kinds of pastry.[23]

Those pastries were what we now call dim sum, from *dim sam*, Cantonese for "dot heart," an expression roughly equivalent to "hits the spot." As in dim sum parlors today, the bill was totaled by adding up the number and size of the small plates on the patron's table. The Guangzhou teahouses were strictly segregated by sex—no women were allowed— and often featured early morning songbird competitions in which patrons vied to see whose pet could sing the sweetest tune. For those with less time to waste, a popular option was to purchase food from the itinerant street vendors who traveled across cities much as the coffee and lunch trucks in modern America do. The basic equipment of these traveling kitchens was a stove and a provisions chest, suspended on either end of a strong bamboo stick that the chef shouldered from spot to spot. Wherever a hungry-looking crowd gathered, he would stop to vend his inexpensive but filling food in bowls that were wiped clean between every customer. This simple, highly portable cuisine could also be transported overseas to new settlements throughout Southeast Asia and even across the Pacific Ocean.

For at least three thousand years, the basic building blocks of Chinese cuisine remained largely the same: ingredients, cooking methods, tools, flavorings (particularly soy sauce, ginger, and scallions), the *fan-cai* dichotomy, and the interlinked concepts of food and health. Nonetheless, all Chinese did not by any means eat all the same food. For truly "national" dishes, we would have to look to the tables of the elite—the delicacies like sea cucumbers and birds' nests that were served in similar preparations on banquet tables across China—and to the codified menus for official celebrations. At other times and on other tables, regional food preferences were as different as, say, the cuisines of Italy, Germany, England, Spain, and France. During the Ming and Qing dynasties, Yuan Mei and other food writers began to recognize and celebrate the culinary differences among the various regions and cities of China. This topic long fascinated, and bedeviled, Chinese gourmets. (For the sake of simplicity, in the following discussion I limit the

Figure 3.3. A "movable chow shop" in Canton, c. 1919. Street vendors have sold noodles and other staple foods since the Sung dynasty.

main regional cuisines to four, based on the points of the compass—with considerable fuzziness around the edges.)

Northern cuisine was centered on Beijing and the North China Plain. At the time of the Qing Dynasty, millet was still eaten there, but the grain staples were wheat breads and noodles. Mutton and lamb were consumed most widely, often with onions, garlic, or scallions or dipped in vinegar or in sweet and savory sauces. Peking duck, especially roasted and dipped in a savory sauce, may have been the invention of a Yuan Dynasty imperial chef. Beijing dining was also heavily influenced by the food of the Manchu, the dominant tribe whose homeland lay to the northeast. This included dairy products and the roast meats Cushing sampled. Eastern cuisine encompassed a huge stretch of China's richest and most populous territory, perhaps from Shandong all the way down to Fujian. This cuisine was based on fresh and saltwater plants and animals, particularly fish and crabs, flavored with ginger, wine, sugar, and vinegar. Specialties included soups and slow-cooked stews with delicate seasonings. The grain staples ranged from millet and breads in the northeast to rice in the southeast. In treaty ports like Shanghai and Fuzhou, foreign merchants and missionaries tasted these specialties at the homes of wealthy merchants and local officials. In Western cuisine, centered on the inland provinces of Hunan and Sichuan, the food was spicy and oily, often featuring a sophisticated blend of intense flavors. Here rice and noodles were the staples, frequently topped with pork, cabbage, river fish, bamboo shoots, and mushrooms. Americans did not acquire a taste for these highly seasoned specialties for over a century.

The southern cuisine was centered on Guangdong Province, the region that for decades defined Chinese food in American minds. Here the people mainly spoke Cantonese and had a long history of rebelliousness—this was the last part of China

Proper to surrender to the Manchu army. The most important part of Guangdong for this discussion is the Pearl River Delta, home to the cities of Guangzhou, Macau, and Hong Kong. Like the roots of a great tree, the Pearl River's three main tributaries meet in the vicinity of Guangzhou, where they divide into a profusion of narrower rivers, streams, and canals. This mesh of waterways shapes the rich, swampy soils of the larger delta, one of the most fertile regions of all China. The Pearl River itself, the main trunk of this riverine system, forms near Guangzhou and flows south to its wide mouth on the South China Sea. To the west of the Pearl River, human settlement marks every square inch of the delta; even the low hills are dotted with stone and concrete grave markers. In the mid–nineteenth century, the Pearl River Delta was a region of crowded cities, bustling market towns, and thousands of villages, interspersed with fields of green vegetables, orchards, rice paddies, and fish ponds. Water connected almost all these communities; there are so many rivers and streams and canals that travelers observed that roads were almost unnecessary. Rice, vegetables, pork, duck, fish, and shellfish were the staples of the delta diet.

The delta's richest region, Sam Yap, or Three Districts (in Cantonese), which surrounded Guangzhou, consisted mostly of farmlands dotted with smaller cities, towns, and villages. The sophisticated chefs of the provincial capital excelled at seafood, which they prepared as simply as possible, often steaming or gently poaching it. The seasonings were usually soy or oyster sauces, fermented black beans, ginger, and scallions. These chefs also skillfully prepared roast meats, particularly pig and duck, as well as slow-cooked casseroles to be served over rice. In Guangzhou, the tradition of teahouse food reached its apex, with dim sum chefs preparing a vast array of sweet and savory pastry snacks. Outside the city's walls, the land was flat, fertile, and green; truck gardens, rice paddies, and fish ponds, often bordered with lychee trees, surrounded most communities. The regular markets that crowded into most of the cities and towns specialized in fish, fruit (lychees, longans, oranges), herbal medicines, spices, pearls, and silk grown on nearby farms. The nearby town of Shunde was a noted restaurant destination where many Guangzhou gourmets went on eating excursions—and found chefs to staff their private kitchens back in the capital. The next region south, Zhongshan, which was hillier, ran all the way down the western riverbank to Macau. Here the main occupations were rice growing and fishing; thousands of seagoing fishing vessels crowded the narrow channels that connected Zhongshan with the sea.

To the west, the Pearl River Delta graded into the more rugged hills of the poorer Sze Yap (Four Districts) region. Here, the largest towns lay along the Tan River; the most important was the city of Xinhui, the center of a fantail palm–growing district, whose inhabitants manufactured ornate fans for the rest of China and abroad. As in Guangzhou, the people spoke Cantonese, but a local dialect of it that the sophisticated residents of Sam Yap found harsh and hard to understand. Away from the river, the countryside was divided between barren, scrub-covered hills and narrow valleys dense with villages and farms that were connected by well-beaten tracks. In each village, several rows of tightly packed houses faced the valley, where lay the village's fish ponds, water buffalo wallows, rice paddies, and vegetable fields: taro with their giant leaves, beans on trellises, cucumbers, squashes, and gourds. On the hillsides stood the orange, banana, and lychee orchards, as well as the pigpens and manure pits. People's meals centered around *fancai*—bowls of rice topped with a bit of vegetable or fish— or mixed stir-fries, made by throwing a bit of everything one had on hand into the wok. Under the broad branches and thick foliage of the village banyan tree, farm families enjoyed the midday shade, processed rice, and conducted meetings. Here the villagers discussed their most pressing issues: how to sustain one's community and one's clan in a region where people could barely produce enough food to survive, bandits roamed the countryside, and the provincial government was alternately weak and oppressive.

For the villagers of the Sze Yap region, the answer was often to seek their fortunes elsewhere—in Sam Yap, Guangzhou, even overseas. For decades, they had joined emigrants from other parts of the South in seeking better conditions elsewhere in Southeast Asia. In 1848, the people of the Four Districts heard of a new and more alluring place of opportunity—across the Pacific Ocean. They would come to call it Gold Mountain.

Chinese Gardens on Gold Mountain

K icking up a cloud of dust and dung, a train of carriages pulled up to the entrance of the four-story Occidental Hotel, San Francisco's finest hostelry, to await the distinguished guests from the East. At six o'clock in the evening, they emerged: Schuyler Colfax, U.S. Speaker of the House; William Bross, lieutenant governor of Illinois; and Samuel Bowles and Albert Richardson, two noted newspapermen intent on publicizing the promise of the American West. They were escorted into the carriages by the evening's Committee of Invitation, a phalanx of the city's white elite, and the procession clattered off toward a destination just a few minutes away. In the heart of the city, where in 1865 few buildings were more than twenty years old, 308 Dupont Street stood out—a gaudy assemblage of balconies, banners, colored lanterns, and signs bearing the words "Hong Heong Restaurant." Here the carriages stopped; their passengers alighted and were ushered through the first-floor kitchen, where the chefs bowed to them, and then up the stairs. In the third-floor reception room, they met their hosts, San Francisco's leading Chinese merchants and the heads of the six main Chinese associations, commonly called the Six Companies. At least sixty men crowded into the room, half of them Chinese and half European Americans. Their dress and appearance were a study in contrasts: the Chinese dignitaries wore loose robes of blue and purple satin, richly embroidered, and silk skullcaps; their faces were smooth and their foreheads shaven, with long plaited queues hanging neatly down their backs. The Americans were dressed in dark woolen jackets, vests, and trousers; black bow ties and white shirts; trimmed beards and moustaches covered their faces; their thick, unruly hair was plastered across their foreheads. After a round of drinks from a table crowded with American and European liquors, a servant announced "The poor feast is ready," and the guests descended to the second-floor dining room.

Everything there had been imported from China—tables, lamps, decorative screens, and place settings. Ornate partitions decorated with colored glass divided the room into three sections, each enclosing three or four circular tables. Six or seven places were set on each table, with ivory chopsticks and porcelain spoons, bowls, plates, and cups; little dishes for soy sauce, mustard, pickles and sweetmeats; and a large Chinese-style flower centerpiece in the middle. Colfax, the guest of honor, was seated next to the head host, Chui Sing Tong of the Sam Yap Company; the other diners took their seats, and the procession of dishes began. Bowles noted: "there were no joints, nothing to be carved. Every article of food was brought on in quart bowls, in a sort of hash form."[1] During the first course, he recorded fried shark's fin and grated ham, stewed pigeon and bamboo soup, fish sinews with ham, stewed chicken with watercress, seaweed, stewed duck and bamboo soup, sponge cake, omelet cake,

flower cake, banana fritters, and birds' nest soup. Some of
the Americans mastered their spoons and chopsticks; others
were given forks with which to sample their helpings of "fish,
flesh, fowl and vegetable substances, in a thousand forms
undreamed of to French cooks and Caucasian housewives
generally."[2] A journalist from the *Chicago Tribune* liked the
shark's fin and ham—"a nice nutty flavor quite pleasant to
taste"—and the bird's nest soup—"which I assure you *is*
a delicacy." Bowles was not so enthusiastic: "every article,
indeed, seemed to have had its original and real taste and
strength dried or cooked out of it, and a common Chinese
flavor put into it."[3] The tea, however, was delicious and
refreshing.

After anywhere from 12 to 136 courses—the attendees'
accounts differ greatly—the guests retired to the reception
room to smoke, stretch their legs, and say goodbye to the
heads of the Six Companies, who departed. The remaining portion of the dinner was hosted by the dozen or so
leading Chinese merchants. After a "peculiar performance"
by a Chinese musical group, everyone returned to the second floor for round two. The diners refreshed themselves
with cups of cold tea and strong, rose-scented liquor, and
the feast resumed: "lichens and a fungus-like moss," more
sharks' fins, stewed chestnuts with chicken, Chinese oysters
("yellow and resurrected from the dried stage"), another
helping of stewed fungus, a stew of flour and white nuts,
stewed mutton, roast ducks, rice soup, rice with ducks'
eggs and pickled cucumbers, and ham and chicken soup,
according to Bowles. Speeches of welcome and appreciation were exchanged. The party moved to the third floor
again for a "Chinese historical recitative song pitched on
a key higher than Mount Shasta." When they returned,
they discovered that the tables had been set for the dessert
course, which was limited to a huge variety of fresh fruits.

At the end, Richardson made a tally: Governor Bross had tasted every dish; he himself had tried around seventy; and Speaker Colfax had tried forty. "The occasion was curious and memorable. Hereafter, upon every invitation, I shall sup with the Celestials, and say grace with all my heart."[4] The *Tribune*'s reporter wrote: "For myself I shall always esteem myself peculiarly happy having made one with the party, in which there was so much to see and think of, albeit there was not much which we who speak only the Saxon tongue, could understandingly write about." But where was Bowles, who had sampled only about a dozen dishes?

> I went to the restaurant weak and hungry; but I found the one universal odor and flavor soon destroyed all appetite; and I fell back resignedly on a constitutional incapacity to use the chopsticks, and was sitting back in grim politeness through dinner number two, when there came an angel in disguise to my relief. The urbane chief of police of the city appeared and touched my shoulder: "There is a gentleman at the door who wishes to see you, and would have you bring your hat and coat." There were visions of violated City ordinances and "assisting" at the police court the next morning. I thought, too, what a polite way this man has of arresting a stranger to the city. But, bowing my excuses to my pig-tail neighbor, I went joyfully to the unknown tribunal. A friend, a leading banker who had sat opposite to me during the evening, and had been called out a few moments before, welcomed me at the street door with: "B——, I knew you were suffering, and were hungry,—let us go get something to eat,—a good square meal!" So we crossed to an American restaurant; the lost appetite came back; and mutton-chops, squabs, fried potatoes and a bottle of champagne soon restored us. My friend insisted that

the second course of the Chinese dinner was only the first warmed over, and that was the object of the recess. However that might be,—this is how I went to the grand Chinese dinner, and went out, when it was two-thirds over, and "got something to eat."[5]

In the 1860s, the white elites of San Francisco had no taste for Chinese food. Once or twice a year, they attended ceremonial banquets like this one, mainly to promote the business interests they shared with the Chinese merchants. They preferred the comforts and pretensions of the city's best French restaurants. (There, waiters who spoke "French to the American and English to the Frenchman" served them the customary menu of soup, "fish, salad, two or three *entrées*, vegetables, roast, dessert, fruit and coffee, in their proper order and succession.")[6] These men were, however, very familiar with the sight of pigtailed Chinese on the streets. Tens of thousands of Asian immigrants lived in the city, many in the "Chinese quarter" centered on Dupont Street (now Grant Avenue). Whites patronized Chinese peddlers and laundry-men, bought Oriental curios and furniture at the Dupont Street dry goods stores, and did business with the big Chinese merchants like those who attended the Hong Heong banquet. For sixteen years, the whites and Chinese of San Francisco had been living in uneasy, but mostly peaceful, coexistence.

It was gold that brought them together on the Pacific coast of North America. During the first half of the nine-teenth century, occasional Chinese sailors had turned up in the coastal towns. In mid-1848, a rumor had whispered across the Pearl River Delta, first brought by clipper ships to Hong Kong and then spreading to Macau and Guangzhou, that in a place called California, gold deposits lay so thick that a man could dig two or three pounds of the yellow metal in a day! Every clipper brought fresh details about the fabulous find. The news was discussed on the balconies

Figure 4.1. A Chinese restaurant on Dupont Street, San Francisco, in 1869. From the décor to the chopsticks, nearly all of its furnishings would have been imported from China.

of the big European trading firms, in the marketplaces, and even out in the country villages under the banyan trees. People from all nations were flocking to California to make their fortunes. There, prospectors became rich with gold but had nothing on which to spend their wealth. They needed food, tools, blankets, clothing, shoes, wood, and stone for houses; furniture, tableware, ornaments for the fine stores and mansions they would surely build; and, of course, food. Those goods took three months or more to arrive from New York or Boston; from Guangzhou, the journey took less than half the time. In the mines themselves and in the burgeoning city of San Francisco, the gateway to the gold fields, adventurous Chinese saw opportunity. So in early 1849, the first few dozen Chinese embarked for the place they called in Cantonese Gam Saan (Jinshan in Mandarin): Gold Mountain.

Departing mainly from Hong Kong, the Chinese adventurers sailed across the Pacific via Manila and the Sandwich Islands (now Hawaii). When the clippers approached the California coast, the land was usually shrouded in fog, invisible except for a few coastal hills and far-off mountains looming above the white. To arrive at San Francisco, the ships sailed through the strait known as the Golden Gate and turned south into a broad bay. There they found boats from all over the world that had been abandoned by crews eager to find their fortunes in the mountains. As the Chinese were rowed ashore with the other passengers, they had a chance to examine the city, such as it was. At midcentury, San Francisco was mostly a raw assortment of canvas tents and one-story wooden houses connected by muddy streets and sand tracks that led off into the dunes. Three years earlier, this place had been an isolated village named Yerba Buena, population two hundred, occasionally visited by ships looking to load water or cattle hides. Now it was the busiest port on the Pacific coast; every clipper that stopped disgorged passengers and goods. There were no real warehouses, so boxes and merchandise piled up in streets crowded with a motley horde of treasure seekers. They were almost all men, from every state in the East, Oregon Territory, Canada, Mexico, the Pacific islands, Peru, Chile, France, England, Germany, Italy, Turkey, and China. All of them were looking for their best chance. On speculation, many had brought all kinds of commodities, from liquor to East Coast newspapers to mining shovels, which they hoped to unload at exorbitant prices. A ship captain on the Pacific route bought lumber in Guangzhou and hired a team of Chinese carpenters to assemble it into houses in San Francisco. Most of the Chinese who disembarked in 1849, however, were not contract laborers but merchants and adventurers who had purchased their own passage. Like the rest of the crowd on the city's sandy streets, they hoped to become rich in this new country, either in the gold diggings or by opening stores or other businesses, such as restaurants.

San Franciscans possessed a lot of ready gold, and they were hungry. Few of these men had real homes, with wives and servants to work in the kitchen, so they customarily took all three meals in restaurants. A young correspondent for the *New York Tribune*, Bayard Taylor, found the culinary offerings far more diverse than plain American fare. "The tastes of all nations can be gratified here," he wrote.

> There are French restaurants on the plaza and on Dupont Street; an extensive German establishment on Pacific Street; the *Fonda Peruana*; the Italian Confectionary; and three Chinese houses, denoted by their long three-cornered flags of yellow silk. The latter are much frequented by Americans, on account of their excellent cookery, and the fact that meals are $1 each, without regard to quantity. Kong-Sung's house is near the water; Whang-Tong's in Sacramento Street, and Tong-Ling's in Jackson street. There the grave Celestials serve up their chow-chow and curry, besides many genuine English dishes; their tea and coffee cannot be surpassed.[7]

The chief attraction of the first Chinese restaurants in North America was clearly the price—all you could eat for $1.00, in the city where food probably cost more than anywhere else on the planet. Even a dish of steak and eggs and a cup of coffee in some grubby tent down by the docks ran $2.50. Another draw was the professionalism of the Chinese restaurateurs:

> I once went into an eating-house, kept by one of these people, and was astonished at the neat arrangements and cleanliness of the place, the excellence of the table, and moderate charges. It was styled the "Canton Restaurant"; and so thoroughly Chinese was it in its appointments, and in the manner of service, that one might have easily fancied oneself deep in the heart of the Celestial Empire. The barkeeper—though he spoke excellent English—was a Chinese, as were also the attendants.[8]

Despite the décor, these restaurants clearly served both Chinese and western dishes. The Englishman William Kelly wrote that "they give dishes peculiar to each nation, over and above their own peculiar soups, curries and ragouts."[9] Eager for novelty in a city where everything was new and strange, many diners sampled the Chinese side of the menu. William Shaw, another Englishman, reported: "the dishes are mostly curries, hashes, and fricasees, served up in small dishes, and as they were exceedingly palatable, I was not curious enough to enquire as to the ingredients."[10] Unfortunately, the descriptions of the food don't get more detailed than that. The "curries" were likely varieties of minced or diced meats in highly seasoned sauces, while the "fricasees" may have been stir-fries. In any case, it's probable that most diners ordered their dinners from the western side of the menu, where they could find "English food" like mutton chops. In short, the restaurateurs made sure that they served nothing that would shock western palates:

> Do not think, reader, that their larders were furnished as at Hong Kong, or Canton, "with rats and mice,

and such small deer," or that they would compel you to eat rice with *chop sticks*, or that they would cram you with birds' nests. I had the curiosity to try them, the hazard notwithstanding, and found, to my gratification, that the viands were served up in true American style, with knives, forks, spoons, and all the other accessories of the table. Their coffee is excellent, and nothing is deficient but their skill in pastry.[11]

From the crosscultural sophistication of these establishments—and the fact that their staffs spoke English—we can guess that their owners probably learned their trade in Guangzhou or Hong Kong, catering to the European tastes and vigorous drinking habits of foreign merchants. In San Francisco, they found a location where customers' desire for good value and service, as well as sense of adventure, helped some restaurateurs amass modest fortunes.

By 1850, when it was recorded that four thousand Chinese were living in California, some merchants and restaurateurs had already amassed enough wealth to pull up stakes and sail back to the Pearl River Delta. The news of their return, and of the wealth one could acquire in California, sent shock waves through South China, where many caught "gold fever." For every dozen Chinese who returned, hundreds departed. In 1851, about twenty-seven hundred Chinese arrived in San Francisco; a year later, the number was almost twenty thousand. Chinese men, dressed in their distinctive wide straw hats, loose jackets and trousers, and oversize boots, streamed off clipper ships. Each carried his bedroll, clothes, and provisions (mainly rice, dried seafood, and seasonings) in baskets suspended on a bamboo rod. During the first years of the Gold Rush, the Chinese came from all parts of the Pearl River Delta and represented a wide variety of social classes, from merchant to artisan to laborer. Later, the immigrants increasingly came from the poor district of Sze Yap and traveled not as free men but as contract workers destined to work off the prices of their tickets in the mines. After they passed through customs, they were met by agents of the big San Francisco Chinese merchants, who were all associated with the "Six Companies" representing different districts of the delta. Taking the place of the traditional clan associations, the Six Companies mediated disputes, administered punishments, acted as insurance companies and banks, shipped the dead back home, and negotiated relations between their countrymen and the larger non-Chinese community. These merchants had usually already contracted the immigrants' labor to American mine owners, and new arrivals spent no more than a few days in San Francisco before they were transported by river boat, wagon, or foot to the harsh terrain of the gold fields.

In California and eventually the rest of the American West, the mining districts were a scene of intense economic competition. Men were drawn to the region not as pioneers or nation-builders but to get rich as quickly as possible. California's governmental institutions were hastily formed—the state capital moved seven times between 1850 and 1854—and could easily be swayed by big business or mob rule. Violence seethed just below the surface, with drunkenness everywhere. The crime rate was sky-high; the only justice was frequently the vigilante's rope. In the gold fields, American prospectors discovered that they had to contend with foreign miners, particularly the more experienced Mexicans, Chileans, and Peruvians. The Americans' response was to hang a few of the foreign miners on trumped-up charges and expel the rest at gunpoint. Their excuse was that the foreigners were likely criminals, the dregs of their native countries and "innately depraved." The real motive was fear that the foreigners would outdig the "freedom-loving" American miners. At first, few Chinese worked in the mines; then in 1852, over the space of a few months, "the surplus and inferior population of Asia" appeared at every gold field. Concerns rose that the big mine owners would hire masses of Chinese and overwhelm the independent operators. Americans immediately noticed everything that made the Chinese different, from their "chattering" language to the way they wore their hair in queues to what they ate.

> If there is one class of "nasty furriners"...more ill-favored, unfortunate and forlorn among us than another, it certainly must be the Chinese.... They are sunk immeasurably lower than the native Indians, in the estimation of the miners. Lower than the beasts that prey upon the flesh of inferior animals, for the bear it is said, will turn from tainted meat, whereas "John" despises nothing of the creeping or crawling kind. Rats, lizards, mud-terrapins, rank and indigestible shell fish, "and such small deer," have been, and continue to be, the food of the "no ways particklar" Celestial, where flour, beef and bacon, and other food suitable to the stomachs of "white folk" abound.[12]

Echoing this sentiment, the authors of the 1855 *Annals of San Francisco* reported that the "manners of the Chinese are very repugnant to Americans in California. Of different language, blood, religion and character, inferior in most mental and bodily qualities, the Chinaman is looked upon by some as only a little superior to the negro, and by others as somewhat inferior."[13] Newspapers reported that the bill of fare in a San Francisco Chinese restaurant read: "Cat Cutlet, 25 cents; Griddled Rats 6 cents; Dog Soup, 12 cents; Roast Dog, 18 cents; Dog Pie, 6 cents."[14] John Bigler, the governor of California, fanned nativist sympathies in a reelection campaign; he was the first American politician to seize on the anti-Chinese issue, pushing bills to ban contract labor and tax foreign workers. These measures were opposed, with more or less success, by a coalition of merchants (both white and Chinese) and ship owners who saw that the Chinese were good for business, and by missionaries trying to save Chinese souls. Californians' anti-Chinese feelings nevertheless continued to fester, fueled by a series of articles by Bayard Taylor that were widely reprinted in the local papers. (He had already earned renown with his 1850 *Eldorado, or Adventures in the Path of Empire*, one of the earliest accounts of the Gold Rush.)

"Tall, erect, active looking and manly, with an aquiline nose, bright, loving eyes, and the dark, ringleted hair with which we endow, in ideal, the head of poets," Taylor was one of the great Romantic figures of nineteenth-century American literature.[15] He considered himself a poet, worked as a journalist and editor, and gained fame as the first best-selling American travel writer. This was the era of Manifest Destiny, when Americans began to explore their place in the larger world. Combining Romantic adventure with a broad sense of cultural superiority, Taylor's travel writings made him a wealthy man (though his florid poetry did not sell nearly so well). His first travel book, *Views A-Foot*, on Europe, was only mildly overheated; *Eldorado*, his second, was a more straightforward journalistic account of his trip to California and Mexico. He described the various races he encountered in San Francisco without bias, and on his return trip via Mexico befriended the portly, smiling Chinese owner of Mazatlan's Fonda de Canton hotel. In August 1851, Taylor embarked on a journey around the world. On this trip, which he turned into three separate books, he let loose his poetic sensibility. In Syria, for example, he donned a burnoose and a turban, strode through the lowest byways of the native bazaars, and ate "hasheesh," which gave him hallucinations worthy of Coleridge. With his poet's eye, he judged the architecture, music, customs, and, perhaps most critically, the physiques of the peoples he visited. His ideal came straight from the muscular symmetry portrayed in Greek sculpture, which he found in Arabs but not in Africans or the Chinese, whom he first encountered in large numbers in Singapore: "Their dull faces, without expression, unless a coarse glimmering of sensuality may be called such, and their half-naked, unsymmetrical bodies, more like figures of yellow clay than warm flesh and blood, filled me with an unconquerable aversion."[16] He nevertheless continued to China, landing first in Hong Kong and then at Shanghai.

There he found two American missionaries to act as his guides: Charles Taylor (whom we met in chapter 2) and M. T. Yates, both Protestants. They piloted the young writer through the narrow streets of Shanghai's Chinese city, feeding him "explanations of the many curious scenes" they passed. He visited temples, shops, pawnshops, tea gardens, street vendors, and prisons; he was even invited to a Chinese banquet, whose dishes he found "numerous and palatable, but hardly substantial enough for a civilized taste." Overall, he was overwhelmed by the "disgusting annoyances of a Chinese city"—the ever-present filth, ragged beggars, and vile smells. Strangely, the encounter that sent him into his greatest outpouring of revulsion was the "absolutely loathsome and repulsive" sight of a prize Chinese flower at a local horticultural show.

> The only taste which the Chinese exhibit to any degree, is a love of the monstrous. That sentiment of harmony, which throbbed like a musical rhythm through the life of the Greeks, never looked out of their oblique eyes.... They admire whatever is distorted or unnatural, and the wider its divergence from its original

beauty or symmetry, the greater is their delight. This mental idiosyncrasy includes a moral one, of similar character. It is my deliberate opinion that the Chinese are, morally, the most debased people of the face of the earth. Forms of vice which in other countries are barely named, are in China so common, that they excite no comment among the natives.... Their touch is pollution, and, harsh as the opinion may seem, justice to our own race demands that they should not be allowed to settle on our soil.[17]

Taylor's missionary guides undoubtedly drew his attention to all those "forms of vice," probably including female infanticide, gambling, eating dogs and cats, and opium smoking (a practice Taylor himself tried out). Declaring China "the best country in the world—*to leave*," Taylor's widely reprinted travel letters first came out in the *New York Tribune* and then in many editions of his 1855 bestseller *A Visit to India, China, and Japan.* For at least the next three decades, his harsh judgments had an outsized influence on the debate over the place of Chinese immigrants in the United States.

Despite this simmering racism, and occasional outbreaks of violence, the immigrants from the Pearl River Delta were by and large tolerated during the late 1850s and early 1860s. Those who arrived in California during this era were determined to earn their fortunes peacefully and by following the traditions they had long practiced in East Asia. The English adventurer Frederick Whymper, who encountered Chinese in both western Canada and California, writes admiringly of their persistence in keeping their culinary culture:

In the mining districts, "John Chinaman" is to be seen travelling through the country, carrying his traps on either end of a long pole, in the style depicted on the tea chests familiar to us from earliest childhood.

In this manner he "packs" much larger loads than the ordinary traveller. The writer well remembers a Chinaman he met carrying at one end of his stick a bag of rice, a pick and shovel, a pair of extra pantaloons, a frying pan, and a billy-pot [for tea]; whilst from the other depended a coop of fowls and chickens, of which "John" is devotedly fond. In this respect he is wiser than his betters; for while the ordinary "honest miner" is feeding on beans, bacon, and tea, he has eggs and chickens with his rice and is very diligent in searching out and utilising wild onions, berries, and roots. In 1865, a number of Chinamen arrived at intervals, in several vessels, at Vancouver, V.I., and a few hours after landing they invariably found their way into the woods, or on to the sea-beach, where they collected shell fish and many kinds of sea-weed, which they stewed and fried in various shapes.[18]

Before leaving China, the immigrants packed provisions for the journey, including rice, dried seafood and sausages, and ceramic jars of condiments like soy sauce and pickled vegetables. Although these provisions ran out quickly after landing in California, the new arrivals did not have to adopt the local, pork-and-beans-based American diet. By the early 1850s, San Francisco was home to a number of Chinese stores specializing in products from the Middle Kingdom, including "hams, tea, dried fish, dried ducks, and other very nasty-looking Chinese eatables, besides copper-pots and kettles."[19] An 1856 directory of the city's Chinese quarter listed thirty-three stores selling "General Merchandise, Groceries, &c." These merchants ordered their wares either directly from China or from the big import-export firms that were already established—branches of Chinese companies in Guangzhou or, more likely, Hong Kong that became known as *gam saan chung*—"Gold Mountain firms." In 1873, the journalist Albert S. Evans recorded the cargo of a ship whose wares were destined for San Francisco merchants:

> 90 packages cassia; 940 packages coffee, from Java and Manila; 192 packages fire-crackers; 30 packages dried fish, cuttle-fish, shark's fins, etc.; 400 packages hemp; 116 packages miscellaneous merchandise, lacquered goods, porcelain-ware, and things for which we have no special names; 53 packages medicines; 18 packages opium; 16 packages plants; 20 packages potatoes; 2,755 packages rice; 1,238 packages sundries,—chow-chow [probably pickles], preserved fruit, salted melon-seeds, dried ducks, pickled ducks' eggs, cabbage sprouts in brine, candied citron, dates, dwarf oranges, ginger, smoked oysters, and a hundred other Chinese edibles and table luxuries; 824 packages sugar; 20 packages silks; 203 packages sago and tapioca; 5,463 packages tea; 27 packages tin.[20]

This was a culinary bounty that could easily supply a gourmet restaurant like Hong Heong; all they needed to complete their banquets were fresh meat and produce (and even the imported "dwarf oranges," either mandarins or kumquats, may have been fresh). The San Francisco import-export firms either sold the ingredients on this list to local restaurants and groceries or shipped them to Chinese stores in the new settlements that were arising in the foothills. In Chew Lung's store in the Chinese mining camp at Camanche, for example, nearly every item—including the scales, cooking pots, bowls, tobacco, rice, tea, sugar, ginger, and cooking oil—came from across the Pacific. The exceptions were the gin and the salt fish, which may have been a local product.

Immigrants from the Pearl River Delta, with its centuries-old fishing tradition, saw the economic and culinary possibilities of California's rich sea life very early. By 1855, they had built dozens of Chinese fishing villages around San Francisco Bay and along the central California coast. They caught Pacific salmon and squid, collected red, black, and green abalone in the intertidal zone, and netted shrimp, minnows, and other fish. They even built Chinese-style fishing junks from which they tended their nets. Some of the catch was delivered fresh to markets and street vendors for retail sales, but most of it was boiled in salted water and dried. It could then be shipped into the mountains, where the Chinese miners used it to season their rice, or more likely packed for transport back to China, where the appetite for dried seafood was nearly inexhaustible. By the 1850s, it was estimated that roughly a thousand Chinese fishermen were working San Francisco Bay. Their methods were so efficient and the mesh on their bag nets so fine that the other fishermen complained that they were clearing every swimming thing out of the bay. Enforcement of fishing laws was impossible: the Chinese simply paid their fines or did their jail time and then returned to the same practices. One journalist estimated that $1 million worth of dried shrimp and fish—including sturgeon sinews, a Chinese delicacy—was being shipped back to China every year. Despite these complaints, and competition from Italian and Portuguese immigrants, the junks sailed in California waters until the twentieth century, when the large-scale Chinese fishing industry finally dwindled away.

From San Francisco's residential districts to the far-flung mining camps, the Chinese produce peddler was a regular sight on the dusty streets and paths:

> We have Chinese vegetable peddlers, who, braving the vicious boys, wicked men, and ugly dogs, visit every part of the city, and travel far out over the sand-hills to supply their regular customers. These men rise long before daylight and go to the great markets and to

Figure 4.2. A painter's depiction of a Chinese fishmonger with his wares, late nineteenth century. White fishermen complained that their Chinese competitors were stripping San Francisco Bay of all living sea creatures.

the market-wagons, fill their panniers and then return home to breakfast; after which they sally out, each man on his regular route, to return to their lodging-houses about noon with a few more dimes in their pockets than they spent at the market in the morning. It would astonish some persons should they look into a pair of these panniers, to see what a variety of articles they may contain—cabbage, beans, peas, and celery; potatoes, turnips, carrots, and parsnips; apples, pears, and the small fruits; with fish, and *bouquets*.[21]

Much of this produce was grown on the small Chinese garden plots that ringed many communities and on larger farms tilled by Chinese owners or leaseholders. Using skills learned on the intensively cultivated plots of the Pearl River Delta, the immigrants had begun to grow vegetables soon after arriving—at first, the greens were for their own use, as they craved fresh toppings for their midday rice. But as they learned the business, and how to grow food crops in the dry but temperate California climate, they came to dominate this agricultural niche; some writers claimed that their labor fed all of San Francisco.

As in the fishing industry, a cultural clash soon arose over traditional Pearl River Delta farming methods. In Auburn, the "miasmata" arising from Chinese gardens supposedly caused diseases:

> The evil consists mainly in the Chinese mode of cultivation, which is filthy and disgusting in the extreme. Their gardens are made on low grounds, and the soil is stimulated to rank productiveness by the application of the most offensive manures. Large holes are excavated in the ground, which are filled with human ordure, dead animals, and every imaginable kind of filth, water is added, and the feculent mass is left to thoroughly decompose, when it is ladled and scattered broadcast over the garden.[22]

The result of these methods was vegetables that "acquire a richness of flavor grateful to Chinese stomachs, but intolerable to most white palates." In fact, most whites were able to overcome their finer feelings and purchase the familiar corn, squash, peas, tomatoes, lettuce, and the like. The farmers also grew elongated Asian radishes, unfamiliar cabbages, bitter melons, foot-long string beans, and so on, destined solely for Chinese consumers.

Thanks to their imports, as well as farming and fishing, the Chinese of California clearly had the raw materials

Figure 4.3. A Chinese peddler sells fruit and vegetables to a San Francisco housewife. These peddlers were a common sight in western cities and towns.

to replicate even the finest dishes of Cantonese cuisine. In 1853, a writer for the *San Francisco Whig* was "escorted to the crack Chinese restaurant on Dupont street called Hong fa-lo, where a circular table was set out in fine style." This eatery may have been the earliest incarnation of Chinatown's famous Hang Far Low restaurant, at 713 and then 723 Grant Avenue, which finally closed in 1960. The evening's host, a merchant named Key Chong, had spared no expense; birds' nests, sea cucumbers, and mushrooms that cost $3 a pound were among the dishes. The other ingredients included fish, dried oysters, "China lobster," ducks, "stewed acorns," chestnuts, sausages, shrimps, and periwinkles. The whites in attendance were often flummoxed as to what they were eating. According to the newspaper, the menu included "Course No. 2—Won Fo (a dish oblivious to us, and not mentioned in the Cook Book). No. 3—Ton-Song, (ditto likewise). No. 4—Tap

Fan, (another quien sabe)." Despite the author's humorous take, he and the other white guests seem to have genuinely enjoyed their meal:

> We came away, after three hours sitting, fully convinced that a China dinner is a costly and elaborate affair, worthy the attention of epicures. From this time henceforth we are in the field for China against any insinuations on the question of diet a la rat, which we pronounce a tale of untruth. We beg leave to return our thanks to our host, Key Chong, for his elegant entertainment which one conversant with the Chinese bill of fare informs us must have cost over $100. Vive la China![23]

It was rare, but not unheard-of, for non-Chinese San Franciscans to initiate a Chinese banquet. In 1857, four "claiming to be white—one a Maj. U.S. Army—two Capts.— and one legal gentleman" decided to enjoy a "dinner got up in the most approved style of the Celestials, laying aside everything like fastidiousness in regard to material or taste, conforming to, and partaking of, the full course, come as it might, whether fricasseed monkey or baked rats made any part of the bill of fare or not." They invited along Lee Kan, a Chinese newspaper editor who arranged the meal, as well as an important Chinese merchant and the head of the Sze Yap Company. The name and location of the restaurant was not recorded, but it possessed a "sumptuous dining-hall, furnished with all the elegancies and appurtenances believed by the Chinese to be indispensable to such an apartment." The first course would have done justice to a wealthy merchant's kitchen back in Guangzhou and included soups of birds' nest and sharks' fin, "calf's throat cut in imitation of mammoth centipedes," quails, duck feet, fish maws, sea cucumbers, crab balls, and herring heads. The whites attempted to down these delicacies using chopsticks and failed. When they saw that their Chinese guests were way ahead of them, they "felt constrained to resort to knife, fork, and spoon, in self defense." Then, on to the second half of the meal:

> Tea; cake made of rice flour; water nuts, called in Chinese Ma Tai and truly delicious; preserved water lily seeds; pomelo, a kind of orange, preserved; Chinese plums; jelly made from sea-weed; ducks' hearts and gizzards with shrimps; cakes of minced pork and other ingredients of doubtful character; fish gelatine; eggs preserved in ley [thousand-year-old eggs?] and oil—very fine; almonds salted and baked; oranges; preserved water melon seeds; two other kinds of cake made from rice flour; cigars; white wine, made from rice; a third proof liquor made from rice; and finishing off with an opium smoke, and Chinese cigaritas.

Those cakes of "doubtful character" are probably dim sum, which often accompanied Chinese banquets of this magnitude. Three days and nine hours after this unique event, a participant wrote, "We are all alive!" He never indicates whether or not he enjoyed the food, but he does give a warning: the bill was $42, an astronomical sum for post–Gold Rush San Francisco. Nevertheless, he says, it was worth it; the memory, and probably the bragging rights, would "last us as long as we live."[24] Of course, these wealthy diners were an exception. The only Chinese-owned restaurants that most whites entered in post–Gold Rush San Francisco were the myriad cheap cafés where they could chew on a gristly steak or plate of pork and beans, not Chinese food.

During the late 1860s and 1870s, San Francisco had well over a dozen Chinese restaurants, including three or four elaborate, multistory establishments whose chefs could prepare banquets featuring the same costly ingredients and sophisticated preparations used by Guangzhou's finest chefs. These did not draw regular customers from the non-Chinese population, as whites picked up on the sentiments first expressed in the *Chinese Repository* decades earlier, that the dishes were on the whole inedible:

> almost everything has the same taste of nut oil sicklied over all, and few western palates can endure even the most delicate of their dishes. Shark's fins, stewed bamboo, duck's eggs boiled, baked and stewed in oil, pork disguised in hot sauces, and other things like these, are the standard dishes of a Chinese bill of fare, though they have an infinite variety of sweetmeats which are really palatable, and of sweetcakes, which are inviting in their quaint, odd forms and decorations, but are ashes and wormwood to taste.[25]

Moreover, a rumor spread that the chefs used the same unclean methods as the neighborhood Chinese laundrymen:

> In the preparation of sauces he even surpasses Soyer's countrymen. The art with which Chinese washermen regulate the fineness and direction of the spray from his [*sic*] mouth upon the garments, has been a source of admiration to the uninitiated. Their admiration would increase were they to witness the dexterity with which the cook would mix the various condiments by blowing from his mouth the exact quantity needed by the dish before him. Many dishes depend entirely on adjuncts for savor; and the taste as a rule inclines to rancid oil and doubtful lard.[26]

Behind this disgust was more than simple differences in taste. Agitation against the presence of Chinese in the West was growing, and it became politically and socially dangerous to admit to having a taste for Chinese cuisine.

In fact, culinary prejudices were so deep that even those few local whites who supported Chinese rights could not stomach their food. The New York–born Methodist minister Otis Gibson had labored for 10 years in Fujian Province. When he moved to San Francisco to continue his mission, he was shocked at the "ignorance, bigotry, prejudice and selfishness" of the anti-Chinese crusaders, who also targeted missionaries like himself. Although his 1877 book *The Chinese in America* does exhibit old missionary intolerance—"the mass of [Chinese] people are untruthful, selfish and cruel"—he strongly defends the Chinese presence in the American West. His reasons were partly economic (the Chinese were good for business) and partly moral (the Chinese in their sins were no worse than the American masses). Nonetheless, he could not bring himself to enjoy the food, due to the same problematic flavor of "rancid oil or strong butter." Yet when missionary guests from the East arrived, he set aside his culinary objections and showed them the wonders of the Chinese quarter:

> In company with the Rev. Dr. Newman, Mrs. Newman, and Rev. Dr. Sunderland, of Washington City, and Dr. J T. M'Lean, of San Francisco, I once took a Chinese dinner at the restaurant on Jackson Street. Dr. Newman took hold and ate like a hungry man, and when I thought he must be about filled, he astonished me by saying that the meats were excellent, and were it not that he had to deliver a lecture that evening, he would take hold and eat a good hearty dinner. Dr. Sunderland did not seem to relish things quite so well. But Mrs. Newman relishing some of the meats, and failing to get the pieces to her mouth with the chopsticks, wisely threw aside all conventional notions, used her fingers instead of chopsticks, and, as the Californians would say, "ate a square meal."[27]

In nineteenth-century America, the idea of a cultured, Christian lady tossing aside manners to stuff herself with strange pagan food was shocking. Then again, these were visitors from the East, perhaps with more sophisticated ideas of right and wrong.

In fact, tourists often eagerly embraced the experience of eating in the quarter now known as Chinatown. San Franciscans only visited the district if they had to; but visitors from the East and Europe considered it a must-see stop on the city's tourist trail. According to one local correspondent, the typical tourist "wants to see it all":

> He wants to be shocked by the Oriental depravity that he has heard so much about, or if he is one of the large class who believes that the Chinese are a much-maligned race of virtuous and enlightened people, he desires to see for himself that John Chinaman has been libeled.... The great majority indulge in this Oriental "slumming." They come out of it with a confused impression of tortuous alleys, underground dens reeking with the odor of tobacco and opium, and faces so villainous that they haunt one's dreams like the Malay that tyrannized over De Quincey's opium-fed imagination.[28]

To see beyond the facades of the curio shops to the "inside" Chinatown, tourists would hire a local police officer, particularly for nighttime tours of the district's netherworld. The itinerary usually included the Chinese temple, a barber shop, the Chinese theater, a "thieves' lodging house" (where one officer amused visitors by "playfully jerking the long cue of one or two Chinamen he could reach without trouble"),[29] a gambling hall, an opium den, and a restaurant or two.

Paying 5 or 10 cents a meal, the mass of Chinese city-dwellers of modest means found regular sustenance at these eateries, which were usually below street level and furnished with benches and tables that served as beds at night. Typically, the kitchen setup was of the most basic kind, "with its rickety little furnace, lumps of pork frying and sputtering, bowls of rice, square bags of sausage meat, fruit, fresh and dried fish, chop sticks of the approved style, and a general flavor of the cook shop grown old and stale."[30] The tourists would never think of eating at one of these establishments, but they did like to peek into the pots:

> The raw material, so far as we could see with our inexperienced eyes, consisted of the sprouts growing out of potato-eyes, pig's (or dog's) ears pickled, and green leeks. (Now, I don't want to say anything mean against the Chinese; but I do believe that the funny little things we saw at the bottom of a deep earthen jar were rat's-tails skinned).[31]

The local Chinese also ate at their places of work, which were equipped with kitchens and dining areas. The employees of a well-to-do merchant enjoyed the traditional communal meals: "Their meat and vegetables are hashed, or cut into small pieces, and are brought to the table in a common dish, from which each one helps himself with his chopsticks. It is the usual custom to have two meals a day, one about eleven o'clock, and the other late in the afternoon."[32] At the opposite end of the spectrum, the district's poorest residents could buy from street vendors who sold "fish, vegetables, rice-cakes and innumerable nameless Chinese comestibles,"[33] or cooked modest meals on small charcoal braziers set up on balconies or even in apartments, creating one more Chinese threat for nativist agitators to attack.

The other culinary sight on the typical Chinatown tour was one of the fancy, three-story banquet restaurants, like Hong Heong. Sometimes the tourists went in simply to stare at the diners, but more often they actually sat down for a bite to eat:

> Try some of this unbaked biscuit with the red letter painted on top. It is a sort of pallid doughball or dumpling filled with dark and finely cut meat: it certainly does not look edible, and its faint flavor suggests—well, nothing at all: it is entirely negative. Then here is a block of pure white marble two inches square, and on its polished top again the red-painted character: this is fairly artistic in its perfect resemblance to a block of stone with clear-cut edges and sharp corners. It is some preparation of rice flour, about the consistency of stiff jelly or blanc-mange, and is of a pleasantly sweetish taste and fairly good, or at least very unobjectionable as food. We are getting reassured and bold: let us try a sample of this yellow affair. It is round like a biscuit, but a brilliant saffron-yellow in color, with of course the omnipresent red character painted on top. Shut your eyes and bite boldly. Dust and ashes! what can this be? Do they use the sacred dust of their ancestors to feed the barbarian on? Bah! this mouldy medicinal taste, this mouthful of dry yellow ashes, is positively nasty. No more, thank you! and please pass the sweetmeats: let us forget in the familiar taste of ginger this tidbit from the tombs. Finish, if you like, with the dried sweets and the pellucid and cloying syrups: I have had enough, and shall be glad to get out.[34]

What this author is describing, of course, is a meal of dim sum—tea with some savory and sweet snacks. The "pallid doughball" is probably *char siu bau*, a steamed roast pork bun, while the block of "marble" is likely an almond-flavored agar jelly, both mainstays of the dim sum table. The tourists usually tried them once—for the adventure and so they could tell their neighbors back home about it—and then returned to more traditional restaurant fare. For the Chinese of San Francisco, these snacks may have been largely an upper-class pleasure. In 1868, the *Overland Monthly* reported that the "tea gardens and tea halls" of the Middle Kingdom had been replaced by "the restaurant and coffee stand": "These are much frequented on holidays and at evening. But California Chinese are frequently seen calling for the cup of coffee and cigar, instead of the tea cup and the long pipe with the mild Chinese tobacco."[35]

Eventually, a few white San Franciscans swallowed their prejudices and began to frequent a handful of Chinese

Figure 4.4. A lavish San Francisco banquet restaurant, c. 1905, the year before the great earthquake. Tourists visited these eateries for Chinese teas and sweets, not full meals. Tourists drawn to the décor of multi-story banquet restaurants were sometimes tempted to try the food, but it was not until after the 1906 earthquake that Chinese cuisine gained traction with California European-Americans.

restaurants, including Tune Fong's at 710 Jackson Street. What drew them was not food but fine, aromatic Chinese tea: "genuine, delicate, strong as old wine of the cob-webbed vintage of '36. This was what our grandmothers who chinked up their hearts on 'washing-days' with Cowper's 'cup that cheers,' sighed for, and like the ancient leader, died without the sight. It sets tongues running."[36] For local artists under the influence of the Orientalist aesthetic, the ritual of tea preparation was also a ceremony worthy of admiration:

> Watch him as he brings the tea, and learn the only true and proper way to concoct the beverage. First, two little pewter holders, in which the cups are set, and so prevented from tipping; then some tea leaves, I don't know how many or how much; then the cups are filled with boiling, fiery, red-hot water, and covered in a trice with saucers fitting just inside their rims. We stand our cups in saucers; he stands his saucers upside down in the cup. The tea-kettle, though, is a regular copper-bottomed Yankee affair, not particularly pleasing, perhaps, to the aesthetic eye, but encouraging, as a sign of the advance of our Western civilization. After waiting five minutes or so, take the cup with the thumb and second finger, with the forefinger resting on the cover, and tilting it gently, pour the tea—real tea it is—into that other cup standing before you. Skillfully done, you will have a cupful of amber, with the perfume of "Araby the Blest."[37]

(Of course, tea came from East Asia, not the Middle East, but never mind.) Chinese restaurateurs learned that white tea-drinkers had no stomach for the savory side of the dim sum menu. With the beverage, they now only served sweets: ginger chow-chow, candied and pickled fruits, and the like. The repast became more like English afternoon tea, an established part of the European American culinary tradition, than the traditional Cantonese morning snack. Most white San Franciscans did not acquire a taste for any other type of Chinatown meal until after Chinatown itself was transformed in the wake of the great earthquake of 1906 (see chapter 5).

Despite their aversion to the food of China, many white city residents had Chinese cooks in their home kitchens and regularly ate western food prepared by Chinese hands. The average middle- and upper-class household needed servants to clean, wash, shop, deal with tradespeople, and cook. In San Francisco in the 1860s and 1870s, the choice was between Irish and Chinese servants, and most chose the latter: "Irish house-servants demand $25 and $30 per month for chamber-work, cooking, or general housework. The Chinese, who as soon as they learn a little English, are much superior to the Irish as servants, ask $12 to $16."[38] The "Bridgets," as the Irish servants were known, had a reputation for being stubborn and wasteful; the Chinese were considered quick and careful, if a little devious. One housewife found her perfect servant in one Hop Sing. After a little glitch was straightened out (he secretly rented his basement room in the family home to "a goodly throng of unwashed Celestials") he became a trusted servant: "And he was such a cook! Beefsteaks tender and juicy, roasts done to perfection, feathery breakfast cakes, and delicious bread regularly proceeded from his bony yellow hands. His teaspoonful of soda or cream of tartar was judiciously piled to the same height at each baking, and the result was that he could always be depended upon." When he had saved $600, his employer wrote, he planned to return home and "live like a grandee on lizard pies and rat catsup for the rest of his life."[39] One couple with three children had a "white woman" to take care of the upstairs tasks and a Chinese cook in the kitchen, where he prepared "a divine salad, an incomparable lemon pie, and coffee that is a continual temptation."[40] In many households, the work in the kitchen was probably more like this lesson from a phrasebook for Chinese immigrants: "Boil some wa-ter. Boil the rice. Cook the meat. Bake the bread. Make tea. Get some bread. Broil some beef. Fry the beef rare. It is not done yet. It is done. Come to din-ner."[41] We never hear of Chinese cooks preparing their own dishes in whites' kitchens, although they presumably cooked rice and toppings and the like for their own consumption. Nor is there any evidence that white employers were curious about whether their Chinese cooks really ate lizard pie and rat catsup. The stereotype of Chinese food as odd, smelly, and repulsive was so ingrained that no housewife would think of tasting it, even in the privacy of her own kitchen.

San Francisco's Chinese community was North America's largest and most vibrant but by no means the only one in California or in the American West. From the earliest days of the Gold Rush, Chinese immigrants pursued opportunities that took them to some of the rawest and most remote outposts in North America and carried their culinary traditions with them. A provision network that transported foodstuffs, kitchen equipment, and tableware extended from the Pearl River Delta to San Francisco, up to the gold fields via Sacramento or Stockton, and further into the interior. In 1856, the missionary William Speer wrote that miners up in the hills could buy Chinese rice, tea, soy sauce, preserves, sugar, and candy, as well as Asian spices like star anise, cassia, "China root" (probably of the sarsaparilla family), cubeb, galangal, and turmeric. In addition to these imports, the miners consumed "potatoes, cabbage, pork, chickens, flour, and almost every article of vegetables raised in this State."[42] The daily diet of the Chinese workmen was the South China staple of rice with a little vegetable or meat as seasoning. Whatever food they bought they supplemented with what they gathered or grew in little gardens next to their camps. On holidays they liked to splurge. In 1857, a miner and storekeeper named Herman Francis Reinhart, who probably lived on salt pork, beans, pancakes, and coffee, was invited to dine at a nearby Chinese camp on Sucker Creek:

> They were called very frugal in their meals and considered close to their provision as to cheapness but these I knew [had] once invited a lot of us storekeepers to a great dinner for the Americans, and they had a special table with the best of victuals, such as pies, cakes, roast pig, oysters in soup, or oyster pie, and all kind of can goods and fresh meats the market afforded in great profusion. And only us white[s were assigned] to the same table; they had their own table to themselves, and they waited on us as gentlemen; after eating they had wine and lemonade and nuts and oranges, figs and raisins and apples—in fact, as well got up as we could have done ourselfs.[43]

From San Francisco, Chinese immigrants also moved north and south along the Pacific coast, finding work in farming, fishing, and logging, and further inland as they followed the trail of gold and silver. In 1859, just as California's gold mines were becoming depleted, an enormous silver lode was discovered just over the border at Virginia City, in what would become Nevada Territory. In the rush that followed, the Chinese came to dig wealth out of the mines or to earn their livings as shopkeepers, vegetable gardeners, laundrymen, servants, or cooks. At its height, Virginia City's "Chinese quarter" had a population of seven hundred (out of a total of twenty-five thousand), mostly living in a jumble of one-story wooden buildings. In 1863 or 1864, a young writer who used the pen name Mark Twain described a tour of this district for the local *Territorial Enterprise*, including a visit to a Chinese store:

> Mr. Ah Sing keeps a general grocery and provision store at No. 13 Wang Street. He lavished his hospitality upon our party in the friendliest way. He had various kinds of colored and colorless wines and brandies, with unpronounceable names, imported from China in little crockery jugs, and which he offered to us in dainty little miniature wash-basins of porcelain. He offered us a mess of birds'-nests; also, small, neat sausages, of which we could have swallowed several yards if we had chosen to try, but we suspected that each link contained the corpse of a mouse and therefore restrained. Mr. Sing had in his store a thousand articles of merchandise, curious to behold, impossible to imagine the uses of, and beyond our ability to describe. His ducks, however, and his eggs, we could understand; the former were split open and flattened out like codfish, and came from China in that shape, and the latter were plastered over with some kind of paste which kept them fresh and palatable through the long voyage.[44]

The latter were probably palatable only to the Chinese, because they sound exactly like thousand-year-old eggs, with their distinct odor of sulfur and ammonia. Despite Twain's obvious biases against Chinese food, he did stop in a "celestial" restaurant to sample some "chow-chow with chop-sticks." This account is a rarity, one of the only descriptions we have of a white eating Chinese food in the western territories. In fact, most of what we know about the diet of Chinese in the interior West comes from archaeological excavations. Even in the most remote mining districts of northern Idaho, with their short growing seasons, the Chinese planted vegetable gardens in which they raised both their own sustenance and cash crops. They also purchased imported provisions from San Francisco. In Pierce, Idaho, a mining camp where hundreds of Chinese lived during the 1860s, archaeologists have found soy sauce jars, ceramic pots for imported pickles, and cans of vegetable oil for cooking. Despite great distance and adversity, the Chinese miners still managed to find ways to enjoy the foods of their native land, somewhat augmented by the miraculous canned American specialties like corned beef and oysters.

In 1865, the railroad magnate Charles Crocker hired fifty Chinese men as an experiment. Construction had just begun on the Central Pacific Railroad, which would link California and the East, and he was having trouble finding workers. The whites he found, mainly Irish immigrants, were often drunk and unruly, so he decided to try Chinese laborers. By 1868, the Central Pacific's workforce included twelve Chinese men who were digging and blasting their way through some of the most treacherous mountain passes in the West. The white laborers had been hired as individuals; the Chinese were hired in work gangs, each with its own Chinese "agent," who mediated with the contractors, and its own Chinese cook. The whites ate the usual frontier diet of company-supplied "beef, beans, bread and butter, and potatoes." The Chinese had their own store in a car that followed them as they laid track. In 1872, Charles Nordhoff, a travel writer and correspondent for the *New York Tribune*, visited a railroad under construction in the San Joaquin Valley and explored the wares of one of these traveling stores:

> Here is a list of the food kept and sold there to the Chinese workmen: Dried oysters, dried cuttle-fish, dried fish, sweet rice, crackers, dried bamboo sprouts,

salted cabbage, Chinese sugar (which tasted to me very much like sorghum sugar), four kinds of dried fruits, five kinds of desiccated vegetables, vermicelli, dried sea weed, Chinese bacon, cut up into small cutlets, dried meat of the abelona [sic] shell, pea-nut oil, dried mushrooms, tea, and rice. They buy also pork of the butcher, and on holidays they eat poultry.... At this railroad store they also sold pipes, bowls, chopsticks, large, shallow, cast-iron bowls for cooking rice, lamps, Joss paper, Chinese writing paper, pencils, and India ink, Chinese shoes, and clothing imported ready from China. Also, scales—for the Chinaman is particular, and reweighs everything he buys, as soon as he gets it to camp. Finally, there was Chinese tobacco. The desiccated vegetables were of excellent quality, and dried, evidently, by a process as good as the best in use by us.[45]

By the 1880s, Chinese workers had helped build thousands of miles of railroads. The American West was now linked to the rest of the country by four main railroad lines, and smaller railways connected many western communities and mining areas. Many of the laborers settled in towns along the tracks, like Tucson and El Paso, where they found work in farming or by opening stores, laundries, and restaurants. Cheap cafés owned by Chinese had been around since the 1850s in California, so it was not a surprise when these eateries sprang up. The waiters or waitresses were often white (or Mexican American in some locations), while the Chinese cook-owner stayed back in the kitchen. The menu was strictly inexpensive American fare—steak and eggs, beans and coffee, though a Chinese customer could probably get a bowl of rice or noodle soup if he stepped back into the kitchen. The local whites along the railroad lines weren't yet ready to convert to Chinese food.

From railroad dining rooms to the chuck wagons that followed cattle drives, Chinese cooks helped feed the American West. During the 1870s, the Central Pacific dining room in Evanston, Wyoming, featured Chinese waiters in native costume serving "excellent" western food prepared by Chinese hands in the kitchen. As in Gold Rush–era San Francisco, Chinese cooks in the remote mining districts learned to prepare American staples just like the natives. At the Polyglot House store and restaurant in Hangville, California, the kitchen churned out dishes that were more fuel than food: "pork, badly baked bread, and beef hardened but not cooked in hot grease," imitating "the American style with a painful accuracy."[46] If the diners didn't like the food, they would often beat the cook. After his work was done, the cook would retire to the Chinese camp nearby, where he would enjoy more civilized fare and company. During the Black Hills Gold Rush of the 1890s, Deadwood, South Dakota, boasted seven Chinese-owned eateries with names like the Philadelphia Café, the Sacramento Restaurant, the Lincoln Restaurant, and the Chicago Restaurant. Although the owners kept bottles of rice wine for their customers to sample, the menu was strictly inexpensive American—T-bone steak and apple pie. Deadwood was a rare western community that was relatively accepting of Chinese, so the owners didn't have to keep to the kitchen and hire white waiters or waitresses to tend to diners. During the great cattle drives of the 1870s and 1880s, Chinese chuck wagon cooks prepared the biscuits, beans, coffee, and bacon that fueled the cowboys. Like all Chinese in the West, the camp cook lived with the possibility that whites could turn against him at any time. Generations later, the 1930s song "Hold That Critter Down" (written by Bob Nolan) described torturing the cook as part of roundup fun:

When the sun goes down and the moon comes
   'round
To the old cook shack we're headin.'
We'll throw the pie in the Chink cook's eye
And tie him up in his beddin.'
And make him run to the tune of a gun
So hold that critter down....

After the Civil War, the anti-Chinese racism that had long simmered in the West came to a boil. The migrants who now streamed into California, many of them from Ireland, discovered that most of the jobs on the major construction projects—the railroads—were reserved for Chinese. These white migrants formed "anti-Coolie" leagues and trade unions that made expulsion of all Chinese people from the West one of their prime goals. Politicians discovered that promoting the cause that "the Chinese must go!" could win elections. Newspapers jumped on the bandwagon, reprinting Bayard Taylor's most incendiary writings and fanning the flames in order to sell more papers. Local governments passed a number of discriminatory laws designed to make the lives of California's Chinese more difficult. The Chinese could not vote, but they did fight back with lawsuits and diplomatic initiatives, which were only partially successful. In October 1871, during a gunfight between two Chinese gangs in the street nicknamed "Nigger Alley," the heart of Chinatown in Los Angeles, a white man was killed in the crossfire. In retaliation, a mob of a thousand white men armed with "pistols, guns, knives, ropes" stormed the quarter and killed over twenty Chinese people. Eight men were eventually found guilty of the murders, but their convictions were overturned. This massacre caused widespread revulsion, but that wasn't enough to stop the anti-Chinese movement, particularly after a financial panic caused record unemployment in California.

Just in time for the 1876 elections, the issue of Chinese expulsion caught the ear of Washington, and a special joint congressional committee was sent to San Francisco to investigate the situation. The congressmen queried a succession of local white "experts," but no Chinese, on such topics as Chinese crime, morality, sanitation, disease, economic competition, and refusal to assimilate, and on "natural" racial hierarchies and the dangers of miscegenation. Food was barely mentioned, except in the testimony that their cheap, rice-based diet was one reason the Chinese could compete so well against white workers, who needed red meat and bread to live. (In 1902, American Federation of Labor president Samuel Gompers expanded on this idea in an essay, "Some Reasons for Chinese Exclusion. Meat vs. Rice. American Manhood against Asiatic Coolieism. Which Shall Survive?") Outside, workers marched and held mass meetings calling for the expulsion of the Chinese from California and the hiring of whites only. The following summer, a big demonstration in sympathy with railroad strikers back East turned ugly when the members of an anti-Coolie group joined in. The demonstrators marched to Chinatown, where they burned buildings, sacked laundries, and left four Chinese dead. White workers gathered in the empty sandlot across from City Hall, where an Irish immigrant named Denis Kearney soon captured leadership of the crowd with his virulent anticapitalist, anti-Chinese oratory. In October 1877, he was elected president of the Workingmen's Party, which demanded the expulsion of all Chinese from the United States, either by law or by force. Kearney became the leader of the anti-Chinese movement, helping Workingmen's Party candidates win local offices and pushing for expulsion. As he barnstormed across the country, California's Chinese citizens endured a spate of threats, beatings, shootings, and arson attacks. "Accidental" fires, in fact, became a favorite method of emptying the state's many Chinatowns. If whites had been unlikely to eat in Chinese restaurants before, now the culture of racial violence made a visit outright dangerous.

Kearney was more rabble-rouser than politician; audiences soon tired of his oratory, and he was reduced to selling coffee and doughnuts in a San Francisco squatter's camp. But the anti-Chinese movement remained one of the most powerful political forces in the American West. In 1882, President Chester A. Arthur, with the strong support of California's congressional delegation and labor unions, signed the Chinese Exclusion Act, which effectively blocked Chinese immigration and naturalization—the first U.S. law to bar a group from entering the country on the basis of its ethnicity. The only exceptions allowed in were merchants, teachers, students, and their personal servants. In 1892, the more onerous Geary Act, replacing the Exclusion Act, imposed even sterner restrictions on Chinese immigration and curtailed Chinese residents' recourse to the courts. Across the West, many whites decided that now was the time for Chinese to leave their cities and towns, as local governments passed even more discriminatory laws. Many California Chinatowns, including in Pasadena, Santa Barbara, Oakland, San Jose, Sacramento, and Sonoma, were emptied under threats. On September 2, 1885, whites in the coal mining town of Rock Springs, Wyoming, decided that the Chinese no longer had any right to live and work there. A mob of men, mostly members of the Knights of Labor, surrounded the local Chinese settlement and opened fire with Winchester rifles. Any Chinese person who ran was shot, and the whites beat with gun butts anyone they could catch. Houses were burned to the ground, some with their Chinese residents inside. By nightfall, at least twenty-eight Chinese were dead, with many more injured and hiding in the hills.

Afterward, sixteen whites were arrested and charged with various crimes, but after a grand jury could find no one to testify against them, they were eventually released, to loud cheers from the community. Although eastern newspapers and politicians strongly condemned the violence, westerners generally supported the murderers. Indeed, the Rock Springs massacre seemed to embolden the anti-Chinese forces. In the coming months, Tacoma and Seattle, Washington, expelled their Chinese populations, and mobs across the Northwest attacked and often killed groups of Chinese miners, loggers, and farmworkers. Most Chinese, excepting those in enclaves in cities like San Francisco and Portland, decided that it was time to leave the West. In the late 1870s, they began to flee—to China on ships, never to return; across the border to Canada or Mexico; or, by the railroads they had built, to the big cities of the Northeast.

CHAPTER FIVE ·

A Toothsome Stew

At the start of 1884, a New York writer named Edwin H. Trafton sent out an invitation to six fellow "connoisseurs of good living":

> Will you join a few other good fellows in chop-stick luck next Saturday night at the Chung Fah Low? As you of course know, this is the Chinese Delmonico's of New York, at No.——Street (upstairs), sign of the Been Gin Law. Apropos of which the *chef* assures me in his most elegant pigeon English, "I cookee allee talkee," which, being freely translated means, "I can cook in every language." I know that you have a cosmopolitan palate and a cast-iron digestive apparatus, else I should not have asked you to come. The first course will be brought on at seven sharp, and stomach pumps may be ordered at nine o'clock.[1]

The point of this dinner, aside from providing Trafton with the material for an article, was to answer the question "How do you do?" Or to phrase it as the Chinese would, "Have you eaten?" To "answer so comprehensive a conundrum,"

Trafton decided, "one must eat Chinese food; to become imbued with the spirit essential to a categorical, succinct and unequivocal response, one must have wielded chopsticks." His six guests had eaten widely in the city, from the fare offered in the dining room of the newest, most elegant hotel—the Windsor on Fifth Avenue—to the pork and beans at Hitchcock's dime restaurant down by the newspaper buildings on Park Row. For these gourmands, this feast would be a once-in-a-lifetime experience, like "going up in a balloon; going down in a diving-bell; the sensation of being hanged, drowned or guillotined; what seasickness is like, or the eating of a Chinese dinner."

A few days before the event, Trafton ventured to Mott Street, the heart of New York's Chinatown. At that time, there were only two Chinese restaurants on Mott, both at the south end of the street close to its intersection with Chatham Square. One was Chung Fah Low, above a Chinese grocery store at number 11. "Dingy, low-walled and ill-lighted," this eatery was a step down from the elegant, three-story establishments of San Francisco's Chinatown. Trafton climbed some rickety stairs and found himself in the restaurant's back office, with two tables, a counter and shelves holding pots, chinaware, and an assortment of dried foodstuffs imported from China. The front room overlooking the street had been turned into the dining room, furnished with a single large table and six smaller ones, where placards with large Chinese characters shared the walls with cheap American color prints. Behind the office was the chef's lair, the kitchen, which Trafton recognized as clean but nevertheless contained "ghastly piles" of plucked ducks, unidentified meats and vegetables, and pots "like witches' caldrons" filled with mysterious broths emitting pungent odors. These sights and smells notwithstanding, Trafton was determined to order his banquet.

"What you want?" the owner asked, suspicious of the white man snooping around. When he heard that Trafton hoped to arrange a dinner party, the "round-faced, moon-eyed" owner turned friendly, offering him a cigar, a cup of Chinese "rice gin," and some tea. Never learning the owner's name, Trafton called him "Ah Sin," after the mild-looking but devious Chinese character in Bret Harte's celebrated and widely reprinted poem "The Heathen Chinee." Trafton and the owner were joined by the chef and the bookkeeper,

Figure 5.1. This second-floor Port Arthur restaurant attracted wealthy white "slummers" to Mott Street in New York's China-town.

and the group attempted to work out the evening's menu. Unfortunately, the language barrier and Trafton's ignorance of Chinese food made their task difficult. "Ah Sin" tried to help him by pulling out samples of the raw materials—"chunks of india-rubber, dried fish of all sorts and sizes, and some things that I could identify and classify a hundred years from now by their odors"—but Trafton could not imagine them made edible. Luckily, the writer's Chinese friend, Hawk Ling, arrived just at this moment to help sort out the muddle. An agent for a wholesale grocer who wore American clothes and spoke "very good" English, Hawk Ling had probably recommended this restaurant as the site for Trafton's dinner. Together, they worked out a menu of bird's-nest soup, pungent-smelling "bull-fish," dried oysters, Chinese codfish, duck, pork, tea, Chinese wine, and rice, for a total cost of $8—a very modest feast compared to what one could get in San Francisco.

When Saturday evening arrived, half the party went missing, giving excuses that "were more ingenious than satisfactory." The dinner went on with four diners, including Hawk Ling. The brave eaters were greeted by a table set with concessions to "American taste and table habits": a white tablecloth, red napkins, slightly tarnished knives and forks of a "primitive farm-house pattern," and little dishes of mustard covered with oil. (Mustard later became ubiquitous on Cantonese American restaurant tables, usually accompanied by plum sauce and deep-fried chop suey noodles.) China plates, bowls, and spoons completed the dinner service. After a little fun with the menu—"Ah Sin" at first handed them a Chinese laundry bill—the Americans learned that duck and pork would not be included in the meal. The restaurant owner had decided that these meats were too common and that his guests would be served only "imported food, mostly fish of some kind, and of the sort only enjoyed by 'high-toned gentlemen in China.' " (Yuan Mei would not have approved.) Assuming a false bravado, Trafton ordered chopsticks to use instead of forks and commenced to eat. Beyond a reference to "lice" (rice), his report skimps on the details of what they ate, attempting only this description:

> The flavors were unlike anything known to our more familiar gastronomy, and the fundamental article of each was so artfully concealed as to defy identification. One course consisted of a hard, white gelatinous substance; another, contained strips of what resembled tripe; another, small rolls of pale-yellow Russia leather, but the *pièce de resistance* was the bowl of bull-fish.[2]

This final item was the imported delicacy that Ah-Sin said "smell heap." As soon as the last course was finished, the guests thanked Hawk Ling and the restaurant's owner and hightailed it to the nearby Astor House hotel on Broadway. Over drinks, they compared notes. Trafton said his "palate testified to having lunched off a rainbow soaked in brine," while a "fashionable New York editor and magazinist" in the party felt as though he had eaten a "rare-done nightmare." They had experienced their Chinese dinner as a novelty, to be boasted about but never to be repeated—an attitude reminiscent of 1844 Macau or 1850s San Francisco.

Ten years later, in one of the greatest cultural shifts in American culinary history, New Yorkers would be flocking to Mott Street to eat Chinese food. The developments that preceded this revolution in taste were gradual, and began with the original founding of New York's Chinese community. The first arrivals began to come in the early nineteenth century in a slow but steady trickle—some from the West, others from Cuba, Peru, and the Middle Kingdom itself. The first to begin to put down roots were sailors who stayed between ships in the boardinghouses down by the East River docks.

Others arrived as members of theatrical exhibitions, including a Guangzhou "princess" named Afong Moy, P. T. Barnum's "Chinese Family," the crew of a Chinese junk that was heading to London's Crystal Palace show, and a Chinese opera company that became stranded when their backers went broke. By the 1850s, New York's permanent Chinese community was based in the Irish boardinghouse district of the Fourth Ward, near the docks. Working as sailors, cigar and candy peddlers, cooks, stewards, and store owners, these men earned modest livelihoods, and many married Irish or German women. In 1873, Wo Kee, a businessman, opened a store and lodging house at 34 Mott Street, just below Pell Street, the first outpost in what became Chinatown. At this time, a *New York Times* reporter estimated that five hundred Chinese lived in the city, most visible as the cigar and candy peddlers who frequented City Hall Park. The centers of the community were three or four lodging houses, a temple and club on Baxter Street, and another club in Wo Kee's building on Mott. Here the reporter encountered some men playing a version of Chinese chess and witnessed meal preparations over a corner stove:

Two men were engaged at this in preparing a meal for some dozen others who were anxiously waiting. What they were cooking is a mystery, only to be fathomed by the brain contained in some "becued" head. It appeared to be a mixture of all the vegetables and meats known to the City markets. The man who seemed to be the head cook first put about half a pound of lard in a monster frying-pan; his assistant in the meantime chopped up a large head of white cabbage, and as soon as the lard was melted threw it, and about half a dozen scraped carrots, into the pan. Salt and pepper were shaken profusely over this, and then came a layer of chopped meat. Cold boiled potatoes followed, the whole being supplemented by what looked like pulled codfish. The fumes that ascended from this peculiar cookery can be better imagined than described.... The Chinese seemed very much offended when it was intimated that the smell of their kitchen was not very pleasant, and that the meal that was being prepared was likely to prove to those of a dyspeptic constitution slightly indigestible.[3]

This one of the earliest accounts we have of the mixed stir-fry, one of the Pearl River Delta's village specialties, that would have an outsized influence on the American perception of Chinese food.

During the 1860s and 1870s, New York journalists predicted the imminent arrival of hordes of Chinese immigrants from the West, and these prophecies became more frequent as work on the railroads ended and anti-Chinese violence spread. In reality, those hordes never materialized, and Chinese immigrants continued to flow in, as they always had, gradually. The journalists, following the lead of the San Francisco newspapers, descended on the city's nascent Chinatown to nose out any signs of gambling, poor sanitation, and particularly opium use. In 1880, a *Times* reporter visited Mott Street's little Chinese community expecting to find "dragons' wings scattered over the floor, and ends of serpents' tails disappearing under the bed" but admitted: "none of these things are there." He had to enlist a police officer to take him behind a combined restaurant and gambling parlor to find one tiny opium den where he could indulge his fantasies of Oriental depravity.[4] Generally, however, these writers couldn't muster as much moral condemnation of Chinese vice as had Bayard Taylor. With more curiosity than outrage, they explored the rules and odds of the Chinese gambling games and sampled a few puffs of opium to learn how it was smoked.

This relative lack of hysteria may have been due to the fact that the thousand or so Chinese in New York were only a drop in the bucket compared to the size of other immigrant groups. In May 1880, the *Times* noted that since the beginning of the year more than one hundred thousand immigrants had passed through the processing facility at Castle Garden on Manhattan's southern tip.[5] The majority were German, English, Irish, French, and Scandinavian. The masses of Italians and East European Jews began to arrive a few years later. Most paused only long enough to collect their baggage before they were whisked off to other parts of the country, but thousands stayed and settled in the crowded immigrant districts of the Lower East and West Sides. The Chinese were certainly the most exotic new immigrants, but they were unlikely to be seen as an economic threat when compared to the flood of Europeans.

Like their compatriots in California, New York City's Chinese residents soon began to remake their environment to suit their culinary needs. By 1878, a pair of Chinese farmers named Ah Wah and Ah Ling were growing Asian vegetables on a three-acre plot in the Tremont section of the Bronx. (Within a few years they were joined by another farmer in the Bronx and then Chinese farms in Astoria, Queens.) Store owners like Wo Kee sold imported specialties like pickled, salted, and dried vegetables as well as the usual array of Chinese dried seafood. In 1880, an agent of the Ichthyophagus Club scouting Chinatown for piscatory oddities for its annual dinner found sharks' fins, dried oysters, salted octopus and squid, sea cucumbers, and birds' nests. The appearance of these alien culinary items soon led to the city's first controversy over Chinese food. In 1883, a "short, stout, excitable Frenchman" named Dr. Charles Kaemmerer accused a Chinatown grocer of cooking cats and rats. He was visiting a saloon at 199 Worth Street when he noticed a "very peculiar odor" in its back courtyard, which it shared with a Chinese grocery at 5 Mott Street. Looking outside, he saw "some Chinamen standing there handling some things that looked like very small cats or very large rats." He told a reporter: "I didn't see them eat the animals ... but I don't know why they shouldn't do so." (After all, a popular street ditty went: "Chink, chink, Chinaman/Eats dead rats, / Eats them up/Like gingersnaps.") A reporter later accompanied Dr. Vermilye, the sanitary inspector, to the premises and found:

> There was no offal in the yard, nor cat or rat skins, and no stench. By the open window a Chinese cook was seen preparing the dinner. He was making a stew, which was composed of salted Chinese turnips, soft-shelled crabs, and pig's ears. These and various other articles of food were washed and sliced on a huge butcher's block with a butcher's cleaver. The cook was as deft as a hotel *chef*, and did his work with as much care and cleanliness. He shelled fresh peas, sliced a wholesome-looking cabbage head, and peeled fresh potatoes whose skins were almost white. There was nothing suggestive of rats or cats about the place, and the doctor said that he should report that there was no cause for complaint.[6]

That wasn't enough for the editor of New York's first Chinese newspaper, Wong Ching Foo, who was very different from the rest of the Chinese population. He had been raised in the Shanghai region, not the Pearl River Delta; he had been educated at an elite academy, not a village school, and had even worked as an interpreter in the imperial court. He was also a sharp-tongued gadfly, not afraid to speak out against the California racist rabble-rouser Denis Kearney or anyone else who wished to deprive the Chinese of their rights. In fact, his aggressive defense of his compatriots may be part of why the anti-Chinese movement failed to gain traction in New York. By 1883, the year he founded the *Chinese-American*, he was the veteran of at least two national lecture tours, one defending his "pagan" beliefs and the other attacking the anti-Chinese movement. When he heard Dr. Kaemmerer's accusations, he offered a $500 reward to anyone who could "prove that a Chinaman ate rats and cats" and threatened a slander suit. In all his travels through China, he declared, he had never heard of anyone eating cats or rats: "They drew the line at dogs."[7] Nobody took Wong up on his challenge, but the event apparently inspired him to write an article on food, the first in English by a Chinese, for the *Brooklyn Eagle*:

> The epicure flourishes in the Orient as well as in the Occident. In Europe he bows down before the genius of France; in Asia, before that of the flowery kingdom. The renown of Chinese food and cooking is more than deserved. For generations the followers of Confucius and Buddha have studied the art which Brillat-Savarin and Blot rendered famous, and have evolved a system which, while it may not in all respects meet the approval of the Western races, yet possesses an individuality and merit of the highest order.[8]

Wong goes on to make the daring suggestion that Chinese cooking may be better, because of its far broader range of ingredients and the mandarin gourmet's preference for "extraordinary" and expensive foods over the European gourmet's cheap and common turkey, duck, lamb, or beef. To further compare the two styles, Wong uses Caleb Cushing's old trope of the Chinese as the opposite of the American:

> Where the Americans use ice water they use hot tea; where we sweeten tea and coffee they drink these beverages plain; where we salt fish they dress it with sugar; with them the dessert comes in the first stages

of the meal; everything in their menu is cooked so thoroughly as to lose entirely its original character, while with us rare meats, raw vegetables, Russian salad, simple fruits, oysters and clams are served almost in their natural condition.

There's a little confusion between "us" and "them" here; the author is Chinese after all. This confused viewpoint appears in a number of places in his article. No Chinese person would have been likely to say that Chinese food is overcooked, because the Chinese considered Westerners the masters of overcooking. In fact, Wong later praises the Chinese practice of steaming, saying that it lets cooks serve vegetables "with every line and point unbroken." Yet Wong certainly had noticed the presence of raw and barely cooked food on New York tables. All this leads one to surmise that it's the editor, not Wong Ching Foo, who speaks in many places in the article.

Wong mentions the Ichthyophagus Club's work in bringing some of China's "extraordinary" dishes to Western palates, and then describes some dishes that could be "well adapted for cosmopolitan use," including hellbenders, sturgeon's swim-bladders, poultry feet, and sharks' fins, which he compares (strangely) to both pickled herring and shad. Finally, he arrives at a list of "other special dishes," giving us the earliest reliable glimpse we have of the ordinary restaurant food of Pearl River Delta immigrants in the United States. Here are sticky rice wrapped in lotus leaf (a dim sum staple), "Wun-hawn," or wonton; "Yak-o-men," wheat noodles with meat in broth; "Sai-fun," seafood with rice noodles; beef, chicken, pork, or bacon balls (popular in soups or as dim sum); curried rice with meat or seafood; "Bo-ahp," duck boiled with orange peel; and "Chop soly," for which "each cook has his own recipe. The main features of it are pork, bacon, chickens, mushroom, bamboo shoots, onion and pepper. These may be called characteristics; accidental ingredients are duck, beef, perfumed turnip, salted black beans, sliced yam, peas and string beans." This, Wong claims, "may be justly termed the national dish of China." Having traveled widely in China, Wong must have known this statement was incorrect. Perhaps he included it because "Chop soly" was already becoming popular with Western diners, who knew the dish also as "chow-chop-sui" and later "chop suey." Wong sums up: "Chinese cooking is better and cheaper than our own. It utilizes almost every part of food animals, and many plants, herbs and trees, both terrestrial and marine, unknown to our pantries." And those stories about cats, dogs, and rats? Fictitious. Poor people will eat them in times of famine, but those animals "are not recognized articles of diet in the great restaurants, any more than at Delmonico's or the Brunswick."[9] That was the kind of white lie that would help protect Chinese from the Kearneys of this world.

Wong Ching Foo's article appeared at a very particular time in the history of Gotham: the middle of the Gilded Age, when the city was awash with money. The newspapers were filled with articles about the lavish homes and outrageous parties of millionaire families like the Vanderbilts, Goulds, and Astors. On Fifth Avenue, old and nouveau riche wealth fought for status against a background of constantly shifting social mores. Those who had "arrived" in high society attempted to keep the socially ambitious out of it by deploying the weapons of snobbery and exclusion. Social arbiters like Ward McAllister limited the elite to four hundred, the number of people who would fit into Mrs. Astor's ballroom, and devised a series of elaborate rules for their behavior. According to McAllister, no expenditures were too great when it came to entertaining, including on the food one provided. The dishes at a dinner party must be classic French cuisine, so the family's chef must of course be French as well. In 1890, McAllister wrote: "twenty years ago there were not over three *chefs* in private families in this city. It is now the exception not to find a man of fashion keeping a first-class *chef* or a famous *cordon bleu*."[10] In preparing for a dinner, the hostess must have a detailed knowledge of French cuisine in order to inspire her temperamental chef to new heights and to decide whether he should follow the truffled *filet*, served with black sauce, with a *riz de veau à la Toulouse* or a *supreme de volaille* with white sauce. If her own dining room wasn't large enough, she would turn to one of the city's palatial restaurants, Delmonico's on Madison Square above all, where she would negotiate the menu with Mr. Delmonico or his famous chef, Charles Ranhofer. If her taste proved correctly exquisite—and if enough money reached the right society columnists and editors—then all New York would recognize and reaffirm her status at the top of the social heap. In this world, encompassing not only socialites but jewelers, florists, dressmakers, and journalists like the "fashionable magazinist" in Edwin H. Trafton's party, there was a right way and a wrong way to comport oneself. You could dine in Chinatown once, and laugh about it over cigars and drinks at the Astor House afterward, but you could not make a habit of it.

However culturally influential the elite were (or thought they were), not all of New York strove to copy their ways. Another group arose that seemed to take pleasure in flouting every rule McAllister's four hundred held dear. They called themselves Bohemians—a name taken from Henri Murger's story "La Vie de Bohème," set in the Latin Quarter of 1840s Paris. Murger's characters were free-spirited but starving artists; the Bohemians of late nineteenth-century New York were free-spirited but frequently well-fed artists and writers. In fact, one way American Bohemians defined themselves was by where they ate. If Mrs. Astor dined at Delmonico's, they chose dark and dingy restaurants down in the immigrant districts where the food was cheap and the clientele disreputable; they were the first "underground gourmets" and "chowhounds." During the 1850s, the favorite haunt of the first generation of city Bohemians (including Walt Whitman) was Pfaff's saloon, a German beer cellar below the sidewalk at Broadway near Bleecker Street, where they drank, talked, sang, caroused, and made love. Twenty years later, a new generation of writers and artists rendezvoused at eateries like the Grand Vatel and the villainous Taverne Alsacienne in the "French Quarter," south of Washington Square. At the former, one could order a filling and "not unpalatable" three-course dinner, along with wine, coffee, and a roll, for a mere 50 cents. The purpose of these Bohemian visits to the immigrant restaurants was not just to enjoy cheap food and the company of fellow artists but also to be transported into a milieu that more accurately reflected the true nature of the city than all the Fifth Avenue ballrooms. So when a little community of Chinese appeared along lower Mott Street in the late 1870s, it became a natural destination for Bohemians. With (relatively) open minds, hungry stomachs, and a metaphoric thumb in the eye of the four hundred, they led the charge across the boundaries of taste.

The journalist and editor Allan Forman was tutored in the delights of Chinese food by a friend, a "jolly New York lawyer of decidedly Bohemian tendencies, who one day suggested, 'Come and dine with me.' " "Where?" Forman asked, knowing the lawyer's taste for reveling in "dirt and mystery and strange viands" down in the immigrant district.

"Oh, over at Mong Sing Wah's, 18 Mott street. He is a Celestial Delmonico," was the reply.

"Thanks awfully. But my palate is not educated up to rats and dogs yet. Let me take a course in some French restaurant where these things are disguised before I brave them in their native honesty," I answered.

"I'm surprised to find this prejudice in you," he exclaimed, rather petulantly. "A Chinese dinner is as clean as an American dinner, only far better. I'll tell you what I'll do. You come with me to Mong Sing Wah's tonight and I'll show you his kitchen. If it is not as clean as that Italian place where you eat spaghetti I'll pay for the best dinner for two you can order at Delmonico's."[11]

So on a bitterly cold night early in 1886, the two white men took the Third Avenue streetcar down to Chatham Square and Mong Sing Wah's restaurant, hidden in a courtyard behind 18 Mott. The lawyer surprised Forman by greeting the owner and then ordering dinner in apparently fluent Chinese: "'Chow-chop-suey, chop-seow, laonraan, san-sui-goy, no-ma-das,' glibly ordered my friend, and the white-robed attendant trotted off and began to chant down a dumbwaiter." This dinner was not a banquet of rare ingredients imported from China but a meal off the menu—the everyday restaurant food eaten by New York's Chinese. When the food appeared, Forman seemed to forget his fears about rats and dogs:

Chow-chop suey was the first dish we attacked. It is a toothsome stew, composed of bean sprouts, chicken's gizzards and livers, calfe's tripe, dragon fish, dried and imported from China, pork, chicken, and various other ingredients which I was unable to make out. Notwithstanding its mysterious nature, it is very good and has formed the basis of many a good Chinese dinner I have since eaten. Chopseow is perfumed roast pork. The pork is roasted and then hung in the smoke of various aromatic herbs which gives it a most delicious flavor. It is cut into small pieces, as indeed is everything at a Chinese restaurant, that it may be readily handled with the chop sticks. No bread is served with a Chinese dinner, but its place is taken by boiled rice, or fan as it is called in Chinese. A couple of bowls of rice is [laonraan], the F being dropped when the number is prefixed, and such rice, white, light, snowy; each grain thoroughly cooked yet separate. Fish is delightfully cooked, baked in a sort of brown sauce, and masquerades under the name of san-sui-goy.

Forman and his friend washed the food down with tea and little cups of "no-ma-das," a Chinese rice liquor. At the end of the dinner, Forman was shocked to realize that he had wholeheartedly enjoyed it: "The meal was not only novel, but it was good, and to cap the climax the bill was only sixty-three cents!"[12] For almost the next century, that would sum up the main attractions of Chinese food for Americans: tasty, exotic, and cheap.

In the 1880s, untold numbers of non-Chinese New Yorkers trekked to Chinatown to eat. In 1885, Wong Ching Foo claimed that thousands of New Yorkers had already tried "oriental" dining; three years later, he declared that at least "five hundred Americans take their meals regularly in Chinese restaurants."[13] Almost all of these were situated on the block of Mott Street between Chatham Square and Pell Street. Wong identified Yu-ung-Fang-Lau at 14 Mott as the only high-class restaurant, the favorite of "Canton importers, Hong Kong merchants, Mongolian visitors from Frisco, flush gamblers, and wealthy laundrymen."[14] The half dozen or so other eateries catered to all the rest of the Chinese: servants, cooks, cigar makers, and most of all laundrymen from the poor Sze Yap district of the Pearl River Delta. Very few of them had wives, so during the week they prepared simple meals (rice with a little meat or vegetable) in their workplaces or rooming houses. On Sundays they came to

Chinatown to shop, socialize, catch up on the news, and have a meal in a restaurant. If they could afford it, they liked to splurge on pricey imported delicacies from the top end of the menu. The Bohemians and other non-Chinese did the opposite: "Many of these Americans have acquired Chinese gastronomical tastes, and order dishes like Chinese mandarins; but as a rule the keepers do not cater to any other trade than Chinese, because the Chinaman frequently orders two-dollar and three-dollar dishes, while the American seldom pays more than fifty or seventy-five cents for his Chinese dinner."[15] Out of the array of dishes the Americans preferred, the earthy mixed stir-fry called "chow chop suey" stood out as their favorite. "Chop suey" is more accurately transcribed as "za sui" (Mandarin) or "shap sui" (Cantonese). "Shap" means mixed or blended together; "sui" means bits or small fragments. Read together, the most common translation is "odds and ends." As a culinary term, "shap sui" refers to a hodgepodge stew of many different ingredients; when this dish is "chow," that means it's fried. You could call it a stir-fried Chinese hash.

Today, chop suey is a relic in most parts of the United States, another food fad that has ended up on the trash heap of culinary history. Those who remember it at all know it only as a preparation of sliced pork or chicken cooked with bean sprouts, onions, celery, bamboo shoots, and water chestnuts until everything is mushy and flavorless, then served with a gummy, translucent sauce over white rice. Yet in nineteenth-century New York, the definition of chop suey was anything but fixed. Most early descriptions tell of chicken livers and gizzards, or perhaps duck giblets, stir-fried with tripe, bean sprouts, "fungi" (probably wood ears), celery, dried fish, and whatever else the cook felt inspired to add, including spices and "seow" (soy sauce). Wong Ching Foo and other reporters describe chop suey as the staple food of the New York

Chinese and even the "national dish of China." In 1893, now an expert on the subject, Allan Forman wrote: "*Chow chop suey* is to the Chinaman what the *olla podrida* is to the Spaniard, or pork and beans to our own Bostonians."[16] Considering the vast, ancient, and complicated tradition of Chinese cuisine, this clearly was not true. But if Forman had only been exposed to Chinese from the Pearl River Delta, then he may have been correct in noting their preference for chop suey. In any case, there's little doubt that this dish—in its manifestation as a stir-fried organ meat and vegetable medley—originated in the Sze Yap area around Toishan. Decades later, a distinguished Hong Kong surgeon named Li Shu-Fan reminisced about a childhood visit to Toishan, which was his ancestral home:

> I first tasted chop suey in a restaurant in Toishan in 1894, but the preparation had been familiar in that city long before my time. The recipe was probably taken to America by Toishan people, who, as I have said, are great travelers. Chinese from places as near to Toishan as Canton and Hong Kong are unaware that chop suey is truly a Chinese dish, and not an American adaptation.[17]

Now launched on a slow but sure path to acceptance, Chinese food, and in particular chop suey, was poised to become a national fad. In the spring of 1896, New Yorkers learned that one of China's most powerful statesmen, the de facto foreign minister, would be visiting their city that year. American China watchers considered Li Hongzhang, the viceroy of Zhili (the provinces around Beijing), as China's best hope for strengthening and modernizing China. The purpose of Li's visit was to shore up relations with the United States and to protest the unfairness of the Exclusion Act as well as the mistreatment of Chinese immigrants. (This might, in turn, shore up his reputation at home, then under a cloud due to the recent humiliation his force had suffered at the hands of the Japanese navy.) In late August, he arrived in New York harbor aboard the steamship *St. Louis*. From Chinatown to Fifth Avenue, all of New York was agog at this elderly and somewhat frail man, wearing a magnificent yellow silk jacket. A troop of cavalry escorted him from the pier up to the Waldorf Hotel, at Fifth Avenue and Thirty-third Street, where he was installed in the royal suite. Every step of the way, teams of reporters from the city's many competing newspapers recorded his actions.

On Mott Street, at Delmonico's, and in the Waldorf kitchens, phalanxes of chefs made preparations to feast the famous visitor. Meanwhile, anxious to pick up any

Figure 5.2. Li Hongzhang's 1896 visit to New York stimulated a craze for Chinese food. However, the one dish he did not eat was chop suey.

scrap of color to entertain its readers, William Randolph Hearst's *New York Journal* planted reporters in the Waldorf's kitchen to record every move of Li's four chefs, who had traveled with him from China. A sketch artist drew them at work, depicting their tools and the lacquer tray that was used to carry the viceroy's food up to his suite. At public events, journalists watched every morsel of food that passed Li's lips—or at least some of them did. The *Times* reporters at the Waldorf banquet in Li's honor wrote that he ate sparingly from the classic French menu but dove in when a servant brought his Chinese food: "It consisted of three dishes. There was boiled chicken cut up in small square pieces, a bowl of rice, and a bowl of vegetable soup."[18] This was the food of either an invalid or a gourmet in the spirit of Yuan Mei. The *Washington Post* reported of the exact same event: "At the table he barely nibbled the delicate dishes before him, and would not touch the wines. This was noticed by his hosts, and in a few moments chop suey and chop sticks were placed before him, and he ate with relish."[19] According to the *Journal*'s careful accounting, Li never ate chop suey during his New York stay, but many other newspapers and the wire services that sent articles across the country repeated the news that he had done so—simply because chop suey, the only Chinese dish most white Americans had tasted, had become emblematic of Chinese food as a whole. (The Chinese diplomats reading those accounts must have been shocked by the idea that a high official from Beijing would stoop to the level of Pearl River Delta peasant food.)

Li Hongzhang spent a little more than a week in the United States, traveling to West Point, Philadelphia, and Washington before heading north to Toronto and then across Canada to take a boat home. (He purposely shunned California because of its mistreatment of the Chinese.)

Meanwhile, New Yorkers went China mad. They flocked to Chinatown to buy curios and eat chop suey. The *Brooklyn Eagle* advised: "The woman who is looking for something in the way of novelty for a dinner may find it in this suggestion: A real Chinese dinner may be gotten up from the favorite recipes of Li Hung Chang's cook, and which were prepared for the great and quaint Chinese statesman during his stay at the Waldorf in New York."[20] Those dishes were lifted from a full-page spread entitled "Queer Dishes Served at the Waldorf by Li Hung Chang's Chicken Cook" that had appeared in the *New York Journal*'s Sunday supplement. These recipes included boiled rice, bird's nest soup, fricasseed giblets ("chow chop sui"), chicken soup, pork sausage, shark's fin soup, and many others; they were almost the first Chinese recipes printed in the United States. Here are the directions for chop suey, a dish the author admits had already achieved some celebrity:

> Cut up equal amounts of celery, and wash and soak some dried mushrooms and bits of raw ginger. Fry the chicken giblets in peanut oil until they are nearly done, then add the other ingredients and a very small quantity of water. A favorite addition to this dish is scraps of pork and slices of dried cuttlefish, also rice which has been left on a damp floor until it has sprouted. These sprouts, about two inches in length, are remarkably tender and palatable. A little soy should be put into the chop sui while cooking and peanut oil to furnish the grease. Eat freely of it. If you can digest it you will live to be as old as Li Hung Chang.[21]

This is still the earthy mixed stir-fry, but not one that was ever prepared for Li Hongzhang. In fact, this list of recipes is remarkably similar to the menus of the Cantonese restaurants that lined Mott and Pell streets in Chinatown, leading one to suspect that it came from a local restaurateur. No matter; that's how the story that Li Hongzhang introduced chop suey to the United States was born—an urban legend that's still repeated today.

Li Hongzhang's visit ushered in an era when American attention was suddenly and aggressively trained on the outside world. The turning point came on February 15, 1898, the day the United States battleship *Maine* mysteriously exploded in Havana harbor. Deliberate or not, journalists and military men seized on that violent event in order to revive the somewhat moribund concept of Manifest Destiny and demand that the United States invade Spain's colonies in the Caribbean and across the Pacific. Their not-so-hidden agenda was to assert America's "God-given" right to expand its territory. One of them, the journalist Margherita Arlina Hamm, a prominent suffragist and one of the first "globe-trotting" woman reporters, had lived in China as the wife of a United States consul. In 1895, an article she wrote for *Good Housekeeping*, "Some Celestial Dishes," presented the first Chinese recipes published in the United States.[22] (Although she claims she has learned these recipes—including one for chop suey—in China, they are thoroughly westernized, containing ingredients like tomato sauce, Worcestershire sauce, and potatoes.)

Hamm had no patience for China's traditional way of life or its system of government. To her, the only hope for civilizing China was for the western powers, including the United States, to divide it up into protectorates. The Chinese, of course, had other ideas. In 1899, the Society of the Right and Harmonious Fists, known in the West as the Boxers, began an effort to violently expel all foreigners and foreign religions from the Middle Kingdom. With the backing of the dowager empress, this movement culminated in 1900 with the siege of Beijing's legation quarter, where, ironically, trapped Westerners were forced to eat taboo foods they'd looked down on for so long: horse meat and rice. The siege was finally lifted, and the Boxers were defeated by an eight-nation force made up of soldiers from Japan, the United States, and the European powers, who promptly went on a looting rampage in the Chinese capital. Back on Mott Street, these events seemed to cause no animosity toward the local Chinese community (whose members had little sympathy for the Manchus who ruled in Beijing). In fact, the episode generated curiosity about the culture, at least to the extent that people bought souvenirs, toured opium dens, and ate Chinese food:

> The streets of Chinatown yesterday resembled Coney Island walks with a few hundred Chinese thrown in. The newspaper prominence which the quarter has had since trouble began in China brought curious crowds from all parts of the city.... The Chinese restaurants, of which there are many, attracted the young men who were showing their best girls through Chinatown. One couple at least knew a great deal more about Chinese food after finishing their first meal than they did when they started. They studied the bill of fare so long that even the lazy stoic who waited on them grew tired.
>
> "We'll have chop suey soup," said the young man at last. "I've heard a lot about that, and I don't believe there are any rats in it."[23]

The rumors about Chinese eating vermin lingered, but whites were able to put them aside as they discovered the "safe" side of Chinese restaurant menus.

That same year the first Chinese restaurants appeared outside Chinatown; rather than wait for customers to come to Mott Street, restaurateurs now took chop suey to them. They opened "chop sueys," as the restaurants became known, on

Third Avenue, along Sixth Avenue in the Tenderloin nightlife district, up on Long Acre (now Times) Square, even in Harlem. Their menus were much shorter than those on Mott Street, focusing on chop suey, chow mein, and yat gaw mein (or yoka-man, yock a main, etc.), a wheat noodle soup containing boiled chicken and hardboiled egg. As cooks catered to the more conservative tastes of uptown diners, chop suey, the dish of odds and ends, lost all of its earthy and mysterious ingredients and became a bland stew of some readily identifiable meat or seafood with a mélange of bean sprouts, bamboo shoots, onions, and water chestnuts, all cooked to exhaustion.

Figure 5.3. The Latest Craze of American Society, New Yorkers Dining in a Chinese Restaurant, *a 1911 magazine announces. Chinese cuisine had by then spread far beyond the bounds of Manhattan's Chinatown.*

Although the chow mein that was cooked in the Pearl River Delta was a distinct dish, as served in the uptown joints chow mein was simply chop suey over fried noodles instead of rice. (In Roy L. M'Cardell's humorous column "Conversations with a Chorus Girl," his attractive but ditzy protagonist touts the wonders of chow mein: "Gee! I like it. You'd think the vermicelli was Saratoga chips [i.e. potato chips] cut into strings.")[24] Customers found these restaurants fit their tastes precisely. They liked the cut-rate, exotic décor of red lanterns and prints of pretty Chinese girls and landscapes; the savory, filling, and inexpensive food (a bowl of chop suey cost a mere 25 cents); and the distinctive ambiance, utterly unlike the rude bustle of the cheap lunch counters or the stuffiness of Delmonico's:

> There is also a free and easy atmosphere about the Chinese eating house which attracts many would-be "Bohemians," as well as a goodly share of the class below the lowest grades of the city's many graded Bohemia. Visitors loll about and talk and laugh loudly. When the waiter is wanted some one emits a shrill yell which brings an answering whoop from the kitchen, followed sooner or later by a little Chinese at a dog trot. Any one who feels like it may stroll into the kitchen and try a little pidgin English on the cook. The proprietor will teach anybody to use the chopsticks and roar with laughter over the failures of the novice. Everybody does as he or she pleases within certain very elastic bounds.[25]

In the Tenderloin and on Long Acre Square, the late hours kept by these "chop sueys" also made them a favorite of both the after-theater set and nighttime revelers who wanted some food in their bellies before they stumbled home to bed. As long as customers behaved themselves—and paid their bills—the proprietors didn't discriminate as to whom they served. In the tenement districts, the cheapest Chinese restaurants catered to "the rounder, the negro and the wandering poor." Indeed, African Americans were the main customers in some neighborhoods: "They seem to like the Chinese," one reporter wrote, "and, indeed, the noise in the kitchen reminds one of the similar condition of Southern kitchens under negro management."[26] Meanwhile, the "real Bohemian" remained down in Chinatown, looking for new culinary adventures:

> It is the Bohemian fad to expatriate himself, to seek strange and bizarre environments. As soon as a place begins to attract civilization he flees it for some new hiding place. When he chooses a Chinese dinner he must have a restaurant where no white man has ever before trod, if he can find one.... As soon as others begin to frequent it also, again he flies.[27]

Up and down the East Coast, chop sueys spread to all the big cities and many of the larger towns, a tribute to both the business acumen of Chinese restaurateurs and the attractions of their food. The Chinese communities of Boston and Philadelphia were founded around 1870, again beginning with a handful of laundries and grocery stores. At first, the natives kept their distance from Chinese food, warned by reports of suspicious sauces, appallingly "fresh" entrees, and odd eating implements. Less than a decade later, the *Boston Daily Globe* admitted that the "chop sui" at Moy Auk's at 36 Harrison was "very palatable." In 1891, one of the *Globe*'s reporters, stopping by another restaurant, heard music from above and investigated up the stairs:

> A door, the upper half of glass, met him. Another rest was taken, when lo, before him and within he caught sight of some of the 400 of Boston, ladies and gentleman, gathered at a feast. The reporter stood entranced. What

next? The cream of society eating Chinese viands in a Chinese restaurant, served by Chinese waiters and breathing in soulful Chinese music.

Among the dozen members of the city's Brahmin elite present were Mr. and Mrs. William Dean Howells, the Orientalists Ernest Fenollosa and Edward S. Morse, and sundry academics and artists dining on bird's nest soup, duck, chicken, sturgeon, rice, and, of course, chop suey. With such a testimonial, the reporter decided, "it's plain, the Chinese must not go."[28] In Philadelphia, meanwhile, the city's Chinatown had formed along Race Street, where by 1899 nearly a dozen "chop sueys" had opened and were very popular with the late-night crowd. As in New York and San Francisco, many of the ingredients were imported, but the fresh vegetables came from nearby Chinese farms that had been established just over the New Jersey state line. The little Chinatown of Washington, D.C., for better or worse, was the social center of the local Bohemian set:

As for this new Bohemia—this imitation of an imitation— I went down the other night to see what it was like. I really have a dark brown taste in my mouth yet. It was simply unutterable.... There were several women in the front room, painted, soggy creatures in loud clothes. In the middle room sat two or three Johnnies, out for the "devil of a time." They were very much frightened and cast apprehensive glances at the men about them. No wonder.... Most of the animals fed on noodle soup and chop-suey. If you want to see a sight, go and watch one of them get hold of the end of a six-foot noodle and commence to consume it. The chop-suey was a nasty-smelling dish, fairly bathed in grease.[29]

A few critics notwithstanding, these restaurants continued to spread into communities that had only small Chinese populations, carrying with them their very particular mix of food, price, customers, and atmosphere. From Atlanta to New Haven to Portland, Maine, eating a bowl of chop suey at midnight among a crowd of ruffians, fallen women, and thespians meant that you had achieved a state of worldly, urban sophistication.

In the Midwest, the arrival and acceptance of Chinese food followed a similar if somewhat delayed timeline. The first Chinese to visit the region were likely a troupe of jugglers who traveled up the Mississippi in the early 1850s. A handful of Chinese opened stores in Chicago and St. Louis during the following two decades, but the first groups of Asian immigrants didn't arrive until after the transcontinental railroad was completed in 1869. They founded little Chinatowns along Clark Street in Chicago and "Hop Alley" in St. Louis, once more earning their livelihoods by running laundries and shops and working as servants. In 1889, the *Chicago Tribune* noticed two Chinese stores in the city, as well as three vegetable farms, two butchers, and a basement restaurant where the owners "welcome Americans if they come to get a meal, but...fear the scoffers who gaze impudently at them, and enter only to ridicule."[30] For the 1893 World's Columbian Exposition, some local Chinese businessmen opened a "Chinese Village," complete with a theater, temple, tea garden, and café. They didn't trust Americans to have a taste for Chinese food: the café menu listed mostly American dishes (cold corned beef, egg sandwiches, potato salad, and the like) along with "Chinese style" rice, "Chinese Cakes & Confections," preserved fruit, and tea—in other words, all the fixings for a Western-style Chinese tea party. The following year, a young writer named Theodore Dreiser (six years shy of publishing his novel *Sister Carrie*) visited St. Louis's Chinese quarter to find some journalistic color. But he couldn't unearth any "opium joints" or gambling dens; he just found a block of South Eighth Street between Walnut and Market Streets where the immigrants liked to mingle on Sundays. Still looking for the unspeakably exotic, he arranged for a meal at one of the district's Chinese-only eateries, sampling duck, chicken, chicken soup, and something called "China dish":

> This dish was wonderful, awe-inspiring, and yet toothsome. It was served in a dish, half bowl, half platter. Around the platter-like edge were carefully placed bits of something which looked like wet piecrust and tasted like smoked fish. The way they stuck out along the edges suggested decoration of lettuce, parsley and watercress. The arrangement of the whole affair inspired visions of hot salad. Celery, giblets, onions, seaweed that looked like dulse, and some peculiar and totally foreign grains resembling barley, went to make this steaming-hot mass.[31]

Maybe this too is chop suey, but who knows? Dreiser is too busy preserving the mystery to bother asking the restaurant owner. The article ran with an engraving showing the restaurant's supposed interior: three Chinese men holding their chopsticks wrong and eating bowls of rats beneath a sign that reads "Stewed Rats Onions 15 Cents." Old stereotypes die hard. Less than a decade later, the *Chicago Tribune* blared "Chop Suey Fad Grows," as midwesterners crowded into Chinese restaurants in Chicago, St. Louis, Kansas City, Minneapolis, and beyond. The *Kansas City Star* remarked: "There are several chop suey restaurants in the city, but in none of them is real Chinese cooking served."[32] It would be decades before anyone would realize what they were missing.

Finally, we retrace our steps to the West, the last holdout against the enticements of Chinese food. In the early 1900s,

Figure 5.4. A postcard for the Guey Sam Chinese Resturant in Chicago, 1958. Chinese-Americans changed little between 1900 and the 1960s.

San Francisco newspapers reported fights that started over "chop suey," usually involving Irish immigrants or African Americans who refused to pay the Chinese owners of cheap eateries, but the actual dishes involved usually turned out to be American specialties like ham and eggs and potatoes. In 1903, the city's most avant-garde hostess, Mrs. Russel Cool, attempted to break cultural barriers by taking guests dressed in Chinese costume to a Chinatown banquet, "from soup to soup again, all the way through chop suey and paste balls and bird's nests." Sadly, she was ahead of her time, as "the few who were brave enough to swallow the courses had difficulty in picking up enough to swallow." "I felt dreadfully guilty about it," she later admitted.[33] The following year, a young society beauty broke numerous taboos by visiting Los Angeles's Chinatown every night, driven by her lust for noodles. At eleven o'clock, she would sweep into a joint "where the chief patrons are outcast negroes and white damsels of no reputation," give the customers a haughty stare, and exclaim: "Pigs! All of you. Pigs!" Then she would order three bowls of Chinese noodles, each "large enough to satisfy a hippopotamus," consume them with fastidious manners, and depart into the night, sated.[34] By 1906, Los Angeles had chop suey restaurants like the Shanghai Chop Suey Café, where the local Credit Men's Association held its annual banquet. The menu included pork soup with vege-tables, ham omelettes, boneless duck with ham, chicken with chestnuts, chicken stuffed with birds' nests, and preserved fruit, tea, and cakes, along with the namesake dish.[35]

Early on the morning of April 18, 1906, San Franciscans were thrown from their beds by the shocks of a massive earthquake. Rushing into the streets, they saw that the initial tremors had destroyed some buildings and damaged many, ruptured gas lines, and sparked fires. As aftershocks rattled the city, property owners set fire to their own buildings to try to recoup their losses (their insurance policies covered fire but not earthquakes). The city caught fire, and five hundred blocks were burned beyond repair. Within hours, troops were called from the Presidio military base and began patrolling the streets with orders to shoot looters on site. Chinatown was not spared the chaos, and eyewitnesses saw many whites, including National Guardsmen and "respectably-dressed women," pawing through the rubble looking for spoils. (Decades later, shame-faced descendants were still donating looted Chinese goods to local museums.) The local newspapers cheered the destruction of Chinatown, which they long had claimed was the city's largest blight, an overcrowded ghetto teeming with crime and immorality. A committee was formed to forcibly remove the entire community from San Francisco, but the Chinese fought back by pointing out that they were property owners, too, and the city would lose huge amounts of trade if they moved their businesses elsewhere. Within weeks, they began to rebuild Chinatown—bigger, cleaner, and with more Oriental flair. Gone, or at least better hidden, were the opium joints and the dark haunts of the hatchet men. This "new look" Chinatown attracted businessmen, tourists, and even local San Franciscans eager for an evening's amusement. In early 1907, the *San Francisco Call* ran a small ad for a restaurant named The China, located at 1538 Geary Boulevard and serving "novel Oriental dishes that please your palate," including chop suey, noodles, tea, and preserves.[36] White San Francisco's fall into the clutches of Chinese food had finally begun, perhaps impelled by the shared suffering during the earthquake and its aftermath. Two years later, chop suey had so overwhelmed the West that the head of the California State Association declared that "if chop suey houses and Chinese laundries were not eliminated from the United States the next century would be one of demoralization and decay."[37] His finger in the dike was not enough; the chop suey flood continued, overrunning even the communities in the West that had been most adamantly opposed to Chinese immigration.

From the distance of over a century, it's hard to understand the reasons behind chop suey's phenomenal popularity. To current tastes, the dish is a brownish, overcooked stew, strangely flavorless, with no redeeming qualities, and redolent of bad school cafeterias and dingy, failing Chinese restaurants. Any redemption is only possible through nostalgia; perhaps a forkful of the dish evokes memories of Sunday evening family meals down at the corner Chinese American eatery. To American diners of a century ago, chop suey was the food of the moment, both sophisticated and enjoyed by everyman. They liked chop suey because it was cheap, filling, and exotic, but there was something more. Chop suey *satisfied*, not just filling stomachs but giving a deeper feeling of gratification. This links it to an important part of the western culinary tradition. Since at least as early as the days of ancient Rome, peasants and urban laborers in the west have subsisted on jumbles of meat and vegetables boiled down to indecipherability: mushes, porridges, burgoos, hodgepodges, ragouts, olla podridas, and the like. Perhaps in chop suey westerners tasted a bit of the same savory primal stew that has fueled them for so many centuries.

Inevitably, just as the craze for chop suey peaked, the backlash began. Its first act was comic, at least in the rendering of a *New York Times* reporter. It seems that in 1904, a cook named Lem Sen, fresh from San Francisco, appeared in a Lower Manhattan lawyer's office claiming that he was the inventor of chop suey. Further, he remarked that "chop-suey is no more a national dish of the Chinese than pork and beans.... There is not a grain of anything Celestial in it." To the contrary, he claimed, he had concocted the dish in the kitchen of a San Francisco "Bohemian" restaurant just before Li Hongzhang arrived in the United States: "The owner of the restaurant...suggested that Lem Sen manufacture some weird dish that would pass as Chinese and gratify the public craze at the time. Lem Sen says that it was then he introduced to the astonished world the great dish." Then, he said, an American man stole his recipe, and Lem Sen wanted compensation: "Mellikan man makee thousand dollar now. Lem Sen, he makee, too, but me allee time look for Mellican man who stole. Me come. Me find! Now me wantee [recipe] back, an' all stop makee choop soo or pay for allowee do same." (American newspapers of the time typically reported the speech of immigrants and African Americans in demeaning dialect.) Lem Sen's lawyer threatened to obtain an injunction "restraining all Chinese restaurant keepers from making and serving chop suey."[38] He never followed through, perhaps because New Yorkers knew that Len Sen's claim was absurd; they had been eating chop suey down on Mott Street for over a decade before Li Hongzhang's visit.

The idea that chop suey was not Chinese, though, had staying power. The following year, the *Boston Globe* ran a photo of six Chinese students at a textile trade school in New Bedford, Massachusetts, each neatly dressed in a Western suit and tie, beneath the headline "Never Heard of Chop Suey in China." The students, two from the Yangzi River area and the others from Guangzhou, claimed that "not one of them had ever heard of chop suey until they came to this country." Rather, it was "a cheap imitation of a dish which pleased Li Hung Chang at a banquet a dozen years ago."[39] Of course, Li actually never ate chop suey, but never mind that detail.

Stories of the "chop suey hoax" proliferated from then on; the gist of the story was always that the dish was a fraud, invented for Americans too ignorant to recognize real Chinese food. The sources were American travelers just back from China or more often Chinese themselves, often highly educated diplomats or businessmen from anywhere but the hinterland of the Pearl River Delta. With their deep knowledge and experience of the Middle Kingdom, they uncovered an alternate tale of the dish's creation. It seems that in China, some beggars carry copper pots and go to the kitchen doors of houses pleading for leftovers. When they have enough scraps, they put their collection over the fire and cook up a miscellaneous "beggar's hash" or, as the Chinese call it, chop suey. The dish was first presented to Americans on some fateful night in Gold Rush–era San Francisco, in a Chinese-run boardinghouse—or was it a restaurant? Carl

Crow, an American businessman in Shanghai, told the most elaborate version of the story, which he got from a Chinese diplomat:

> Soon after the discovery of gold the Chinese colony in the city was large enough to support a couple of restaurants conducted by Cantonese cooks, who catered only to their fellow-exiles from the Middle Kingdom. The white men had heard the usual sailor yarns about what these pigtailed yellow men ate, and one night a crowd of miners decided they would try this strange fare just to see what it was like. They had been told that Chinese ate rats and they wanted to see whether or not it was true. When they got to the restaurant the regular customers had finished their suppers, and the proprietor was ready to close his doors. But the miners demanded food, so he did the best he could to avoid trouble and get them out of the way as soon as possible. He went out into the kitchen, dumped together all the food his Chinese patrons had left in their bowls, put a dash of Chinese sauce on top and served it to his unwelcome guests. As they didn't understand Cantonese slang they didn't know what he meant when he told them that they were eating chop suey, or "beggar hash." At any rate, they liked it so well that they came back for more and in that chance way the great chop suey industry was established.[40]

According to a *Philadelphia Inquirer* headline, the moral of this tale was "The Origin of Chop Suey Is an Enormous Chinese Joke."[41] Even today, the dish is described as the "biggest culinary joke played by one culture on another."[42] In every version, the butts of the joke were the Americans who were too stupid to know that they were essentially eating garbage.

In reality, of course, the Sze Yap–born residents of Chinatown apparently liked chop suey just as much as the barbarians, and there is no evidence of white San Franciscans eating chop suey before 1900. So why did the "experts" repeat a story that appears to have no basis in fact? Well, the tale about the bullying of the Chinese restaurant owner does ring true, and the punch line about eating garbage suggests a veiled revenge (analogous to the chef spitting in the soup) for decades of mistreatment. Call it a myth that conveys a larger historical "truth." Despite these stories, the hungry American masses kept on gobbling chop suey with gusto, for now.

American Chop Suey

*I*n 1909, Elsie Sigel, age nineteen, lived in New York City's Washington Heights and liked Chinese food and, apparently, Chinese men. Elsie's mother, devoting her energies to converting the Chinese to Christianity, regularly visited a mission down on Mott Street. Both mother and daughter frequented two "chop sueys"—the one in their Upper Manhattan neighborhood and a high-class Chinese restaurant down on Mott Street named the Port Arthur. The Sigels' apartment was decorated with vases, tea sets, and other curios from Chinatown. Elsie's father, Paul Sigel, a government clerk whose father had been a revered general in the Civil War, detested his wife's mission work and often threatened to eject any Chinese men he found visiting the Sigel household. In fact, Chinese men often did visit; they came to ask for Mrs. Sigel's help and to court her daughter. Though not considered a beauty—she had a broad, flat nose and bad teeth—Elsie was pleasingly plump, dressed well, and possessed an agreeable, soft-spoken nature. Attracted by these qualities, both Leon Ling, the suave and well-dressed ex-manager of the Washington Heights chop suey, and Chu Gain, the manager of the Port Arthur, were among her suitors. Mrs. Sigel favored Chu Gain, who was rumored to be wealthy, but Elsie preferred Ling and had been writing steamy notes to him for over a year. Many guessed that she and Ling were having an affair. However, in the spring of 1909 Elsie seemed to be tiring of Ling and, swayed by her mother, turning her affections to Chu Gain. Those who knew the trio sensed that something bad might happen: Leon Ling was persistent and known to have a violent streak.

Figure 6.1. Elsie Sigel's unsolved 1909 murder, dubbed the "Chinatown Trunk Mystery" by the national media, reinforced misgivings about the exotic world of that neighborhood. The police description of the main suspect as a "Chinaman" who "usually dresses like an American" and "talks good English" did not allay unease.

On the morning of June 9, 1909, Elsie Sigel told her mother that she was going to visit the grocer, the butcher, and then her grandmother in the Bronx. She made the first two stops but never arrived at her grandmother's. By evening, the family was worried, their fears only partially alleviated by the arrival of a telegram from Washington, D.C.: "Don't worry. Will be home Sunday noon. E.J.S." Sure that her daughter had eloped, most likely with Leon Ling, they nevertheless hurried to Chinatown the next morning to see if they could locate her. (Fearing a scandal, they didn't report the disappearance to the police.) They scoured the neighborhood between Broadway and the Bowery, running into Chu Gain, who joined the search for Elsie, but not Leon Ling. Sun Leung, the owner of a restaurant over a bicycle store at Eighth Avenue and Forty-eighth Street, was also looking for Leon Ling, who worked there as a waiter. Ling shared an apartment with two other Chinese men on the fourth floor of the restaurant's building. Sun Leung knocked on the door of his room again and again over the next few days, until on June 18 he smelled a foul odor coming from behind the door. He ran for a policeman, who soon arrived with a locksmith to open the room. Inside the small, neat bedroom, they found a black trunk bound with rope. The policeman cut the rope, pried open the lid, and uncovered the decaying corpse of a young woman, wrapped in a blanket. Nothing in the trunk identified the body, but investigators found a letter in a bureau addressed to a "Miss Elizabeth Sigel." They hurried to Washington Heights.

Paul Sigel admitted that his daughter was missing, but on viewing the body, neither he nor his two sons would confirm that the young woman was Elsie. Positive identification came from Mrs. Florence Todd, the head of the Mott Street mission, and two days later the Sigel family held a private funeral at the Woodlawn Cemetery. Afterward, Mrs. Sigel retired to a sanatorium in Connecticut, and Elsie's father and brothers refused to make any further comment about the frightful case. Throughout the city and indeed across the nation, an uproar arose about the murder. "Chinaman Is Supposed to Be the Murderer of Young Girl" blared the *Ogden Standard* out in Utah, one of the many newspapers that led with the story. In response to the outcry, the police began an intensive manhunt for Leon Ling, wiring descriptions of him around the country. They rounded up all the Chinese people associated with the case and submitted them to questioning that sometimes turned brutal. Out on the street, any Chinese man who looked "Americanized"—in Western clothes and without a queue—was viewed with suspicion. In upstate New York, Pennsylvania, Chicago, California, and elsewhere, local whites turned in dozens of Asian men, both Chinese and Japanese. Despite a watch kept at every major railroad station and the Pacific Mail steamship docks in San Francisco, the presumed murderer remained elusive. The New York police declared that they would soon get their man, but William M. Clemens, the *Chicago Tribune*'s "Famous Expert in Crimology," thought otherwise: "The New York sleuths did not reckon with the Chinese mind.... A race that drinks its wine hot, shakes hands with itself in greeting, eats its eggs and melon only when old and dried—such a race in criminal things can be looked upon for unexpected cunning."[1] Ling was never caught, and the real story of how Elsie Sigel died remains a mystery.

The case received such widespread publicity partly because "white slavery" was a prominent issue at the time. Many influential people, including politicians, policemen, religious leaders, and feminists, believed that an epidemic of prostitution was sweeping across the country and young women were being forced into lives of shame. This conviction had many roots, including the fact that thousands of women were

finding jobs and a new financial independence in cities, prejudice toward the masses of European immigrants (including
many single young women) then arriving, and a few actual
prostitution cases. The outcry over Elsie Sigel's murder helped
link the nation's Chinatowns and their thousands of chop suey
joints to the white slavery issue. Like public dance halls,
brothels, gambling houses, and disreputable hotels, reform-
ers declared that Chinese restaurants were places where
unmarried women could be lured into depravity. On Mott
Street, where the restaurants did the bulk of their business
late at night, the police forced early closing times and tem-
porarily barred unaccompanied white women from the district altogether. In her book *The Market for Souls*, Elizabeth
Goodnow describes her tour of Lower Manhattan's fleshpots,
ending with Chinatown: "We entered a house that had a chop
suey place on the first floor. The rest of the house was filled
with women and the fumes of opium came down the stairs."[2]
Goodnow ascends to the bordello and finds a small room
furnished with gaudy Chinese embroidery and a Chinese idol.
On the bed lies a white prostitute who has killed herself with
an overdose of opium, another victim of the path to ruin that
began with an innocent visit to Chinatown. The *Chicago
Tribune* reported:

> More than 300 Chicago white girls have sacrificed
> themselves to the influence of the chop suey 'joints'
> during the last year, according to police statistics....
> Vanity and the desire for showy clothes led to their
> downfall, it is declared. It was accomplished only after
> they smoked and drank in the chop suey restaurants
> and permitted themselves to be hypnotized by the
> dreamy, seductive music that is always on tap.[3]

Meanwhile, in South Bend, Indiana, the Board of Health
was more direct, calling that city's Chinese restaurants

"nothing but opium joints with chop suey attachments."[4] The police and other groups continued to associate chop sueys with sin for almost a decade, and news of Chinatown raids dominated headlines.

Back on the women's page, something very different was happening. Instead of joining in the anti–Chinese food frenzy, syndicated columnists like Marion Harland and Jane Eddington published numerous recipes for chop suey and other dishes, apparently due to public demand. As Eddington wrote in 1914 in the *Chicago Tribune*, "there is always a demand for chop suey recipes." One of the most prolific women writers of her time, Harland was always game to try new things, even at age eighty-three:

> So many nationalities unite to make up the American people that it is only natural we should have diversities in our bill of fare. For myself, I like it. I enjoy trying new dishes and adding to my table combinations which have had their birth on the other side of the ocean.... We have gone further afield and eaten and enjoyed chop suey, and from a number of our constituency have come requests for full and minute directions for making this Chinese dish, for instructions how and with what to serve it.[5]

The first Chinese cookbook for American readers, *Chinese Cookery in the Home Kitchen*, had been written two years earlier by another newspaperwoman, Jessie Louise Nolton of the *Chicago Inter-Ocean*. The recipes replicated the menu of the average downtown Chinese restaurant: boiled rice, multiple kinds of "chop sooy," "eggs fo yong," roast pork and chicken, fried rice, and so on.

For more sophisticated housewives, preparing a bowl of chop suey for the family meal was not enough. In 1913, *Harper's Bazaar* published a series of articles on how to cook and serve a Chinese dinner, luncheon, and tea party. These pieces were written by one Sara Eaton Bossé, the daughter of a Chinese mother and English father, who lived a distinctly Bohemian lifestyle as a painter and artist's model in New York. For her, these Chinese parties were theatrical events, a way of escaping from middle-class existence into the realm of East Asian exotica: "A Chinese dinner, properly served, proves a delightful and novel form of entertainment. It should be served, of course, in the purely Chinese fashion, which lends an added charm and mystery to the dishes themselves."[6] Preparation for these parties took days, beginning with trips to Chinatown (those in New York, Chicago, Boston, San Francisco, and Montreal are listed) to purchase the proper furniture, table settings, decorations, and finally ingredients. Luncheon hostesses seeking more "authenticity" required guests to come in Chinese costume and acquired a Chinese "boy" to wait on table (if not, the maid could be dressed in Chinese fashion and instructed to shuffle noiselessly). Wisely, Bossé advises her readers to first taste the dishes in Chinatown before trying to cook them. The menus are fairly straightforward, resembling the set feasts that restaurants like the Port Arthur served to wealthy white slumming parties. Her Chinese dinner includes bird's nest soup, sweet and sour fish, pineapple chicken, duck chow mein, "Gar Lu Chop Suey," sautéed cucumbers, Chinese mushrooms with green peppers, and the usual assortment of preserved fruits and Chinese cakes for dessert. The following year, Bossé and her sister Winnifred, writing under the pseudonym Onoto Watanna, published their groundbreaking *Chinese-Japanese Cook Book*. This milestone (the first Japanese cookbook written in English and perhaps the second Chinese), representing the cutting edge of cuisine at the time, was a perfect source for the hostess who sought to re-create a bit of Bohemia in her home.

We get another glimpse of how American women used these recipes and the suggestions for Chinese-themed parties in Sinclair Lewis's 1920 novel *Main Street*. Born in the small town of Sauk Centre, Minnesota, Lewis excelled at describing Middle America in the post–World War I era. In much of his work, Chinese restaurants ("lanterns painted with cherry-blossoms and with pagodas, hung against lattices of lustrous gold and black") appear prominently as part of the downtown landscape of midwestern towns and cities.

The protagonist of *Main Street* is Carol Kennicott, a young woman from Minneapolis who marries a doctor and goes to live in his dreary, conservative hometown, Gopher Prairie. A few months after arriving, she decides to throw a house-warming party, as people do in the city. She spends weeks on preparations, going to Minneapolis to buy supplies, new furniture, clothes, and a Japanese obi to hang on the wall. Her guests consist of Gopher Prairie's entire "aristocracy"— doctors, lawyers, businessmen, and their wives. They expect a prim and proper entertainment, followed by a filling meat-and-potatoes meal, but Carol Kennicott has another idea: something "noisy and undignified." After making her guests play a game she learned in Chicago—in the dark, with no shoes, and on their hands and knees no less—she produces paper Chinese masquerade costumes she has bought for everyone to wear. She also changes her dress, becoming "an airy figure in trousers and a coat of green brocade edged with gold; a high gold collar under a proud chin; black hair pierced with jade pins; a languid peacock fan in an outstretched hand; eyes uplifted to a vision of pagoda towers."[7] After regaling her guests with an impromptu "Chinese" concert, she leads them "in a dancing procession" to the dining room, where they find blue bowls of chow mein, with lychee nuts and ginger preserved in syrup. "None of them save that city-rounder Harry Haydock had heard of any

Chinese dish except chop sooey. With agreeable doubt they ventured through the bamboo shoots into the golden fried noodles of the chow mein."[8] The eating guests allow Carol to rest for a minute, and she briefly considers one more gesture to shock them—smoking a cigarette—before dismissing the thought as "obscene." In the social column of the local weekly, the editor (who attended the event) praises the party and its novel diversions, including the "dainty refreshments served in true Oriental style." But a few days later, Carol's best friend tells her what the guests really thought: the party was too expensive, and the Chinese theme too novel: "And it certainly is unfair of them to make fun of your having that Chinese food—chow mein, was it?—and to laugh about your wearing your pretty trousers."[9] Carol bursts into tears, and no more Chinese food is served in Gopher Prairie. (A few chapters later, however, Carol and her husband escape for a quick trip to Minneapolis, where they visit a "Chinese restaurant that was frequented by clerks and their sweethearts on paydays. They sat at a teak and marble table eating Eggs Foo yung, and listened to a brassy automatic piano, and were altogether cosmopolitan.")[10] The Chinese restaurant experience is something only urban sophisticates appreciate, at least in Minnesota in the 1920s.

Mechanical pianos, fixtures in many chop suey joints by World War I, propelled some Chinese restaurant owners into a new phase of business. These machines were the jukeboxes of their day: you put a nickel in the slot, and the piano's mechanism played fox-trots, jazz tunes, and popular songs. Unsettled by one such piano's "whang and pulse," the members of the Women's Christian Temperance Union chapter in Hammond, Indiana, drilled holes in the floor of the apartment above the King Honk Low restaurant and poured dirty mop water onto the patrons in 1913. The mechanical piano's quick rise to popularity soon inspired entrepreneurial restaurant owners to bring entertainment—music, dancing, and a floor show—into their establishments. (They had been best known as *after*-theater joints.) One of the earliest of these new nightclub-restaurants was the Pekin, at Broadway and Forty-seventh Street, which a 1916 New York City guidebook listed as "an elaborate Chinese show restaurant; cabaret, music, dancing."[11] This trend only accelerated when the Volstead Act banning the sale of alcoholic beverages went into effect in early 1920. In the first years of Prohibition, tens of thousands of restaurants and nightclubs across the nation, from Manhattan lobster palaces to Los Angeles cantinas, went out of business. Chinese restaurants, however, thrived, because they had never served alcohol—tea had always been their most potent beverage.

By 1924, Broadway between Times Square and Columbus Circle was home to fourteen big "chop suey jazz places." One Chinese nightclub owner, a former Essex Street laundryman, supposedly wore a huge diamond ring, rode in an imported car, and squired around a bottle-blond burlesque dancer. In San Francisco, most of these new nightspots were in Chinatown, probably beginning with Shanghai Low in the 1920s. Featuring all-Chinese singers, musicians, chorus lines, and even strippers, clubs like the Forbidden City attracted a clientele of politicians, movie stars, and businessmen out for an exotic good time. In smaller cities, the entertainment at Chinese restaurants, still revolving around the player piano, was more modest. On Atlanta's Auburn Avenue, the heart of the African American district, the Lum Pong Chop Suey Place had the danceable "I'll Be Glad When You Are Dead, You Rascal You" cued up on the piano.

Nearly all of these Chinese restaurant-nightclubs catered strictly to mass tastes; there was never a Chinese version of El Morocco or the Stork Club. A 1934 New York restaurant guide describes Chin Lee's, one of the largest of these

Figure 6.2. From 1938 to 1962, San Francisco's Forbidden City nightclub featured performances by Asian-American musicians, dancers, strippers, and magicians. Performers were given such nicknames as the "Chinese Sinatra" to attract non-Chinese clients.

joints at Broadway and Forty-ninth Street, as "chop suey chef to the masses and dispenser of dim lights, ceaseless dance music, undistinguished floor shows, and tons of chow mein." As for its patrons, they were young, numerous, and hungry:

> Here at any hour of the day, from eleven to midnight, you may find the girl who waits on you at Gimbel's, her boy friend, who is one of Wall Street's million margin clerks, noisy parties of Bronx handmaidens babblingly

bent on a movie and subgum spree, college boys from
Princeton (slumming, of course), and, perhaps, even
your next-door neighbor. Within the not-so-occidental
confines of Chin's, the girls dance with other girls,
and the boys dance with anyone handy. The prices are
scaled down to suit the toiling thousands, and Chin
Lee's offers its clientele, for 55 cents or 85 cents, their
idea of a $5 floor show. Though their idea may be a
bit vague and thin, the customers seem to like it and
applaud lustily between mouthfuls of fried noodles
and oriental onions.[12]

These restaurant owners were all too aware that they weren't
selling caviar and champagne but chop suey, ham and cheese
sandwiches, and the like—food everybody liked but nobody
wanted to spend much money on. The real profits were in
volume and in liquor; the businessmen rented the largest
possible spaces and featured a wide array of exotic cocktails
on their menus.

The specialties of the Chinese American menu, from
chop suey to moo goo gai pan to pepper steak, eventually
lost their exotic associations. In his 1916 novel *Uneasy
Money*, P. G. Wodehouse listed chop suey among the "great
American institutions," up there with New Jersey mosqui-
toes, the Woolworth Building, and corn on the cob. In big
cities like New York, the most popular Chinese restaurant
dishes had become everyday food:

[Chop suey] has become a staple. It is vigorously vying
with sandwiches and salad as the sometime nourishment of the young women typists and telephonists of
John, Dey and Fulton Streets. It rivals coffee-and-two-
kinds-of-cake as the recess repast of the sales forces of
West Thirty-Fourth Street department stores. At lunch
hour there is an eager exodus toward Chinatown of

the women workers employed in Franklin, Duane and Worth Streets. To them the district is not an intriguing bit of transplanted Orient. It is simply a good place to eat.[13]

In midwestern towns like those Sinclair Lewis used as models for Gopher Prairie, Chinese food probably held on to its mystery through the 1930s. (For small-town sophisticates, the local Chinese restaurant was often the only eatery where they could find both glamour and late closing hours.) Beyond these establishments, chop suey was now served in soda fountains, coffee shops, school cafeterias, military messes, church suppers, and even Manhattan's ultrasophisticated Stork Club (whose version was made with wild rice, butter, celery, spinach, and big rib steaks). Forty years after its appearance on Mott Street, chop suey had become cheap, fun, and filling American food.

Americans' embrace of chop suey was impelled by more than the assemblage of ingredients, style of preparation, and lingering whiffs of the far-off East: chop suey penetrated the larger culture, mutating and changing its meaning depending on the context. Cookbooks gave housewives one way to prepare chop suey and other Chinese dishes, but soy sauce, bean sprouts, and the like remained hard to find outside big cities. By 1915, regional companies like Chicago's Libby, McNeil & Libby had started canning chop suey and selling it in grocery stores; apparently, these products were bland and unappealing and didn't really take off. In 1920, two men in Detroit, Wally Smith and Ilhan New, began growing bean sprouts in Smith's bathtub and canning them. Within four years, their company, which they named La Choy, had a whole line of canned Chinese foods on the market: bean sprouts, mushrooms, crispy chow mein noodles, Chinese vegetables (mixed water chestnuts and bamboo shoots),

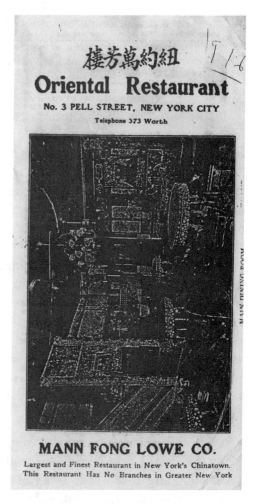

樓芳萬約紐

Oriental Restaurant

No. 3 PELL STREET, NEW YORK CITY

Telephone 373 Worth

MANN FONG LOWE CO.

Largest and Finest Restaurant in New York's Chinatown.
This Restaurant Has No Branches in Greater New York

Figure 6.3. The 1916 menu for the Oriental Restaurant in New York's Chinatown contains dishes like birds' nest soup and sharks' fins, as well as "chop sooy" and chow mein.

"Chinese Sauce" (soy sauce), and "Brown Sauce," a kind of savory, molasses-based gravy. The labels claimed you could now make "genuine Chop Suey or Chow Mein in ten minutes." According to the millions of recipe booklets La Choy distributed, all you had to do was fry up some meat, onions, and celery; mix in La Choy vegetables; spoon in the Chinese Sauce and Brown Sauce; and serve the resulting stew over rice or chow mein noodles. Semi-homemade chop suey tasted better than the canned version, and La Choy soon dominated the grocery aisles. (Now owned by ConAgra Foods, it remains the leader in canned Chinese American provisions today.)

In the early twentieth century, chop suey also took a lexical jump from Chinese restaurants onto other kinds of menus—a testament to its penetration of the culture. Soda fountains began offering "chop suey sundaes," described as "chopped dates, cherries, figs, raisins, citron and different kinds of nuts, all forming a cherry colored syrup, [and] poured over a round allowance of cream; then...sprinkled with more nuts."[14] Two decades later, this concoction had become a mélange of chopped tropical and fresh fruits flavored with cherry syrup and served over ice cream with sliced bananas, nuts, and whipped cream. "American chop suey," another faux version of the dish, was invented around the same time. The *Alton (IL) Evening Telegraph* called the Chinese dish "the high water mark of the delicacy" and then described the American version as perhaps more satisfying to less sophisticated appetites. Here's the recipe:

> Place in a spider a lump of butter, size of a walnut; in this, when hot, brown one and one-half pounds of Hamburg steak; heat a can of tomatoes, fry four medium-sized onions, and boil two cups of macaroni or spaghetti; seasoning each article well; drain macaroni and add it, with the onions and tomatoes, to the meat, and simmer five minutes. No side dishes are needed if this is made for lunch, as it makes a palatable, substantial lunch for six or seven people.[15]

Home cooks in rural New England and the Midwest today still prepare nearly the same recipe—filling food for hardworking people. As the writer for the *Evening Telegraph* admitted, chop suey was just another word for hash.

Away from the restaurant counter and home dinner table, the practitioners of the other popular arts also embraced chop suey as a concept. As early as 1900, Chinese food was considered fun and lively, with plenty of mass appeal. Why not throw it into a song, a movie, or a vaudeville show? That year, chop suey was the centerpiece of a twenty-four-second short entitled *In a Chinese Restaurant*. Produced by the American Mutoscope and Biograph Company, it showed the Bowery personality Chuck Connors and two Chinese men seated at a table and eating chop suey while having an animated conversation—a scene of intercultural fraternization that probably shocked many in the audience. Over the next few decades, Chinese restaurants appeared in a number of movies, usually as the quintessential urban, working-class eatery—the kind of place where hard-bitten showgirls discussed their men, or the cop fell in love with the gangland moll. A few of these films also played with the old white slavery stereotypes. In Harold Lloyd's 1919 short *Chop Suey & Company*, a heroic but hopelessly naïve policeman becomes convinced that evil Chinese are plotting to abduct a young woman eating in a chop suey joint. After many gags, it's revealed that she's really an actress rehearsing scenes for a play. Others traded in chauvinism, like Gale Henry's 1919 comedy *The Detectress*, featuring special glasses that allow a character to see what's really in chop suey: dead dragonflies, rope, the sole of a shoe, and a puppy. One of the rare films to apply these stereotypes more seriously to the Chinese restaurant setting was the 1930 potboiler *East Is West*, starring Lew Ayres. In it, young Ming Toy (played by Lupe Vélez!) is rescued from slavery and brought to San Francisco, where she attracts the attention of evil Charlie Yong (Edward G. Robinson), the city's chop suey kingpin. In the nick of time, they discover that Ming Toy isn't Chinese at all but the child of white missionaries and can finally marry Lew Ayres after all. (The *New York Times* reviewer noted that even pulp magazines would hesitate to publish such a trashy story.)

Race also figured in some of the early song lyrics that referred to Chinese food. The 1909 "Chink, Chink, Chinaman," by Bert Williams, a popular African American vaudeville performer, begins: "One time have chop suey house / on street where heap white boys, / all time sing 'bout chink chink chinee / all time make heap noise." The narrator decides to move to the African American neighborhood but discovers that even there the residents sing "Chink chink chinee." By the 1920s, these stereotypes had become stale and overused, at least in their most blatant form. The era's most popular dance was the jazz fox-trot, inspiring tunes like the 1923 "Hi Lee Hi Lo—I Love You Chop Suey a la Foxee" and Louis Armstrong's famous "Cornet Chop Suey," an instrumental with a bright and lively melody. Two years later, Margaret Johnson recorded Sidney Bechet's humorous "Who'll Chop Your Suey When I'm Gone?"

> There is something, honey baby, that grieves my mind.
> I'm thinking about your future, when I leave you
>   behind.
> It's got me up a tree—here's the thing that worries me:
> Who'll chop your suey when I'm gone?
> Who'll corn your fritters Sunday morn?

Borrowing from African American artists, white songwriters used food-related motifs for novelty songs, for example, "A Bowl of Chop Suey and You-ey," from the 1934 Jack Oakie musical *Shoot the Works*:

> Take a look at this place that we've wandered into,
> It's not Arabian, it's not Hindu,
> It's just a Chinese eat place, not a swell or elite place,

I won't order rice or tea, here's what appeals to me.
All I want is a bowl of chop suey, a bowl of chop
  suey and you-ey,
A cozy little table for two-ey with a bowl of chop
  suey and you-ey.

(It goes on like this for far too long.) This stew of Chinese food, fun, and romance continued into the 1950s with songs like Louis Prima and Keely Smith's "Chop Suey, Chow Mein" ("Chop suey, chow mein, tufu [sic] and you, / I've got the craziest feeling... "). Perhaps something about food as a theme encourages frivolity. Only Rogers and Hammerstein's song "Chop Suey," from their 1957 musical *Flower Drum Song*, resists cartoon imagery and addresses racial themes more earnestly, reflecting an era when these issues were beginning to be treated more seriously.

Visual artists also began using Chinese restaurants in their paintings and drawings: the chop suey joint was now a quintessential urban setting. Images ranged from the stylized *Vanity Fair* cartoons by the Mexican artist Miguel Covarrubias to the earthier and more realistic work of Reginald Marsh. His 1929 etching *Chop Suey Dancers* #2 portrays three all-female couples dressed as flappers practicing their dance moves in a Chinese nightclub, probably during their lunch hour. A series of booths lines the wall in the background, where a shadowy figure in black, maybe a Chinese waiter, flits across the scene, appearing to leer at the women. Arguably the most famous of all Chinese restaurant paintings is Edward Hopper's 1929 painting *Chop Suey*. As in many of his works, a strong dose of melancholy infuses the scene. In the foreground we see two women, both in cloche hats, sitting at a little table in the dining room of a second-floor Chinese restaurant. Through the window we see the fragment of a large sign saying "SUEY" and a slice of fire escape ladder. It may be wintertime, because a woman's yellow coat hangs on a peg. One of the women, in a lilac blouse, has her back to us. Opposite her sits a woman in a green sweater, its color made pale by the sun. Under her hat, her face is stark white, with bright red lips and luminous eyes that seem to be stunned or saddened by something her tablemate has said. On the table between the two women stand a pale pink teapot and an empty blue bowl. Perhaps this unusual scene for a painting, the chop suey joint, was meant to help create a jarring suggestion of tension and loss.

By the 1920s, chop suey and chow mein had claimed a place in the national diet alongside ham and eggs, coffee and a slice of pie, and the Sunday pot roast. For those who were not part of the mainstream culture, eating Chinese food offered one way to join it, to prove one belonged. For the sons and daughters of Jewish immigrants, growing up in New York, Chicago, and many other urban areas, all the chop suey joints up one flight of stairs on side streets proved particularly attractive. By 1925, the United States was home to well over a million Jewish immigrants, the majority from Eastern Europe and Russia. Most of these immigrants continued to follow the religious practices of Old World Orthodox Judaism, where food and spirituality mingled: eating was another way of celebrating the divine. Each meal began with blessings over the wine, the bread, and the rest of the dishes. Of course, Jewish food was as much about what it was *not* as about what it was. The laws of *kashrut* (kosher practice) forbid a long list of foods, including pork, rabbit, eel, shrimp, lobster, insects (except for certain grasshoppers), and any meat that has not been ritually slaughtered by a kosher butcher. Meat and dairy products cannot be served together or heated in the same pot, and one is forbidden to consume many cooked foods unless they have been prepared by Jewish hands or under rabbinic supervision. Compare this with the anything-goes tradition of Chinese food, as Lin Yutang described it: "We are too over-populated and famine is too common for us not to eat everything we can lay our hands on."[16] In spite of—and perhaps also because of—this fundamental difference, for second- and third-generation American Jews, Chinese restaurants became a home away from home.

During the 1920s and 1930s, Jews coming of age were being pulled in many directions. First, there was the weight of religious custom as practiced by their immigrant parents. After arriving, many settled in densely populated Jewish districts of the big cities. On New York's Lower East Side, synagogues could be found on nearly every block, and Yiddish, not English, was the lingua franca. These were insular neighborhoods, cultural ghettoes with little contact with the larger society—in fact, these Lower East Siders rarely even visited nearby Chinatown. But for their American-educated children, this Old World Jewish identity was in many ways a dead end. Jews who emigrated from Europe had been cut off from their ancestral homes in the cities and shtetls by war, political unrest, and anti-Semitism. Their children born in the United States would probably live there for the rest of their lives. If they wanted to succeed, they had to speak English and drop the outward signs of being observant Jews—beards and sidelocks for men and headscarves for women. The necessity to assimilate grew as their families moved from the urban ghettoes out into newer and more ethnically mixed middle-class neighborhoods away from the city center. Part of that assimilation was becoming accustomed to the alien eating habits they were exposed to in schools—a ham sandwich and a glass of milk—and workplaces. Their immigrant parents had rarely, if ever, eaten out; they only felt comfortable with food they had cooked themselves. But young Jews employed in factories and offices were on occasion invited to go out with their workmates. Their destination was a place called a restaurant, with alien customs like ordering from a menu and mysterious food that didn't conform to kosher standards. During this era, the most popular restaurants to visit for a fun, after-work meal were Chinese.

We get a picture of the difficulty second- and third-generation Jews faced in crossing the culinary gulf to eating Chinese food from Herman Wouk's bestselling 1954 novel *Marjorie Morningstar*. Its story begins around 1933; the lead character is the daughter of successful immigrants from Eastern Europe who have already made the jump from the Bronx to the comfort of the El Dorado, a big apartment building on Central Park West. She attends Hunter College, where her beauty and talent land her the lead in a production of *The Mikado*. While working on the play, she meets Marsha Zelenko, and one night early in their friendship, Marsha takes Marjorie out to dinner:

> They went to an old brownstone house on a side street, and up a flight of stairs to a doorway framed by a huge grinning gilt dragon mouth; *Mi Fong's Jade Garden*, the sign over the dragon's ears read. They passed through the fanged jaws into a crimson-lit room smelling of incense and strange cookery. Marjorie was very glad she had not committed herself to eat. She half believed that cats, dogs, and mice were cooked in Chinese restaurants. The pervading odor seemed more or less to confirm the idea.[17]

Marsha, the personification of the adventurous, intellectual, assimilated Jewish New Yorker, tells her that the food is sublime, "and it costs next to nothing. If you have forty cents on you, you can have a feast." The first dish arrives with their Singapore slings: a plate "full of fat brown curved

Figure 6.4. Started in 1959, Bernstein-on-Essex on New York's Lower East Side was the pioneer of Chinese-kosher cuisine. From its menu you could order both moo goo gai pan and pastrami sandwiches.

things"—shrimp. Marjorie demurs; she's never eaten shrimp. Marsha asks, "You're kosher, aren't you?" "Well, hardly," Marjorie replies. "My folks are. But pork or shellfish—it's just the idea." Finally, Marsha cajoles Marjorie into trying some Chinese food, starting with the soup: "Marjorie took a few spoonfuls, straining the liquid. The taste was very spicy, not bad. But when she found herself chewing what seemed to be a couple of rubber bands, or possibly worms, she emptied her mouth and pushed away the dish."[18] Then comes "Moo Yak with almonds," a main course made up of a "number of greasy objects, some vegetable, some animal" piled on white rice. The restaurant owner claims that the meat is lamb, but Marjorie knows what pork smells like. Nevertheless, she eats:

> Not wanting to insult Marsha by seeming to call her a liar, Marjorie made a hearty show of enjoying the dish, whatever it was; she scooped the rice from under the meat and ate that. But the light was dim and her instruments greasy for such delicate work. She soon found herself chewing a large piece of rubbery meat. She went into a coughing fit, got rid of it in her handkerchief, and pushed the food around her plate without eating any more.[19]

Despite her discomfort, the dinner is a watershed moment for Marjorie, because during it Marsha convinces her to make the theater her career.

Almost four hundred pages and perhaps three years later, Marjorie indulges in a second Chinese meal. Now she's a successful, world-traveled theater actress with a Bohemian playwright boyfriend named Noel Airman. After a dress rehearsal of his musical masterwork, there's a small party in his apartment where everybody drinks highballs and eats Chinese takeout:

> It was quite a supper. A plate of sliced pink pork was part of the buffet, along with egg rolls, chow mein, fried lobster and rice. Marjorie had become quite free about the food she ate; but she had never yet deliberately helped herself to pork, though she had suspected more than once that she was eating it, and had gone on eating. It occurred to her now, when she saw little Mrs. Lemberg piling pork on her plate, that it was high time she shrugged off these hypocritical little distinctions of hers. She took a couple of pork slices; and by dipping them completely in mustard sauce she got them down without any trouble. Eating the pork gave her an odd sense of freedom, and at the same time, though she suppressed it, a twinge of disgust.[20]

Here we understand that Marjorie has finally cast off ances-tral customs and become assimilated fully into American life. Later that night, after a few more highballs, she loses her virginity. This experience, too, gives her simultaneous feelings of liberation and disgust. By the novel's end, she has finally jettisoned her no-good boyfriend, married a nice but boring lawyer named Milton Schwartz, and settled down to raise a family in the Westchester suburbs.

Wouk's ending implies that Mrs. Milton Schwartz, now a kosher-keeping mother of four, has left the sinful, sexu-ally tinged realm of Chinese food behind. But in the real world, most American Jews, including the observant ones, found chop suey, chow mein, fried shrimp, roast pork, and all those other forbidden foods too tempting to avoid. In 1936, the *Sentinel Jewish Cook Book*, published in Chicago, included recipes for chop suey from scratch, chop suey from cans, and egg foo young. The same year, a Jewish newspa-per noticed that Chinese restaurants had taken over even the Lower East Side; there were eighteen within blocks of Ratner's dairy restaurant and Katz's Delicatessen. Out in the sprawling neighborhoods of two-story row houses and middle-class apartment buildings that were covering the Bronx and Brooklyn, the neon signs of chop suey joints vied with Italian red sauce restaurants and American cof-fee shops to attract patrons. Within their walls, the children and grandchildren of eastern European immigrants were attracted by the same qualities that had drawn the rest of society: Chinese food was cheap, filling, and just mysterious enough. Ordering a plate of chow mein showed sophistica-tion, setting one apart from the Old World immigrants with the odors of the shtetl still clinging to their clothes. Still, the match between the two cultures was not completely con-summated. In the 1930s, there was still something absurd about the idea of Jews eating Chinese food.

In the 1938 movie *Mannequin*, Joan Crawford plays a tough girl from Hester Street who marries her no-good boyfriend. The wedding takes place in a Chinese-Jewish restaurant, where a waiter named Horowitz is garbed in Chinese clothes and carries a platter of Chinese-style gefilte fish to the newlyweds' table. (Stranger things actually happened; many of the waiters at Ratner's on Delancey Street were Chinese and could trade rapid-fire witticisms with the largely Yiddish-speaking clientele.) In the story "A Man Will Do Anything to Make a Living," by the Yiddish writer Sam Liptzin, a couple considers what to do after failing at a "candy store, a grocery, a boarding house, a marriage broker's business, a restaurant, a bakery, a 5-and-10-cent store."[21] Finally, the wife decides: a Chinese restaurant. So the husband adopts the name Yu Fang, learns to eat gefilte fish with chopsticks, and opens a restaurant with Chinese cooks, waiters, and dishwashers. They wait and wait, but after two months nobody comes. "Yu Fang!" says the wife. "We must give up the business. We are Jews, not Chinese, we can't compete with them!"[22]

Over time, American Jews noticed many similarities between their food and Chinese cuisine, including the use of garlic, onions, celery, and chicken and the avoidance of milk. Nevertheless, they still had to address the issue of kashrut and the prevalence of shellfish and pork. For those who followed the letter of Jewish law, Chinese food was definitely *treyf* (unclean). But there is a tradition in Judaism of devising interpretations that find loopholes in the law in order to allow people some room to live. When faced with the question of how to eat Chinese food and keep their Jewish identity, hungry and creative minds came up with the idea of "safe treyf"—food that is unclean but okay. A pork chop was still forbidden, but pork chop suey was okay, because the meat was sliced into little pieces and hidden under a mound of sauce-drenched vegetables. (There's definitely a streak of humor running through the concept of safe treyf.) Though almost always flavored with ham, Chinese soups were also permitted, because the pork was invisible. As for the shrimp and lobster? Somehow serving them in a Chinese restaurant converted them into acceptable foods, perhaps because the cooks and waiters were both non-Christian and even more alien in America than Jews. They would have felt much less comfortable eating in, say, a neighborhood Italian restaurant, because the memory of Europe's long history of Christian persecutions of Jews was fresh in their minds. The very newness of Chinese food gave them room to find a way to make it their own. During the next three decades, American Jews came to be identified as the minority group with a taste for eating Chinese.

As chop suey became Americanized, one group was relegated to the sidelines and almost forgotten: the Chinese themselves. Compared to the days in the 1880s when the Chinese had feared for their lives, this was an improvement. They had the ability to run their businesses without fear that a mob was around the corner ready to burn their homes and drive them from town. A new vision of the Chinese gradually supplanted the old prejudices—particularly after Japan invaded China in 1937, when Americans began to see the Chinese first as victims and then, as they fought back, plucky freedom fighters. At the movies, wise, old Charlie Chan supplanted evil, hissing Fu Manchu. However, Chinese Americans still led lives on the margins of society. The Exclusion Act remained in force; immigration from China was banned, and Chinese still could not become American citizens. After the onset of the Great Depression, travel back to mainland China became much rarer. The ratio of males to females had improved (4:1 versus 25:1 in 1890), but the majority of Chinese residents still died childless. If trends continued, the country's Chinese population would dwindle away to nothing.

The one exception to this gloomy picture was the Territory of Hawaii, where Chinese had for decades dominated the restaurant industry. Chinese had begun to arrive in Hawaii back in the late eighteenth century. Between 1850 and 1882 (the advent of the Chinese Exclusion Act), thousands of contract laborers from Guangdong Province were brought to work in the islands' sugar industry. They were joined by South Chinese entrepreneurs who founded trading companies and stores, many based in Honolulu's nascent Chinatown. The Chinese Hawaiians were mainly Cantonese from the Zhongshan district (near Macau) of the Pearl River Delta and members of the Hakka ethnic group from eastern Guangdong. Like the Chinese adventurers who traveled to other parts of the New World, they brought their cuisine with them, mainly Cantonese and Hakka peasant fare. In the countryside, they opened general stores that also served Hawaiian and American food. In Honolulu, they owned most of the city's cheap cafés. For the Chinese themselves, the place to eat was Chinatown, where they could enjoy the rural fare of the Pearl River Delta, mainly various kinds of soups, congees, noodle dishes, and dumplings. The Wo Fat restaurant, opened in 1882, was reputed to be the favorite of a young Zhongshan native named Sun Yat-Sen, who became one of China's most revered revolutionary leaders. In 1901, at least one Honolulu restaurant existed where one could order more sophisticated banquet food—"preserved chicken, shark's fin, fresh lotus nest, duck, edible bird's nest with chopped chicken, preserved yellow fish heads, preserved snow lichen, almonds and fresh turquoise [turtle?], gold coin chicken, [and] Chinese fancy tarts"[23]—but this was the exception.

In 1890, 20 percent of Hawaii's population were Chinese; thereafter, their numbers slowly dwindled due to harsh immigration restrictions. Nevertheless, the Chinese retained an important role in the islands' life, mainly as farmers, merchants, and factory owners. Many intermarried with local Hawaiians, with an accompanying blending of cultures, and missionaries were pleased to note a surprisingly large number of Chinese converts to Christianity. As tourism from the mainland boomed, the demands and expectations of the visitors necessitated changes in the local businesses: most Chinese restaurants added "chop suey" to their name—Wo Fat became Wo Fat Chop Suey—so that the tourists would know what to expect. Nonetheless, the Chinese Hawaiians relied on their numbers, cultural strength, and proximity to China to keep their traditions alive. In 1941, the Chinese Committee of the Honolulu YWCA compiled a cookbook entitled *Chinese Home Cooking*; it was probably compiled by Mary Li Sia, a cookbook author and the YWCA's Chinese cooking instructor. The book's well over a hundred recipes unabashedly exhibit local Chinese tastes, including gingered pigs' feet, bitter melon with beef, abalone with vegetables and gluten balls, numerous "long rice" (rice noodle) dishes, and nine varieties of chop suey. Their mode of preparation might not have been exactly what the tourists remembered from back home, but they were outnumbered by the palates and wallets of Chinatown residents. The Chinese Hawaiians retained their distinctive culinary culture far longer than their compatriots on the mainland.

During the 1930s and 1940s, Chinese Americans continued to rely on restaurants and family laundries for their economic survival. However, they now had competition; big mechanized laundries were putting the Chinese laundrymen out of work. And they had lost their monopoly on chop suey and chow mein as Americans learned to cook the dishes, and with Prohibition over, non-Chinese nightclubs were now crowding out the vast chop-suey-and-dancing halls. There were still twenty-eight Chinatowns across the country, but the only ones where the populations were increasing were those in San Francisco and New York. In a striking reversal, the largest, in San Francisco, was now famous not as a dingy and mysterious ghetto but as a bright, modern tourist trap:

> Indeed, Chinatown today is not only clean but quaint, a sort of permanent exhibit of the Orient, colorful and exotic, set down amid the gray uniformity of American city life. The architectural and decorative embellishments of its buildings are often typically Oriental in color and design. Here are shops which allure tourists with displays of Oriental art, and joss-houses on the upper floors of "benevolent association" buildings, where friendly guides sound deep-voiced gongs, burn incense, shake the fortune-telling sticks before the gloriously carved and colored shrine of Kwan-yin, the goddess of mercy, and dispense souvenirs—for a consideration![24]

The main streets of the two most important districts—Grant Avenue in San Francisco and Mott Street in New York— were lined with blinking chop suey signs and curio shops. In the side streets, the Chinese themselves conducted their business—in grocery stores, tea shops, doctor's offices, noodle factories, printing shops, and bakeries. Indeed the Chinatowns of these two cities were the central manufacturing and distribution points for a wide range of products necessary for Chinese eateries, from imported tea and soy sauce to almond cookies and restaurant menus. These goods were shipped from New York to restaurants east of the Mississippi; San Francisco handled the trade for the western half of the country.

The Chinatown restaurants of New York and San Francisco were of two types: those catering to Chinese diners and

KING HONG LAU CO.,

The Leading Chinese Restaurant,

16 MOTT STREET, NEW YORK, N. Y.

SOUPS.

Main, with meat and egg..	$0 10
Main, extra, with meat	20
Main, ex. with boneless chicken	25
Noodle	10
Bird's Nest	2 00
Shark's Fin	2 00

FRIED.

Chop Sooy	15
Ham & Eggs, with herbs, etc.	25
Main, with meat	50
Main, with boneless chicken	70
Pork, with onions	15
Beef, with onions	15
Mushrooms Chop Sooy	25
Ly Chee duck	70
Ly Chee chicken	70
Ly Chee with boneless chicken	70
Mushrooms, squab	70
Sweet & pungent Chop Sooy	25
Fried chicken	1 50
Fried squab	1 50
Plain broiled chicken	15
Roast duck	15
Loin of pork	05
Rice, per bowl	05

PRESERVED FRUITS.

Pears	25
Pineapple	25
Ly Chee	25
Carambola	25
Ginger	25
Oolong tea	10
Sui Sinn tea	10
Long Sue tea	15

30. Jan. 1900 SPECIAL NOTICE.

The arrangements can be made with the Manager for private parties. Special rates will be furnished on application, and the order must be given the day before.

Figure 6.5. In 1900, Mott Street's King Hong Lau served white patrons noodle soups and chop suey, with tea and sweets for dessert.

those primarily feeding everyone else. In 1939, the Chinese needed big banquet restaurants as much as the Chinese in 1865 San Francisco had—for events like holidays, weddings, anniversaries, and business gatherings. That year, the Committee to Save China's Children hosted a fundraising banquet at the China Clipper restaurant on Doyers Street in New York's Chinatown that featured bean curd soup, brown stewed duck with almonds, diced squab with Chinese veg-etables, chicken with "Chinese brown cheese" (bean curd), Cantonese noodles, sweet and pungent shrimp, rice, dessert soup, and lotus wine. This was real Cantonese banquet fare, albeit the relatively restrained Sze Yap version. Meanwhile, at Lum Fong's over on Canal Street, the mainstays were chop suey, chow mein, egg foo young, yat gaw mein, fried rice, tomato beef, pepper steak, and egg rolls—an item Lum Fong claimed to have introduced to American menus. For a dollar or two more, diners could order moo goo gai pan (chicken with mushrooms), lobster Cantonese, shrimp with lobster sauce, and a few other specialties. Some eateries also listed fried wontons, which they described as *kreplach* (Yiddish for small, meat-filled dumplings). In other parts of the United States, the Lum Fong's type of Chinese American menu was the only game in town. If one wanted more interesting dishes, one could usually call ahead and order off the menu. A Chinese family in Omaha, Nebraska, could probably find a reasonable Cantonese meal in that city. But you had to know that possibility existed and want to act on that knowl-edge. Around the early 1940s, the menus in Chinese res-taurants stopped evolving. Their food stagnated into bland and unexciting dishes that were now far removed from the preparations of the Pearl River Delta; and they were losing ground to the competition. The magic and excitement were gone from Chinese food. Unless something changed, Chinese restaurants were in danger of fading away into obscurity.

Devouring the Duck

*I*n the decades following World War II, Chinese restaurant owners hung on by adapting their businesses to changes in the larger society. They followed Americans out of the center cities, opening eateries in new suburbs like Levittown, New York, and Park Forest, Illinois. There they encountered competition from the new fast food hamburger stands, fried chicken restaurants, and pizza parlors that were catering to hungry, busy Americans. To compete, Chinese restaurants capitalized on one of their longtime strengths: the ability to sell large portions of inexpensive food. The centerpiece of their menus was the "family dinner," a multicourse meal of Cantonese American favorites for one low price. The cheapest two-person family dinner at New Joy Young in Knoxville, Tennessee, featured four courses: wonton or Chinese vegetable soup, egg foo young or fried rice, subgum chow mein, and egg rolls, all for $3.20. (Some restaurants divided the choices into columns; hence the "one from column A and one from column B" that many associate with eateries from this era.) For only $1.25, you could enjoy fried rice, one egg roll, and chicken chow mein. You could also order à la carte dishes: lobster Cantonese, moo goo gai pan, American steaks, lobster Newburg, and sandwiches. For better or worse, the cheap, familiar Chinese dinners drew the most customers.

The trials of the Chinese restaurant business were outlined in a 1958 article in the *Washington Post*. There were 110 Chinese eateries in the District of Columbia, and for most of them business was not good: "A few restaurants turn a tidy profit; others supply a comfortable income; many furnish a bare subsistence." The leaders of the local Chinese community considered the restaurant business moribund, an enterprise that had less and less to do with the Chinese-ness of its product. One businessman complained to the reporter about the restaurant owners: "They have to do a job of public relations. They have to improve their food, their service, their atmosphere. A Chinese restaurant should have

4509 Kingston Pike, at Lyons View Road
On U. S. Highway 11 & 70
Knoxville, Tennessee
Telephone 6-1081

New Joy Young Family Dinners

$3.20 For 2 Persons

Wonton or Chinese Vegetable Soup
Egg Foo Young or Fried Rice
Subgum Chow Mein
Egg Rolls

$4.80 For 3 Persons

Wonton or Chinese Vegetable Soup
Fried Rice
Subgum Chicken Chow Mein
Lobster Cantonese Style
Egg Rolls

$6.40 For 4 Persons

Wonton or Chinese Vegetable Soup
Lobster Cantonese Style
Egg Foo Young or Fried Rice
Sweet and Pungent Pork
Chicken Chop Suey
Egg Rolls

$8.00 For 5 Persons

Wonton or Chinese Vegetable Soup
Lobster Cantonese Style
Chicken Chop Suey
Egg Foo Young or Fried Rice
Sweet and Pungent Pork
Chun Far Chow Mein
Egg Rolls

$9.60 For 6 Persons

Wonton or Chinese Vegetable Soup
Lobster Cantonese Style
Moo Goo Gai Pen
Egg Foo Young or Fried Rice
Sweet and Pungent Pork
Chun Far Chow Mein
Egg Rolls

$11.20 For 7 Persons

Wonton or Chinese Vegetable Soup
Lobster Cantonese Style
Egg Foo Young or Fried Rice
Moo Goo Gai Pen
Chun Far Chow Mein
Sweet and Pungent Pork
Roast Pork Chinese Vegetable
Egg Rolls

$12.80 For 8 Persons

Wonton or Chinese Vegetable Soup
2 Lobster Cantonese Style
Fried Rice
Almond Dice Cut Chicken
Chun Far Chow Mein
Sweet and Pungent Pork
Moo Goo Gai Pen
Subgum Egg Foo Young Chinese Style
Egg Rolls

TEA SERVED WITH FAMILY DINNERS

Our Special Combination Platter

(1)	Fried Rice, 1 Egg Roll, Chicken Chow Mein	$1.25
(2)	Fried Rice, 1 Egg Roll, Shrimp Chow Mein	1.35
(3)	Fried Rice, 1 Egg Roll, Chicken Chop Suey	1.40
(4)	Fried Rice, 1 Egg Roll, Subgum Chow Mein	1.50
(5)	Fried Rice, 1 Egg Roll, Sweet and Pungent Pork	1.60
(6)	Fried Rice, 1 Egg Roll, Shrimp and Lobster Sauce	1.75

Do not ask for substitute on family dinner.

WE WILL BE HAPPY TO ASSIST YOU IN SELECTING
DIFFERENT CHINESE DISHES FOR A SPECIAL DINNER

Extra plate service .25

Not Responsible for Lost Articles Unless Checked

Figure 7.1. Inexpensive "family dinners," like these offerings at New Joy Young in Knoxville, Tennessee, were the mainstay of 1950s Chinese-American restaurants.

pleasant Chinese surroundings—not chrome and neon and juke boxes. Why look how Washington has grown. But the Chinese restaurants haven't."[1] One of the many problems was that young cooks with any ambition refused to work for $4,000 a year, so most of the food was prepared by old-timers whose methods were mired in the past. Some of the larger restaurants had attempted to import trained chefs from Hong Kong or Taiwan but had run into prohibitive immigration restrictions.

In a 1954 *Mad* comic strip entitled "Restaurant!" by the artist Will Elder, Dad decides to take the family for lunch on a typical Sunday afternoon in America.[2] Elder packed the piece with what he called "chicken fat," visual gags that filled every corner of his panels. A lot of these are at the beginning: the nebbishy Sturdley family waits to be seated in a crowded restaurant filled with shouting, fighting customers, pets, flies in the soup, kids running around with chamber pots on their heads, stray characters from other comic strips, and so on. Next come the usual indignities: getting a booth, waiting for the greasy dishes of previous diners to be cleaned away, waiting for the waiter, and waiting for Uncle Smurdley to make up his mind. Finally, the chow mein arrives. Dad savors the aroma of crisp noodles, stewed onions, bean sprouts, strips of chicken, and snowy rice. Just as he's about to put the first chopstick-full into his mouth, Baby announces that he has to go to the bathroom. Finally Dad is able to eat, but further humiliations ensue, including getting smacked on the head by the cute kid in the next booth. Afterward, the family vows to stay at home, only to find themselves once again—"eyeballs protruding, tongues gently lolling"—waiting for a booth at the same eatery the next Sunday. What's remarkable about the scene Elder depicts (aside from his manic visual imagery) is how un-Chinese the restaurant is. You have to look closely to notice the red lanterns scattered here and there. Only one of the waiters appears to be Asian, and a peek into the kitchen reveals no Chinese but a bunch of sweaty, unshaven hash-joint cooks. Despite all this, habit—and price—still pulled diners back to the Chinese American restaurants.

In and around cities like New York, Chicago, and San Francisco, some restaurant owners with deeper pockets experimented with changes in design and new menus. The classic Chinese restaurant aesthetic had not changed in decades: booths along the wall, tables in the center, lanterns hanging from the ceiling, a few cheap Chinese prints on the walls, a counter for the cash register, and a display of cigars and cigarettes by the entrance. In the late fifties, owners began to hire architects to convert their interiors into something dramatic and modern. Sometimes, they became a little too modern; the *New York Times* described Manhattan's Empress restaurant as a "distracting" blend of contemporary Danish with Chinese influences: "the walls are of black and scarlet, the banquettes are of gold and the napkins of rich pink."[3] This trend reached a peak in 1973, when the firm of Gwathmey Siegel Associates renovated Pearl's Chinese Restaurant, then popular with Manhattan movers and shakers. The *Times*'s architecture critic praised the design's elegance, sophistication, and simple geometric forms (which made the dining room reverberate with noise). However, at most restaurants where the modern décor was meant to complement the clientele's taste, the menus remained the same.

In 1934, an ex-bootlegger and beach bum named Ernest Raymond Beaumont Gantt opened in Hollywood a nightspot he called Don's Beachcomber. He served exotic rum drinks—including the Zombie, a concoction he'd invented—from a bar decorated with tropical motifs. Three years later, he revamped his establishment as the Don the Beachcomber restaurant, serving Cantonese food with a few Polynesian touches, mostly on the pupu platter. The concept was so successful that he changed his name to Donn Beach. The buzz about it caught the attention of Victor Bergeron, the young owner of Hinky Dink's Tavern, a bar in Oakland. He copied Don the Beachcomber's rum cocktails, tropical look, and Cantonese menu and renamed his restaurant Trader Vic's. He also added such creations as rumaki, crab Rangoon, and Calcutta lamb curry to his menus. However, the main culinary offerings of both restaurants were Cantonese: egg rolls, wonton soup, barbecued pork, almond chicken, beef with tomato, fried rice, and so on. By the 1950s, branches of Don the Beachcomber and Trader Vic's had opened across the country, followed by a host of imitators, including many with Chinese owners. The Kon-Tiki Club in Chicago advertised: "Escape to the South Seas!" You could also enjoy a complete Cantonese dinner there for $1.85 to $3.25. (The low food prices were offset by bar profits and turnover in the large, often full dining rooms.) This craze for "Polynesian" restaurants with Cantonese food continued well into the 1970s, particularly in suburban New Jersey, where the commercial strips were dotted with colorful eateries like the Orient Luau, featuring a popular all-you-can-eat "Hawaiian smorgasbord." (Today, the few that remain are patronized largely by senior citizens, baby boomers on nostalgia visits, and devotees of the revived Tiki bar cult.)

These gimmicks were not enough to save the classic Chinese American restaurant formula. By the 1960s, it was clear that chop suey, chow mein, egg foo young, and the like were ageing along with the Chinatown old-timers. The last of the "bachelor" generation (almost all male), who had grown up during the early decades of the Exclusion Act era and had manned Chinese kitchens across the United States, were slowly dying out. Restrictions had been eased, so new immigrants from China were finally beginning to enter the country. These changes had been incremental. First, the Magnuson Act of 1943 ended Chinese Exclusion and allowed the Chinese people who were living in the United States to become naturalized citizens at last. Alien wives of citizens were admitted in 1946. In 1947, the War Brides Act opened the door to approximately six thousand Chinese brides of Chinese American soldiers. In San Francisco, the number of births to Chinese couples more than doubled. After the Communist takeover in China, further changes were made in immigration laws, allowing some political refugees from China to gain citizenship. In 1965, the Immigration and Nationality Act abolished quotas based on national origin and made reunification of families a priority, and thousands of immigrants streamed into the United States from Taiwan and Hong Kong, all of them bringing with them their food traditions. Increased communication between the Chinese American community and their families in East Asia reinforced the economic and cultural ties between the two regions. Slowly at first, Chinese food in the United States began a transformation.

The first glimmerings that Chinese food consisted of more than a small set of Cantonese American specialties came from a cookbook. In 1945, a Chinese immigrant, Buwei Yang Chao, published a little cookbook, *How to Cook and Eat in Chinese*. Trained as a doctor, Chao was born in 1889 in Nanjing, a large city in the lower Yangzi basin. She married a professor of philology, and they raised four daughters while her husband held teaching positions in China, Europe, and the United States. By World War II, the family was settled in Cambridge, Massachusetts, where he taught at Harvard, and she began work on the cookbook. She had been raised in an upper-class family and had not learned to cook as a child. In a note, she tells us that she only began cooking while studying medicine in Japan: "I found Japanese food so uneatable that I had to cook my own meals. I had always looked down upon food and things, but I hated to look down upon a Japanese dinner under my nose. So by the time I became a doctor, I also became something of a cook."[4] Accompanying her husband on his research trips around China, she had studied regional cuisines while he studied regional dialects. She says she began to write her cookbook at the urging of a fellow faculty wife, but it's clear that the suggestion struck some deeper chord within her, because *How to Cook and Eat in Chinese* is far more than a compendium of favorite dishes she served at faculty parties. With the help of her husband and her daughter Rulan, Chao set a more ambitious goal for herself: re-creating the traditional Chinese way of eating on United States soil.

She discusses this topic for fifty pages before presenting any recipes. First, she describes how the Chinese organize their meals, from breakfasts at home to big restaurant banquets. Here many readers first discovered congee and dim sum—"dot hearts," in Chao's translation—and learned of the intricacies of communal family meals and dinner party etiquette. Chao also delineates a number of China's regional cuisines—for nearly the first time in English. Next, she broaches a delicate question: "Do you get real Chinese food in the Chinese restaurants outside of China? The answer is, You can get it if you ask for it.... If you say you want real Chinese dishes and eat the Chinese way, that is, a few dishes to eat in common and with chopsticks, then they know that you know." She mentions the existence of only three eateries that are not Cantonese—Tianjin restaurants in New York and Washington and a Ningbo one in New York. Regarding the fare offered in the typical Cantonese restaurant, she comments:

> Many times the trouble is that because the customers do not know what is good in Chinese food they often order things which the Chinese do not eat very much. The restaurant people, on their part, try to serve the

public what they think the public wants. So in the course of time a tradition of American-Chinese food and ceremonies of eating has grown up which is different from eating in China.[5]

That's a nice way of saying she doesn't recognize chop suey and chow mein as Chinese, although she does include a recipe for American-style egg foo young. She goes on to systematically discuss raw materials, seasonings, utensils, and cooking methods. Finally come the recipes; in this part of the book, she subverts the normal cookbook order of rice, soup, and main dish by beginning with meats and ending with rice and noodles. The sense of unfamiliarity is further heightened by the book's many word coinages, for example "wraplings" (pot sticker–type dumplings) and "ramblings" (wontons), which enhance the reader's sense that this isn't the Chinese food they've tried but something new and interesting.

When *How to Cook and Eat in Chinese* appeared, Jane Holt, a *New York Times* food writer, called it "something novel in the way of a cook book." Although she disavowed expertise on the subject, Holt said "the book strikes us as being an authentic account of the Chinese culinary system, which apparently is every bit as complicated as the culture that has produced it."[6] Repeatedly cited in succeeding years as the best cookbook for those interested in Chinese cuisine, the book continued to sell; after the 1968 third and final edition, reprints appeared well into the 1970s. It's difficult to judge how many people actually prepared the recipes in *How to Cook and Eat in Chinese*, but it's clear that fans often returned to the book to help them understand the culture of Chinese food and guide them toward new eating experiences.

In the years after World War II, restaurants opened that pioneered a new taste in Chinese food. The entrepreneurs behind them were often either Chinatown businessmen frustrated with the low profits and cultural embarrassment of the chop suey joints or members of China's elite, mainly academics and diplomats, who had been stranded abroad by war and then the Communist takeover. The Peking Restaurant on Connecticut Avenue in Washington, D.C., one of the first, was founded in 1947 by C. M. Loo—once a Chinese diplomat's chef and later the butler at the Chinese Embassy—along with four partners. The menu featured "Peking Style Native Foods," including moo shu pork and the house specialty, Peking duck. Patrons included members of the local diplomatic community and many "China hands" who had fallen in love with Chinese food during their service in mainland China. The groundbreaker in San Francisco was Kan's, the brainchild of Johnny Kan, a local businessman:

> Our concept was to have a Ming or Tang dynasty theme for décor, a fine crew of master chefs, and a well-organized dining room crew headed by a courteous maitre d', host, hostesses, and so on. And we topped it off with a glass-enclosed kitchen. This would serve many purposes. The customers could actually see Chinese food being prepared, and it would encourage everybody to keep the kitchen clean.[7]

Kan's sought to revive the tradition of the high-end banquet restaurants that had flourished in San Francisco in the nineteenth century. Customers who wanted to order chop suey were not so gently encouraged to order something else. The thick menu, not limited to Cantonese cuisine, listed expensive dishes like bird's nest soup and Peking duck. Soon enough, culinary tourists streamed to Chinatown for dinner at Kan's or upscale competitors like the Empress of China and the Imperial Palace. Many were locals: a century after its arrival, San Franciscans were now eager to spend serious money for Chinese food.

In 1961, a new restaurant called the Mandarin opened up in a hard-luck location outside Chinatown. Its owner, Cecilia Chang, had lived through the some of the most dramatic events in modern Chinese history. Born into a wealthy family, she had been forced by the Japanese invasion to flee for 2,500 miles, largely on foot and wearing dirty peasant clothes as a disguise. She married a Nationalist diplomat and then fled again, this time to Japan to avoid the Communist takeover. By 1958, she had arrived in San Francisco, where she decided to open a restaurant: "I named the restaurant the Mandarin, and selected dishes for the menu from northern China, Peking, Hunan and Szechwan: real Chinese food, with a conspicuous absence of chop suey and egg foo young."[8] With the backing of influential columnists like Herb Caen, the Mandarin was a success, introducing dishes like tea-smoked duck, pot stickers, and sizzling rice soup. By 1968, the restaurant had expanded to three hundred seats and become even more elaborate, featuring fine Chinese paintings and embroideries and an open Mongolian barbecue. Meanwhile, other restaurants bearing the name Mandarin and featuring non-Cantonese food were opening across the country, with a large cluster in Chicago. In New York, the first was Mandarin House, owned by Emily Kwoh, a Shanghai native. She had entered the restaurant business in the mid-1950s with the Great Shanghai at Broadway and 103rd Street, serving food from three menus: Cantonese, American, and Shanghai. (For the next three decades, the stretch of upper Broadway from Eighty-sixth to 110th Street was a mecca for Chinese food aficionados.) At Mandarin House, which opened in 1958, Kwoh served non-Cantonese specialties like beggar's chicken, sesame-sprinkled flatbread, and, most important, *mu xu rou* (moo shu pork).

The menu quickly caught the attention of someone who didn't know much about Chinese food, except that he liked it: the *Times*'s food editor, Craig Claiborne. In the late 1920s, when he was seven or eight years old, Claiborne had been taken on a family trip from his home in tiny Sunflower, Mississippi, to the bright lights of Birmingham, Alabama:

> I remember—to tell the truth, it is the only thing I do remember about that trip—being taken to a Chinese restaurant. There were hanging Chinese lanterns and foreign waiters and real Chinese china and chopsticks and very hot and exotic tea. I cannot recall the menu in precise detail, but I did eat won ton soup and a dish that contained bean sprouts.... It is reasonable to suppose that the food I ate then was quite spurious, adapted to the Southern palate, and dreadful. But it kindled a flame.[9]

Thirty years later, when Claiborne went to work at the *Times*, he knew little more about Chinese food than he'd picked up that day in Birmingham. But he was eager to expand his horizons beyond chop suey and chow mein. He apprenticed himself to a series of Chinese cooking instructors, most notably Grace Chu (who taught classes at Mandarin House) and Virginia Lee (with whom he wrote a cookbook). He also befriended and learned from many of the chefs who were beginning to open the non-Cantonese restaurants. He filled his pages with glowing reviews, and the exposure helped make Chinese cooking schools, cookbooks, and above all, eateries hugely popular.

Perhaps the restaurant that benefited most from Claiborne's promotion was Shun Lee, owned by its chef, Tsung Ting Wang (from Shanghai via the Peking Restaurant in Washington), and Michael Tong, its Shanghai-born manager. When Shun Lee first opened in the early sixties, Claiborne described it as "a large, bustling and physically colorless Chinese restaurant with unadorned walls and artificial flowers."[10] Inside, diners could eat cheap chicken chow mein luncheon specials or order more elaborate dishes like squab in casserole. Two years later, the restaurant reopened at Second Avenue and 49th Street as Shun Lee Dynasty, with a spectacular interior by the designer Russel Wright. Egg rolls and chow mein were still offered, but now what Claiborne really was interested in was the Sichuan side of the menu: chicken in hoisin sauce, shrimp in "Szechuan sauce," and the like—the hotter the better. He complained, however, that the "Szechuan foods...are not so highly spiced as they should be, which is a concession to the public's taste." Just as with chop suey seventy-five years earlier, the newly arrived dishes were being adapted to the dominant American palate. No matter; Claiborne's infatuation with the food at Shun Lee continued unabated, reaching its apotheosis when he gave Shun Lee Dynasty four stars in the 1969 *New York Times Guide to Dining Out in New York*, the highest ranking ever for a Chinese restaurant in the United States.

The new climate of receptivity to adventurous Chinese restaurants drew a small group of chefs from Taiwan to New York City. They had trained under the great master chefs who had fled the Communist takeover and opened restaurants in Taipei. When the Immigration Act of 1965 opened the door to the United States, they decided to seek out new opportunities there. Many of them opened restaurants serving Shanghai and Sichuan specialties, like the Four Seas on Maiden Lane in New York, which were primarily aimed at a clientele of China hands and expatriates. But then, led by Claiborne and *New York* magazine's column "Underground Gourmet," a new group of culinary Bohemians began to patronize restaurants serving Sichuan food and demand dishes that were hot, hotter, hottest. Claiborne warned diners that some dishes could literally bring tears to their eyes, but that didn't seem to matter. Eateries like Szechuan Taste on Chatham Square, David Keh's Szechuan on Broadway and Ninety-fifth Street, and Szechuan East on Second Avenue and Eightieth Street flourished and spread as chefs followed opportunities. Fans of Chinese food relished the thrill of the hunt, finding out where the top chefs were cooking and which restaurants were serving the newest and most "authentic" dishes. When aficionados learned that chef Wang Yun Ching had moved from the Szechuan Restaurant to the Peking Restaurant just down Broadway, the lines moved to the Peking for his lamb with scallions.

In the New York food world, Chinese was hot; and it was just at this moment that President Nixon made his groundbreaking trip to Beijing. One frigid February evening in 1972, television lights shone brightly inside the Great Hall of the People, the vast banquet room and meeting chamber on the western side of Beijing's Tiananmen Square. The lights illuminated a large O-shaped table situated next to the stage in the Great Hall's main banquet room. A low mass of greenery dotted with orange kumquats filled the table's center. On the white tablecloth, twenty places were set with plates, chopsticks, knives and forks, tea cups and glasses, and artfully arranged servings of cold appetizers. In the host's seat, with his back to the stage sat Communist China's premier, Zhou Enlai, soberly dressed in his dark grey Mao suit. On either side of him sat the guests of honor: President Richard M. Nixon, his face incongruously brightened with pancake makeup, and Mrs. Nixon, her blonde bouffant hairdo glowing in the bright light. Premier Zhou unfolded his napkin onto his lap and picked up his chopsticks—the signal that the banquet had begun.

The more than six hundred American and Chinese guests seated at the room's smaller tables began to reach for their food. President Nixon fitted his chopsticks into his hand, plucked a morsel of appetizer from one of the plates, gazed

Figure 7.2. President Richard Nixon shares a meal—and a turning point in history—with Premier Zhou Enlai on February 21, 1972. The event was watched by millions of TV viewers around the world.

at it quizzically for a moment, put it into his mouth and began to chew. As a bank of television and movie cameras whirred, millions of people around the world watched the president of the United States eat Chinese food.

Nixon's trip to China was one of the great turning points in world diplomatic history, when two implacable foes met on the road to friendship. The enmity between the two countries dated to 1949, when the Communist Party under Mao Zedong had completed its takeover of the mainland. Diplomatic relations were soon cut off; American soldiers fought Red Army battalions during the Korean War; and the People's Republic of China aligned itself with the Soviet Union. But by the 1960s, the Soviets and the Chinese had become bitter enemies, their troops facing off along their long mutual border. As a presidential candidate in 1967,

Nixon proposed resuming relations with China as a way of breaking up the Communist bloc and bringing the billion or so Chinese out of self-imposed isolation. After he became president, it took two years of veiled messages and secret meetings for the two sides to overcome their mutual distrust and begin serious negotiations. Journalists, scholars, and the participants themselves have amply documented the complicated road to this new relationship. They have not discussed the importance of food, particularly Chinese food, during this whole affair. Nixon's China trip not only changed the course of American foreign relations but also helped instigate a revolution in Americans' perception of Chinese food.

Nixon conceived the opening of relations with China, but the mastermind who turned it into a reality was his Machiavellian national security advisor, Henry Kissinger. Operating with utmost secrecy, Kissinger oversaw the delicate diplomatic dance whose purpose was to convince the Chinese that the United States was serious about rapprochement. Both sides were hampered by the fact that they knew remarkably little about each other's country. Nobody in Washington had any firsthand knowledge of conditions inside the People's Republic; most of the knowledge the CIA had was gleaned from defectors and from reading the Chinese press at the CIA's monitoring station in Hong Kong. For American journalists and scholars, visas for China had been essentially impossible to get, particularly since the start of the Cultural Revolution in 1966. The exception was the old American "fellow traveler" Edgar Snow, who had been invited to visit Chairman Mao and was photographed with him reviewing a parade. (The Americans learned only later that the Chinese had been trying to send a message to *them*.) For help, Kissinger relied on two trusted advisers: his right-hand man, Winston Lord, who was married to a Chinese woman (the novelist Bette Bao Lord), and Charles "Chas" Freeman, a China expert at the State Department who had spent years studying, and eating, in Taiwan. When the time came, the White House turned to experts like Lord and Freeman for advice on how to handle a pair of chopsticks.

In July 1971, Kissinger, three aides, and two very nervous Secret Service agents found themselves on a Pakistani airliner flying over the Himalayas into Chinese airspace. The secret trip, code-named Polo I, was a leap into the void. As Kissinger looked out at the stark, snow-clad summits of the Rooftop of the World, his mind was filled with questions: How would they be received? Would the trip be a success or an international embarrassment? Would they meet Chairman Mao himself? How would they handle the delicate issue of Taiwan? And what would they eat during their allotted fifty hours in China?

The Americans had heard that the decades since the Communist takeover had not been good for Chinese cuisine. The best chefs had fled and their restaurants closed; both peasants and city folk had been forced to give up their family-centered meals and eat in communal dining halls. By the 1960s, the quality of the food had sunk to little better than livestock feed. During the Cultural Revolution, the chefs who remained became targets of denunciations and beatings by Little Red Book–waving mobs. But then Chairman Mao decided to temper the devastation of the forces he himself had unleashed. He sent the angry mobs to the countryside, where they could focus their energies on tilling the soil, and he ordered Premier Zhou Enlai to reestablish contact with the non-Communist world by wining and dining foreign leaders. Within a few months, the Chinese read of state banquets again being held in the Great Hall of the People. There were limits, of course: the meals were kept to six or eight courses, not the hundreds typical of the old Qing imperial era.

Still, not everyone agreed with the change in policy: "Class struggle exists even at the tips of one's chopsticks," one radical wrote in *Red Flag* in 1970. "As the common saying goes, if you eat the things of others you will find it difficult to raise your hand against them."[11] Nevertheless, the chairman had given the order, so the banquets continued. There was one ironclad rule, which reflected Chinese nationalism more than Communism: only Chinese cuisine was allowed on the menu. Serving Western food to American guests would be left to imperialist lackeys like Taiwan's Chiang Kai-shek. In the People's Republic, foreigners adapted to Chinese tastes, not the other way round.

The Pakistani jet touched down in Beijing on July 9, 1971. Kissinger and his aides were met on the runway by the stern-faced Marshal Ye Jianying, a vice-chairman of the Chinese Communist Party. A closed motorcade whisked the party to the secluded Diaoyutai guesthouse where the most important foreign visitors usually stayed. There, the aged Marshal Ye hosted a multicourse feast for the Americans—their first meal on Chinese soil. It was all a bit unreal. The Americans, jet-lagged and culture-shocked, were unable to believe that they were actually in Beijing sitting down at a table with a group of friendly Red Chinese. Kissinger, probably exaggerating, told Nixon that the dishes had been of "staggering variety and quantity"; Winston Lord remembers that it was merely a "good meal." Either way, it was quickly overshadowed by the next event of the afternoon: the arrival of Premier Zhou Enlai, unaccompanied, at the guesthouse. Elegant, cultured, ruthless, and brilliant, Zhou was the nation's main contact with the outside world. While living in Chongqing, the capital of Nationalist China during World War II, he had met and entertained many Americans and learned how they thought and how they ate. The Chinese and the Americans repaired to a meeting room, and for the next seven hours Kissinger and Zhou debated and discussed the future of U.S.-Chinese relations. In his memoir, Kissinger would call Zhou one of the two most impressive world leaders he ever met (the other was Charles DeGaulle). Discussions resumed on a much harsher note in the Great Hall of the People the next morning. Zhou gave a "scorching" lecture on the state of the world, emphasizing China's great differences with the United States. Kissinger felt he had to respond in kind, but just as he was getting warmed up for his tough talk, Zhou interrupted: "I believe the second item which you wanted to go into is Indochina, which is also very long. I suggest rest now and relaxation. Otherwise, you will be under tension and the duck will be cold."

"That would be most calamitous," Kissinger replied. "Tension we can take."[12]

Zhou escorted the Americans to a dining room next door, where they were seated at a large round banquet table. White-jacketed waiters began to pass around the plates of what would be their most memorable meal in China. "If I could choose a last meal on Earth," said Lord, "it would be Peking duck"; and this meal featured not just one serving of duck; it was a complete, traditional Peking duck dinner, with duck parts for every course, including the crispy skin, feet, gizzards, and brains and a soup made from the bones. The pièce de résistance was tender, juicy duck meat dabbed with a rich, salty-sweet-tart sauce and wrapped in a thin pancake with scallions or slivered cucumbers. The consummate Chinese host, Zhou himself deftly wrapped these succulent packages for the enjoyment of his honored guests. As they ate, the tension of the meeting mellowed, carried away on a sea of duck fat. Zhou steered the conversation to the subject of the Cultural Revolution, which he said had caused immense disruption in the country and killed many, including party officials. Used to the image of the implacable, inscrutable Chinese Communist, the Americans felt that with this statement Zhou had bared something of his soul, his deepest anguish.

After lunch, the premier insisted that his guests pile into a tiny elevator and ascend to a special kitchen, apparently designed for the sole task of preparing Peking ducks. Its only occupant was a soldier scrubbing the floor of the spotless room. John Holdridge, a Kissinger aide, wrote: "The stunned look on his face when he saw a band of foreigners in his kitchen guided by none other than the Chinese premier was alone well worth the trip."[13] Zhou showed them the special ovens for roasting the ducks and explained how apple and cherry wood coals helped give the birds their flavor. The Americans were impressed, according to Holdridge: "This whole episode shows the great hospitality, graciousness, and effort to put us at ease displayed by Premier Zhou Enlai, surely one of contemporary China's greatest leaders."[14]

When the two sides returned to the conference room, Kissinger resumed his forceful rebuttal of Zhou's speech. However, his heart—or should we say his stomach?—wasn't in it. A mood of duck-fueled geniality pervaded the room, and the talk soon returned to the more welcome subject of President Nixon visiting China. In fact, this meal set a pattern that was followed again and again during the Americans' advance trips to China. Whenever the discussion became a little too heated, or the Chinese felt that the Americans needed to unwind a bit, Zhou would suggest another duck dinner. During Kissinger's "Polo II" trip in October 1971, Zhou invited the Americans to dine on roast duck just as negotiations bogged down over the wording of an important Chinese-American communiqué. He decided that his two guests of honor would be Kissinger, of course, and, as the youngest American present, Nixon aide Dwight Chapin (later a bit player in the Watergate scandal).

"Premier Zhou did our pancakes for us," Chapin recalls, "because that's what a gracious Chinese person does. I had no knowledge this was going to happen. So delicious: I don't have the words to express the taste delight. Then at the end, they bring out the topper—the head of the duck, split in half. Zhou gives one half of the head to Kissinger and one half to me. He tells us to eat the brain. I can tell you that I touched it to my lips, but didn't eat it."

Afterward, the premier suggested to a duck-happy Kissinger a radically different organization for the communiqué, one that laid out the Chinese and American positions side by side without any attempt at synthesis. "It was unprecedented in design," Kissinger wrote. "It stated the Chinese position on a whole host of issues in extremely uncompromising terms.... But as I reflected further I began to see that the very novelty of the approach might resolve our perplexities."[15] Stuffed with duck, Kissinger agreed to Zhou's proposal.

Unfortunately, one cannot subsist on Peking duck alone. The American advance parties had to endure almost daily Chinese banquets, with their complicated etiquette and dizzying array of dishes. Acting as a stand-in for Nixon, for whom he had worked as a glorified gofer since the early 1960s, Chapin wrote notes to his boss counseling him on how to handle the river of unfamiliar dishes he would encounter. Eat light from the start, he advised, because it keeps coming. The president should also be prepared to use chopsticks and to expect his host to place choice pieces of food on his plate. In addition, it was proper etiquette to try everything. If they were in Shanghai, that "everything" could be particularly dangerous. During the Polo II trip, the Party leaders in Shanghai served Kissinger and his team a dish they called "Dragon, Tiger, Phoenix" that turned out to be a stew of snake, cat, and chicken. During the January 1972 advance trip headed by General Alexander Haig, the standout dish in Shanghai was a plate of tiny brown deep-fried birds. "Gentlemen," their host gleefully announced, "this is a salute to spring—a sparrow! Yes, the sparrow that flies." Chapin only hesitated a moment: "I just threw one in my mouth. It was very crunchy, but not bad." (Only much later did the Americans learn that their Shanghai hosts weren't exactly warm to renewing relations with the United States. After Mao's death, they would become key members of the radical Communist group known as the Gang of Four.)

Another challenge the Americans faced was chopsticks. Although they found forks and knives at each table setting, Lord advised them to use chopsticks to show respect for their Chinese hosts. Unfortunately, Kissinger proved utterly incompetent at wielding chopsticks during the Polo I trip and had to resort to his fork. To make matters worse, the Chinese waiters removed it at the end of each course, and he further lost face by having to ask for another. His clumsiness became a running joke. When he and his aides were in Hawaii at the start of the Polo II trip, Holdridge saw his chance and pounced. He called everyone together and formally presented Kissinger with "a handy, dandy practice kit for using chopsticks," consisting of "three types of chopsticks—wood, ivory, and silver—plus an assortment of different items to be picked up by the chopsticks: mothballs, marbles, and wood chips. I can't recall any other occasion in my tenure with him during which he was absolutely speechless," Holdridge recalled.[16] Four months later, Chapin sent a pair to everyone on the White House staff going to China, along with the suggestion: "Borrowing from the Chairman the old 'Practice makes perfect,' I suggest you become acquainted with using the enclosed chopsticks."

In early February 1972, when the final advance team was holed up in Beijing's Hotel of the Nationalities and working virtually around the clock to prepare for the presidential visit, the Chinese head of protocol posed a question to Ron Walker, director of the White House Advance Office: "What is President Nixon's favorite Chinese food?" The query was relayed by satellite phone back to Washington, where Chapin brought it to H. R. Haldeman, Nixon's chief of staff. A veteran ad man who had worked on Nixon campaigns since 1956, Haldeman understood the real question: what did they want the world to see him eat?

If Americans knew one thing about Richard M. Nixon's eating habits, it was that he ate cottage cheese, and lots of it. He was obsessed about his weight and not looking fat on national television. His regular lunch, which he ate either alone or with Haldeman, was a scoop of low-fat cottage cheese with some pineapple (the California touch) or a splash of ketchup for flavor. But on the occasions when this tightly wound man allowed himself to indulge, he had sophisticated tastes—for a politician. He liked rich, meaty food. At home, this meant steak, meat loaf, spaghetti and meatballs, lasagna, and chicken fricassee. Eating out, he liked to frequent the best French restaurants in Washington and New York, where he ordered dishes like beef stroganoff and duckling a l'orange. All washed down with copious amounts of the best wine and liquor; the manifest for Air Force One showed, among other bottles, thirty-year-old Ballantine's Scotch, Chateau Margaux 1966, Chateau Lafite Rothschild 1966, Chateau Haut-Brion 1955, and Dom Perignon champagne, mostly for the president's consumption. To put it bluntly, the most powerful man in the world was a very heavy drinker (and particularly at the end of his presidency). One cuisine he apparently didn't eat much of was Chinese. The main Washington hangout for the younger Nixons was the nearby Trader Vic's, but the president and first lady did not take their much-publicized walk over to the Tiki Temple for another year. At this moment, Nixon had more important concerns than gustatory satisfaction, like winning the upcoming election. Haldeman and Nixon mulled over the question for a while and then sent word back to Chapin. Within a few hours, Walker had his answer for the Chinese: "The President will eat anything served to him."

Haldeman had decided that Nixon's trip would highlight visual image over political substance. The reason was twofold: they wanted to distract the public from the pesky details of any treaty the United States and China might sign—particularly one involving the hot-button question of Taiwan's status. And for the campaign, they needed to show Nixon as a confident, sophisticated world leader: negotiating international agreements, conversing with Chairman Mao, contemplating history at the Great Wall of China, and eating authentic Chinese food (while Democratic opponents Edmund Muskie and George McGovern were choking down stale doughnuts in New Hampshire coffee shops). They didn't tell the public that when Air Force One took off from Andrews Air Force Base on February 17, 1972, its hold was stuffed with frozen steak, hamburger, lobster tail, Campbell's bean and bacon soup, Wishbone salad dressing, ketchup, white Pepperidge Farm bread, apple and cherry pies, and three flavors of ice cream. On short notice, Zosimo Monzon, the Nixons' personal steward, could turn all this into a good American meal. When cameras were present, though, the only food that would pass the president's lips during his week on foreign soil would be Chinese.

The passengers on Air Force One that day dutifully carried their chopsticks and their fat briefing books stamped with the presidential seal. These contained everything they needed to know for the upcoming trip, from a history of U.S.-Chinese relations to a description of what they would encounter on the table: "Banquet food served in the Peoples' Republic of China is to the 'Chinese food' served in restaurants in the U.S. as Beef Wellington is to a cafeteria hamburger." One might be served things like sharks' fins, birds' nests, sea cucumbers, snake, dog, bears' paws, and who knows what else. "Fortunately, one's taste buds are a more reliable guide to the excellence of these delicacies than one's imagination. Most Westerners are surprised to find, once they have tasted them, that they like them very much." As for the tricky question of Chinese etiquette, which promised to be radically different from what one was used to at Washington's state banquets and embassy dinners, "the Chinese relish their cuisine," Mrs. Nixon read. "You should not be offended at the noisy downing of soups, or even at burping after a meal. These are unconscious table habits accepted in Chinese society."[17] There would be toasts at the banquets, of course—with fiery mao-tai, a 106-proof liquor distilled from sorghum. Nixon was warned not to actually drink it during toasts; just touching it to your lips would be enough. Finally came the delicate matter of table topics: What do you talk about with the ageing Long March veteran who is your tablemate? Why, food, of course: "While citizens of many countries regard their native cuisine as the finest in the world, the Chinese have more basis than most for their pride. They react with much pleasure to compliments about the truly remarkable variety of tastes, textures, and aromas in Chinese cuisine." There was one caveat: "It is wise not to say a particular dish is 'good' or 'interesting' when in fact you do not like it, as your hosts, in an effort to please, may serve you extra portions to your embarrassment." The best course was to remember the experience of Caleb Cushing's party more than a century earlier—"gape, simper, and swallow!"

As Air Force One approached Beijing on February 21, Nixon and his aides still had no idea whether their China trip would succeed or fail. The first signs were ominous: no welcoming crowd awaited them at the airport, just forty officials in dark coats and a military honor guard. While a burly aide kept everyone else inside, President and Mrs. Nixon, who wore a flaming red coat, descended alone the stairs to the tarmac. There, Nixon and Zhou shook hands for a long minute, both to ensure that every camera got the shot and to erase an old diplomatic slight. (In 1954, secretary of state John Foster Dulles had refused Zhou's handshake at a peace conference.) The Americans were

Figure 7.3. Adroitly wielding her chopsticks, Mrs. Nixon enjoys some spicy eggplant on her visit to the kitchens of the Peking Hotel, February 1972. The White House used the interest in Chinese food to distract attention from more substantive issues.

then hustled into a motorcade and driven to the now familiar Diaoyutai guesthouse for lunch. We are told only (by Kissinger again) that the spread was "opulent." Afterward, Zhou pulled Kissinger aside and informed him that Chairman Mao wanted to meet Nixon at his residence, immediately. Ageing and seriously ill, Mao was still China's paramount leader and was obsessed with his place in history. There wasn't much substance to their hour-long discussion, but one clear message was sent: Mao bestowed his blessing on the process of rapprochement. Afterward, Nixon barely had time to change into a fresh suit for what promised to be the biggest media event of the trip, the official welcoming banquet.

For the Chinese, the evening was far more than just another state dinner; it was also a coming-out party, a signal to the world that the People's Republic was emerging from twenty-two years of self-imposed isolation. They planned every phase of the event with meticulous care, mobilizing their nation's limitless human resources, shipping in the best ingredients, and requisitioning the top hotel and restaurant chefs for the kitchens at the Great Hall of the People. While there had never been any question whether the banquet would follow Chinese standards of cuisine and service, certain limits had been imposed. For the past seven months, the Chinese had been testing the culinary sophistication of the Americans visiting China on the advance trips. After these trials, the Chinese protocol staff had given the Americans one guarantee: President Nixon would not have to eat sea cucumbers during his China visit.

The Nixons arrived in a boxy, Chinese-made "Red Flag" limousine and entered the Great Hall of the People, passing under a huge portrait of Chairman Mao. Zhou Enlai escorted them up a grand staircase for photographs and then down a long receiving line into the banquet hall itself. Here the American TV networks picked up the story. Back in the States, millions of Americans eating breakfast watched the cameras pan over the empty tables and the white-jacketed waiters standing at attention, as the reporters desperately tried to fill the time. Barbara Walters of NBC commented to Ed Newman back in New York: "We had our first taste of food and, Ed, you know what? It tasted like Chinese food! We had been told that it was so very exotic and so different that we might not recognize it, but we did indeed—it's just better than the Chinese food that we get in our country." She also revealed that the Chinese serve their "most esteemed" foreign guests nine-course banquets, while lesser visitors receive fewer courses.

Finally President Nixon and Premier Zhou Enlai entered, and the meal began under the glare of the television lights at the big round table next to the stage. In addition to the cold hors d'oeuvres—salted chicken, vegetarian ham, cucumber rolls, crisp silver carp, duck slices with pineapple, three colored eggs (including thousand-year-old eggs with their aroma of sulfur and ammonia), and Cantonese smoked salted meat and duck liver sausage—a sharp-eyed viewer could spot big rosettes of butter and slices of white bread at every place. The barbarians would not have to sneak loaves in their pockets. Walters was awed at what she was seeing: "Mrs. Nixon using chopsticks!" The perfect Chinese host, Zhou selected a delicacy from one of the dishes and gave it to Mrs. Nixon. She gingerly pushed the food around her plate for a minute or two, finally inserted something into her mouth, and ever-so-slowly began to chew. Watching from New York, Ed Newman observed: "I think we can also see that President Nixon is using chopsticks and apparently doing very well with them." Over on ABC, Harry Reasoner was also impressed: "Here is a tremendous picture: the President of the United States with chopsticks!" The next day, the *New*

York Times television critic wrote: "Some images were simply beyond words or still photographs," including the sight of "Mr. and Mrs. Nixon carefully wielding chopsticks."

Chopsticks were quickly forgotten as Zhou rose to toast the friendship of the Chinese and American peoples. The reporters declared that he was "warm and gracious" and had dispelled the chill that had descended at the airport. Then Nixon took the stage and read his toast, suggesting that the two nations should, in the words of Chairman Mao, "seize the day, seize the hour." After complimenting the chefs for preparing such a magnificent banquet, Nixon descended to toast each top Chinese official with mao-tai. He didn't forget his instructions: the level of drink in his glass hardly dropped. The president, Dan Rather opined, looked "energetic and triumphant." For two more hours, the meal continued, through entrées including spongy bamboo shoots and egg-white consommé, shark's fin in three shreds, fried and stewed prawns, mushrooms and mustard greens, steamed chicken with coconut, and a cold almond junket for dessert. These were served with assorted pastries, including purée of pea cake, fried spring rolls, plum blossom dumplings, and fried sweet rice cake. Finally came a simple dessert of melon and tangerines, and then the banquet ended. For those present, it had been an amazing, history-making evening, even if the details were a bit vague after all those firewater toasts. Of all the Americans present, only Charles Freeman, the veteran of Taipei's dining scene, opined the meal's offerings had merely been "very good, standard Chinese banquet food."

The American television audience did not see the entire banquet because the networks cut back to their regular programming right after the toasts. Before that happened, the viewers received a message from their sponsors. On CBS, McDonald's promoted its deep-fried cherry pies to celebrate

Washington's Birthday. Meanwhile, over on NBC was heard the bouncy jingle "East meets West. La Choy makes Chinese food *swing* American. La Choy makes Oriental recipes to serve at home." A crisply coiffed nuclear family sat in a spotlessly white dining alcove. A baritone voice-over announced: "Let East meet West at your home. Enjoy La Choy Chicken or Beef Chow Mein. Exotic recipes from scratch? Use La Choy ingredients: Chinese vegetables, bean sprouts, water chestnuts, soy sauce." The camera closed in on the family smiling down at a serving platter in the center of the white table: a mound of steaming chicken chow mein. Given the moment, La Choy's ad buyers may have thought this savvy marketing. They did not realize, however, that the coming fad for Chinese food would include everything but chop suey and chow mein.

Even before Nixon departed, Americans had been going crazy for things Chinese—a reprise of the China fad during Li Hongzhang's visit. People were swarming to classes in Mandarin and in Chinese cooking; department stores sold Chinese handicrafts (the Mao suits quickly sold out at Bloomingdale's in New York); publishers rushed books on the People's Republic into print; and Chinese restaurants suddenly began to fill up. After they saw the images of Nixon eating banquet food in Beijing, customers began to use chopsticks and ask about sharks' fin soup and Peking duck. In New York, Chicago, and Washington, D.C., restaurant owners anxious to cash in on the trend quickly whipped up special nine-course menus that supposedly replicated Nixon's meal with Zhou Enlai. In response, Taiwan's government flew in a team of chefs to show that they were the true guardians of Chinese culinary tradition. Banquet fever lasted for weeks—the first time Americans chose that most sophisticated format for a Chinese meal. Yet as they threw themselves into new eating experiences, they discovered that they needed a new set of skills to properly enjoy Chinese cuisine. That included ordering the right balance of contrasting (soft vs. crunchy, fried vs. boiled, etc.) dishes, selecting the correct beverage, using chopsticks, eating communally, and making sure that the food was prepared to Chinese and not American tastes. The ability to read and speak a little Chinese couldn't hurt either. If all else failed, the *Wall Street Journal* advised: "put yourself in the chef's hands by letting him decide the menu based upon what's fresh in the kitchen that day and what he feels like creating. But be sure to let him know you are capable of enjoying his extra efforts. Chinese chefs, perhaps the most artistic in their profession, love appreciative clients."[18]

And diners appreciated the food. During the recession of the 1970s, when many high-end restaurants, including the famous Le Pavillon, went out of business, Chinese eateries flourished and expanded, particularly those serving adventurous new menus. Shortly after Nixon's trip, the owners of the Shun Lee restaurant empire further jolted the food world by introducing a new Chinese regional cuisine: Hunan, which they advertised as "hot-hot-hot."

Their restaurant, called Hunam, immediately earned four stars from the *New York Times* and was followed by imitators like Uncle Tai's Hunan Yuan. In 1974, Henry Chung opened his Hunan Restaurant in San Francisco, probably the first such eatery west of the Mississippi. The original list of Hunan specialties served in the United States included harvest pork, beef with watercress, and honey ham with lotus nuts. Soon diners also began to notice a dish of chicken chunks in a savory, spicy sauce. Shun Lee called it "General Ching's Chicken"; other eateries called it "General Tso's Chicken." The restaurant impresario David Keh told Roy Andries de Groot of the *Chicago Tribune* a complicated story of how General Tso, a real military hero, had invented

Hunam Specialties

* ▲ 1. **SLICED LEG OF LAMB, Hunam Style** 5.15
  Choice spring lamb with scallions and hot pepper sauce

* ▲ 2. **GENERAL CHING'S CHICKEN** 5.15
  General Ching, the renowned General of the Chung Dynasty trained the famous Hunam Army. Chicken chunks with tingling Hot Sauce

* 3. **LAKE TUNG TING SHRIMP** 5.25
  Giant Shrimp marinated with broccoli, ham, bamboo shoots and mushrooms in a white sauce (Lake Tung Ting is the largest lake in China)

* ▲ 4. **HUNAM BEEF** 5.25
  Fillet of beef garnished with fresh water cress in a hot sauce

* 5. **HUNAM'S HONEY HAM** 6.25
  China's finest preserved ham, honey glazed with lotus nuts

* ▲ 6. **SPICY CRISPY WHOLE SEA BASS** 7.50
  Sea Bass, deep fried till crisp coated with Hunam hot sauce

* ▲ 7. **BAMBOO STEAMER'S SPARERIBS** 5.15
  An authentic Hunam specialty. Baby spareribs marinated in hot sauce coated with rice flour. Steamed in a bamboo steamer

* 8. **NEPTUNE'S PLATTER** 6.75
  An assortment of culinary sea treasures with crisp Chinese vegetables

* 9. **HUNAM PRESERVED DUCK** 5.25
  Young preserved duckling steamed on a bed of marinated lean pork patties

* ▲ 10. **FILLET OF SEA BASS with SHRIMP ROE SAUCE** 5.25
  Sea Bass fillet sauteed in a hot shrimp roe sauce

* ▲ 11. **SHREDDED LAMB TRIPE** 4.50
  Authentic Hunam country style cooking. Shredded lamb tripe sauteed in hot Hunam Sauce

* ▲ 12. **GENERAL GAU'S DUCKLING** 5.15
  Boned Duckling with button mushrooms and Chinese five spices in red hot sauce. (General Gau was a famous Governor of Hunam during the Chung's Dynasty)

湖南羊肉
國藩雞球
湘綺蝦片
岳陽牛柳
湘蓮雲腿
湖南翠皮魚
粉蒸排骨
湘江第一菜
蒸臘雙味
長沙魚脯
椒麻羊肚絲
宗棠鴨麟

Figure 7.4. In 1972, the Hunam restaurant introduced diners to the "hot-hot-hot" caisine of China's Hunan province. General's chicken and Lake Tung Ting Shrimp are now served by Chinese restaurants across the country.

the dish in his retirement, when he had "turned his creative energies to the development and improvement of the aromatic, peppery, spicy Hunanese cuisine."[19]

In reality, however, the chef who invented General Tso's chicken, Peng Chang-kuei, was then cooking on East Forty-fourth Street in Manhattan. Born in 1919 in the capital of Hunan Province, Peng had been apprenticed to one of Hunan's most prominent chefs and ended up, after the Communist takeover, in Taiwan. There he met President Chiang Kai-shek, who appreciated his cooking skills and invited him to prepare banquets for VIPs and foreign visitors. During this period, he invented a number of signature dishes, including General Tso's chicken, made from chunks of dark meat chicken marinated in egg whites and soy sauce. After being quickly deep-fried, the chunks are stir-fried with ginger, garlic, soy sauce, vinegar, cornstarch, sesame oil, and dried chili peppers. Chef Peng named it after the general because he admired this hero from his home province. Many young chefs who later moved to the United States learned how to make his dishes, including Chef Wang of Shun Lee and Uncle Tai. Word of their success reached Chef Peng, and in 1974 he decided to try his luck in New York. His first restaurant, Uncle Peng's Hunan Yuan on East Forty-fourth Street, quickly went bust, leaving him nearly broke. Unwilling to return to Taiwan in shame, he borrowed from friends and opened the Yunnan Yuan restaurant on Fifty-second Street. Before long, its prime patron was Kissinger, fresh from opening China. Building on this hard-earned success, Chef Peng returned to the Forty-fourth Street location and opened his most famous U.S. restaurant, simply called Peng's. In 1984, he decided he had proved his mettle and that it was time to return home. He sold his restaurants and moved back to Taiwan, where he started his chain of highly successful Peng Yuan restaurants. His most famous dish had already spread from Manhattan to the suburbs and then across the United States, changing every time a new chef prepared it. Already in 1978, a dish of General Tso's served in New Jersey was described as "slightly peppery, batter-fried chicken."[20] The adaptation of Hunan and Sichuan food to American tastes was well under way.

While Americans celebrated their love affair with spicy Chinese food, another great change was taking place. For the first time in a century, waves of Chinese immigrants began arriving in the United States. They came not only from Hong Kong and Taiwan as in decades past but also from Vietnam, Malaysia, Singapore, Burma, Thailand, and, most significantly, the People's Republic of China. The Cantonese among them, already linked to the United States by family and clan associations, usually settled in existing Chinatowns— most importantly, in Manhattan and San Francisco. Others sought a fresh start, building Chinese communities in neighborhoods like Flushing, Queens, and Sunset Park, Brooklyn, both a quick subway ride from jobs in Manhattan. On the West Coast, the most vital Chinese district was founded in Monterey Park, a city in Los Angeles County's San Gabriel Valley. Wherever these Chinese immigrants settled, they opened restaurants. Filled with Taiwanese, Monterey Park was dubbed Little Taipei and boasted dozens of Taiwanstyle eateries catering primarily to recent immigrants. Other parts of the country saw the appearance of establishments specializing in dishes from Shanghai, Fujian, Chaozhou, Dongbei (China's far northeast), Xinjiang, the Hakka ethnic group, and the Chinese communities in Singapore, Vietnam, Malaysia, and even Cuba. Not to be outdone, the Cantonese opened sprawling banquet halls doubling as lunchtime dim sum parlors, like New York City's HSF (short for Hee Seung Fung). (San Franciscans yawned at this development—they had been eating Chinese tea pastries for a hundred years.) From the 1980s on, Chinese food flourished wherever new immigrants congregated.

Meanwhile, the owners of the Sichuan and Hunan restaurants improved their business skills, smoothing out the uncertainties. The epicenter of this transformation was "Szechuan Valley" (also known as "Hunan Gulch"), the stretch of Upper Broadway in Manhattan where nearly every block had its Sichuan or Hunan restaurant. Now managers standardized their menus so that they didn't need a temperamental and high-priced artist to make the dishes, just a team of competent Chinese cooks. The offerings at Empire Szechuan, which grew into a chain that covered

Figure 7.5. Many storefront Chinese restaurants, like this one in Bedford-Stuyvesant, Brooklyn, are run by recent Fujianese immigrants. Like the chop suey joints of the 1920s and 1930s, they serve Chinese food adapted to American tastes.

Manhattan, included not only Sichuan-style dishes like Ta Chien chicken, Kung Pao shrimp, and beef with broccoli but lobster Cantonese, egg drop soup, and chicken chow mein. (By 1993, you could also order sushi, teriyaki chicken, dim sum, and low-fat steamed vegetables with brown rice at Empire Szechuan.) And the recipes were altered once more to appeal to local, non-Chinese tastes. Shun Lee's Michael Tong noticed that "Americans like anything spicy, anything sweet, anything crispy."[21] At many eateries, chefs now dunked their cubes of meat in a thick all-purpose batter, deep-fried them, and served them in different slightly spicy, cloyingly sweet sauces. In order to maximize trade, owners also began offering delivery, slipping thousands of folded paper menus under apartment doors across Manhattan. No longer did you have to wait in line on a freezing winter night to get a table: one phone call, and the food would be at your door in twenty minutes. Business boomed, but the connection with customers was lost—it was far too easy to eat at home.

In the late 1980s, the restaurant business attracted the attention of one of the largest new groups of Asian immigrants, those from the province of Fujian, just up the coast from Guangdong. After Deng Xiaoping unleashed his free market reforms in the late seventies, the new development zones around the provincial capital of Fuzhou experienced a massive influx of people looking for capitalist opportunities. The economic upheaval caused widespread social dislocation in the region as the old Communist way of life broke down. Like their adventurous South China forebears, many decided to emigrate in order to look for better prospects. Unable to get visas, they paid "snakeheads" tens of thousands of dollars to smuggle them into the United States. Once they landed in New York's Chinatown, they were steered to a warren of tiny employment offices in the blocks under the Manhattan Bridge, where they found listings for jobs in restaurants throughout the East, from Florida to Maine. After a phone call, they were put on the next bus for Baton Rouge, Pittsburgh, or Winston-Salem, to work as dishwashers and busboys for $1,000 a month.

For these Fujianese immigrants, like others before them, restaurants became a stepping-stone to success. After years of working long hours, a family could amass enough money to buy a storefront Chinese eatery in some Alabama town or across the street from a housing project on Chicago's South Side. Like the chop suey joint owners of the 1920s and 1930s, these immigrants aspired to nothing more than earning a living. Their menus hewed to the formula of the tried and true: spring rolls, chicken lo mein, beef with broccoli, fried rice, barbecue spare ribs, pork chow mein, and so on. Meanwhile, behind the counter, the Fujianese restaurant workers enjoyed their staff luncheons of noodle soup, greens, and a bit of seafood over steamed rice—the traditional South China family meal. Today, these restaurants represent the vast majority of Chinese eateries in the United States.

The status of Chinese food in the American culinary scene has always been linked, albeit often loosely, to the state of international relations between the two countries. In 1989, the brutal squashing of the Tiananmen Square protest shattered any illusion of China evolving into an American-style democracy. Cultural exchanges ground to a halt; tourists canceled their China trips; and the U.S. government instituted economic sanctions against the Communist government. At the same time, the American culinary world's attention was directed elsewhere, particularly toward the Japanese and New American restaurants that dominated the white-tablecloth end of the market. These places often paired the French techniques taught at cooking schools like the Culinary Institute of America with Asian or American dishes and ingredients. Still, many in the business believed that Chinese food could continue to draw customers, with a little tweaking. Entrepreneurs started Chinese food franchises like Panda Express (founded in 1973), Manchu Wok,

City Wok, and the more ambitious P. F. Chang's China Bistro. Featuring streamlined Chinese-American menus, they vied for diners' dollars wherever the storefront Fujianese eateries were not, particularly in places like malls, airports, and train stations. These competed with either fast food franchises like Taco Bell and Pizza Hut or more upscale "casual dining" chains like Olive Garden and T.G.I. Friday's. With higher ambitions, cooking school graduates began to "update" Chinese cuisine by applying French techniques to classic dishes like Peking duck. The pioneer in this movement was probably the California-trained chef Ken Hom, who wrote the 1987 cookbook *Ken Hom's East Meets West Cuisine*. Chinese "fusion" restaurants like Wolfgang Puck's Chinois-on-Main and Patricia Yeo's AZ opened on the East and West coasts, featuring food that was adventurously Asian yet accessible. This food was not always very Chinese. The menus at two prominent Chinese fusion restaurants, Susanna Foo's in Philadelphia and Blue Ginger outside of Boston, listed dishes like goat cheese wontons and sesame Caesar salad with Chinese cruller croutons. Nevertheless, today when gastronomes want to splurge on a "Chinese" feast, they often gravitate toward these more culturally familiar choices rather than the nearest Chinatown.

In August 2008, when an army of American athletes, journalists, and fans descended on Beijing for the Summer Olympics, the world media focused on China once again, reporting on not just the sports but on the nation's people and culture. For the Chinese government, the Olympics was far more than an athletic event: it was a show of political, cultural, and economic might by a country whose exports of manufactured goods now exceeded those of the United States. The stunning new venues for the Olympic events, designed by the world's top architects, were just one symbol of China's arrival as a world power. The integration

Figure 7.6. With hundreds of locations across the country, P.F. Chang's offers upscale Americanized Chinese food in an exotic "Chinese village" setting. Its menu includes dishes such as Singapore street noodles, "Sichuan from the Sea" scallops, and a "Great Wall of Chocolate" dessert.

of China into the world economy meant that to visiting American athletes and tourists—unlike the New England traders who landed in eighteenth-century Guangzhou—the culinary landscape was somewhat familiar. McDonald's was the official restaurant of the Summer Games, and Kentucky Fried Chicken already had almost fifteen hundred franchises across China. Nevertheless, cultural barriers remained, particularly that language. Few Americans spoke Chinese, and tourist menus in local restaurants contained literal translations of fancifully named dishes like "husband-and-wife lung slices" and "chicken without sexual life." This increased the visitors' tendency to see Chinese cuisine as a collection of absurd and exotic dishes, an inclination that was magnified by visits to the Wangfujing Night Market, where grilled scorpions, lizard tails, and horse stew were among the offerings. The *South Florida Sun-Sentinel* ran the headline "From Pig's Liver to Sheep Penis, Authentic Chinese Food Is Tough to Stomach." A small contingent of aficionados did scurry down the *hutong* alleyways to find the best local dumplings and restaurants serving obscure regional cuisines unheard-of in the States. But for most, it was enough to eat burgers at the McDonald's next to the hotel and sample the bland options on display in the Olympic Village canteen. Operated by the American food service giant Aramark, the canteen offered a rotating menu of 460 dishes from all major cuisines, including Chinese. At the start of the Olympics, three hundred roast ducks were delivered every day. The number was raised to six hundred when they began selling out by early evening. Somewhat unexpectedly, it seemed that the whole world loved Peking duck.

Over two centuries have passed since the *Empress of China* sailed up the Pearl River and American traders sampled their first bites of Chinese food. How much has changed in that time? Since 1789, numerous waves of Chinese immigration and cultural influence have profoundly affected American life. Today, more than forty thousand Chinese restaurants dot this country and are a routine part of the American environment, as exciting as the corner gas station or the Super 8 Motel down by the highway entrance. Supermarkets sell an array of Chinese ingredients, from soy sauce and ginger to Napa cabbage, bean sprouts, green tea, and rice noodles. Communities with large enough Chinese populations are also home to markets like the West Coast–based 99 Ranch Market chain, selling a huge variety of products aimed at immigrant cooks and eaters. Many American diners can handle a pair of chopsticks and aren't afraid to use cooking techniques like stir-frying and steaming in their home kitchens.

Despite this progress, one also sees an incredible resistance to Chinese food—at least as it's served in China. The editor of *Chinese Restaurant News* has estimated that 80 percent of those forty thousand or so eateries serve a limited Chinese American menu—a short roster of dishes like Kung Pao chicken, hot and sour soup, egg rolls, beef with broccoli, and General Tso's chicken. Americans have the same taste for spicy, sweet, crispy food that Michael Tong remarked on back in the 1980s, and, just as in the days of chop suey and chow mein, expect Chinese food to be priced low. More adventurous tasters can find alternatives to that menu in the other 20 percent of the restaurants, usually located in immigrant communities. In places like Flushing and the San Gabriel Valley, the food can be exciting, meticulously prepared, even expensive. Think Shanghai soup dumplings made with foie gras.

Diners still need to watch one crucial marker to see how a restaurant will evolve: the ratio of Chinese to non-Chinese diners. Whichever group dominates the seats will inevitably have the most influence on what is served, and how. The restaurant owner has to survive. If you don't see any immigrants or their descendants at the tables, then you know that American tastes will rule the meal—for spicy but not too spicy food, for steamed vegetables and brown rice, for sushi and Pad Thai noodles. (It's all Asian, isn't it?) Like their ancestors fifty and a hundred years ago, most Americans still expect Chinese food to be cheap, filling, familiar, and bland.

PHOTO CREDITS ·

NOTES ································

Chapter 1

1. Samuel Shaw and Josiah Quincy, *The Journals of Major Samuel Shaw* (Boston: Wm. Crosby and H. Nichols, 1847), 111–2.
2. Shaw and Quincy, *Journals*, 155.
3. Shaw and Quincy, *Journals*, 167–8.
4. Shaw and Quincy, *Journals*, 168.
5. Shaw and Quincy, *Journals*, 338.
6. Shaw and Quincy, *Journals*, 180–1.
7. Philip Dormer Stanhope Chesterfield, *Lord Chesterfield's Advice to His Son* (Philadelphia: Thomas Dobson, 1786), 52.
8. Shaw and Quincy, *Journals*, 182.
9. Shaw and Quincy, *Journals*, 179.
10. Shaw and Quincy, *Journals*, 179.
11. William Hickey, *Memoirs of William Hickey*, 4 vols. (New York: Knopf, 1921), 1:224.
12. Shaw and Quincy, *Journals*, 199–200.
13. *Li Chi: Book of Rites*, trans. James Legge, 2 vols. (New Hyde Park, N.Y.: University Books, 1967), 1:229.
14. Jean-Baptiste Du Halde, *The General History of China*, 4 vols. (London: J. Watts, 1751), 2:201.
15. *The Chinese Traveller* (London: E. and C. Dilly, 1772), 204.
16. *Chinese Traveller*, 118.
17. *Chinese Traveller*, 37–8.
18. Du Halde, *General History*, 201.
19. "Walks about the City of Canton," *Chinese Repository*, May 1835, 43.
20. Lawrence Waters Jenkins, *Bryant Parrott Tilden of Salem, at a Chinese Dinner Party* (Princeton: Princeton University Press, 1944), 18–21.
21. Eliza J. Gillett Bridgman, *The Pioneer of American Missions in China* (New York: A. D. F. Randolph, 1864), 43.
22. Bridgman, *Pioneer*, 97.

23. Edmund Roberts, *Embassy to the Eastern Courts of Cochin-China, Siam, and Muscat* (New York: Harper, 1837), 151.
24. Frederick Wells Williams, *The Life and Letters of Samuel Wells Williams* (New York: Putnam, 1889), 64.
25. Williams, *Life and Letters*, 69.
26. "Diet of the Chinese," *Chinese Repository*, February 1835, 465.

Chapter 2

1. Josiah Quincy, *Memoir of the Life of John Quincy Adams* (Boston: Crosby, Nichols, Lee, 1860), 341.
2. Quincy, *Memoir*, 340.
3. Claude M. Fuess, *The Life of Caleb Cushing*, 2 vols. (Hamden, Conn.: Archon Books, 1965) 1:414.
4. William C. Hunter, *Bits of Old China* (London: K. Paul, Trench, 1885), 38–9.
5. "Mr. F. Webster's Lecture on China," *American Penny Magazine*, November 15, 1845, 645–6.
6. "Mr. Fletcher Webster's Lectures," *Niles' National Register*, November 15, 1845, 170–1.
7. Earl Swisher, *China's Management of the American Barbarians* (New Haven, Conn.: Far Eastern, 1953), 160.
8. Swisher, *China's Management*, 174.
9. John R. Peters, Jr., *Miscellaneous Remarks upon the Government, History, Religions, Literature, Agriculture, Arts, Trades, Manners, and Customs of the Chinese* (Boston: John F. Trow, 1846), 162.
10. "China," *Wisconsin Herald*, December 11, 1845, 1.
11. "Miscellaneous," *Niles' National Register*, November 1, 1845, 9–10.
12. "Too Good," *Sandusky (OH) Clarion*, May 24, 1845, 2.
13. Mayers, William F., N. B. Dennys, and C. King, *The Treaty Ports of China and Japan* (London: Trübner, 1867), 397.
14. Charles M. Dyce, *Personal Reminiscences of Thirty Years' Residence in the Model Settlement Shanghai* (London: Chapman and Hall, 1906), 95.
15. Arthur Ransome, *The Chinese Puzzle* (London: Allen and Unwin, 1927), 29.
16. Samuel Wells Williams, *The Middle Kingdom*, 2 vols. (New York: Wiley, 1849), 1:xv.
17. Williams, *Middle Kingdom*, 1:3.
18. Williams, *Middle Kingdom*, 2:47–8.
19. Williams, *Middle Kingdom*, 2:50.
20. Frederick Wells Williams, *Life and Letters* (New York: Putnam, 1889), 172.

21. William Dean, *The China Mission* (New York: Sheldon, 1859), 271.
22. Dean, *China Mission*, 7–8.
23. Charles Taylor, *Five Years in China* (New York: Derby and Jackson, 1860), 133–4.

Chapter 3

1. Arthur Waley, *Yuan Mei* (London: Allen and Unwin, 1956), 191.
2. Waley, *Yuan Mei*, 53.
3. Waley, *Yuan Mei*, 52.
4. Waley, *Yuan Mei*, 196.
5. Herbert A. Giles, *A History of Chinese Literature* (New York: F. Ungar, 1967), 410.
6. Giles, *History*, 411.
7. Giles, *History*, 412.
8. Anne Birrell, *Chinese Mythology: An Introduction* (Baltimore: Johns Hopkins University Press, 1993), 49.
9. *Li Chi: Book of Rites*, trans. James Legge, 2 vols. (New Hyde Park, N.Y.: University Books, 1967), 1:369.
10. David, R. Knechtges, "A Literary Feast: Food in Early Chinese Literature," *Journal of the American Oriental Society* 106, no. 1 (January–March 1986): 53.
11. Fung Yu-Lan and Derek Bodde, ed., *A Short History of Chinese Philosophy* (New York: Macmillan, 1948), 289.
12. Birrell, *Chinese Mythology*, 57.
13. Dominique Hoizey and Marie-Joseph Hoizey, *A History of Chinese Medicine* (Edinburgh: Edinburgh University Press, 1993), 28–9.
14. *The Yellow Emperor's Classic of Internal Medicine*, trans. Ilza Veith (Berkeley: University of California Press, 1972), 206.
15. Knechtges, "Literary Feast," 49.
16. H. T. Huang, *Fermentations and Food Science*, vol. 6, pt. 5 of *Science and Civilization in China*, ed. Joseph Needham (Cambridge: Cambridge University Presss, 2000), 68.
17. Silvano Serventi and Françoise Sabban, *Pasta: The Story of a Universal Food* (New York: Columbia University Press, 2002), 273–4.
18. Jonathan Spence, "Ch'ing," in *Food in Chinese Culture*, ed. K. C. Chang (New Haven, Conn.: Yale University Press, 1977), 277.
19. John Minford and Joseph Lau, *Classical Chinese Literature* (New York: Columbia University Press, 2000), 223.
20. Buwei Y. Chao, *How to Cook and Eat in Chinese* (New York: John Day, 1945), 35.
21. Michael Freeman, "Sung," in Chang, *Food in Chinese Culture*, 161.

22. John Henry Gray, *China: A History of the Laws, Manners, and Customs of the People* (London: Macmillan, 1878), 64.

23. Gray, *China*, 72.

Chapter 4

1. Samuel Bowles, *Our New West* (Hartford, Conn.: Hartford, 1869), 410.

2. Bowles, *New West*, 411.

3. "From California," *Chicago Tribune*, September 28, 1865, 3.

4. Albert D. Richardson, *Beyond the Mississippi* (Hartford, Conn.: American, 1867), 440.

5. Bowles, *New West*, 412–3.

6. "Restaurant Life in San Francisco," *Overland Monthly*, November 1868, 471.

7. Bayard Taylor, *Eldorado* (New York: Putnam: 1850), 116–7.

8. John Frost, *History of the State of California* (Auburn, N.Y.: Derby and Miller, 1851), 100–101.

9. William Kelly, *An Excursion to California* (London: Chapman and Hall, 1851), 244.

10. William Shaw, *Golden Dreams and Waking Realities* (London: Smith, Elder, 1851), 42.

11. *Notes on California and the Placers* (New York: H. Long, 1850), 100.

12. "The Chinese," *Weekly Alta California*, June 18, 1853, 4.

13. Frank Soulé, *The Annals of San Francisco* (San Francisco: Appleton, 1855), 378.

14. "Chinese Dinner and Bill of Fare," *Charleston (SC) Mercury*, September 30, 1853, 2 (from the *San Francisco Whig*, August 16, 1853).

15. Albert H. Smyth, *Bayard Taylor* (Boston: Houghton, Mifflin, 1896), 70.

16. Bayard Taylor, *A Visit to India, China, and Japan, in the Year 1853* (New York: Putnam, 1855), 285.

17. Taylor, *Visit*, 353–4.

18. Frederick Whymper, *Travel and Adventure in the Territory of Alaska* (London: J. Murray, 1868), 280.

19. J. D. Borthwick, *Three Years in California* (Edinburgh: W. Blackwood, 1857), 75.

20. Albert S. Evans, *Á la California* (San Francisco: A. L. Bancroft, 1873), 320.

21. "How Our Chinamen Are Employed," *Overland Monthly*, March 1896, 236.

22. Auburn *Stars and Stripes,* 1866 (in *Bancroft Scraps,* Vol 6), p. 28.
23. "A Dinner with the Chinese," *Hutchings' California Magazine,* May 1857, 513.
24. Noah Brooks, "Restaurant Life in San Francisco," *Overland Monthly,* November 1868, 472.
25. Hubert Howe Bancroft, "Mongolianism in America," in *The Works of Hubert Howe Bancroft, vol.* 38, *Essays and Miscellany* (San Francisco: A. L. Bancroft, 1890), 331.
26. Otis Gibson, *The Chinese in America* (Cincinnati: Hitchcock and Walden, 1877), 71–2.
27. George H. Fitch, "A Night in Chinatown," *Cosmopolitan,* February 1887, 349.
28. Josephine Clifford, "Chinatown," *Potter's American Monthly,* May 1880, 353.
29. *New York Journal of Commerce,* December 14, 1869, clipping, in "Chinese clippings," vols. 6–9 of *Bancroft Scraps,* Bancroft Library, University of California, Berkeley.
30. Clifford, "Chinatown," 354.
31. Ira M. Condit, *The Chinaman as We See Him* (Chicago: F. H. Revell, 1900), 43.
32. Ralph Keeler, "John Chinaman Picturesquely Considered," *Western Monthly,* May 1870, 348.
33. J. W. Ames, "A Day in Chinatown," *Lippincott's,* October 1875, 497–8.
34. "The Old East in the New West," *Overland Monthly,* October 1868, 365.
35. Benjamin F. Taylor, *Between the Gates* (Chicago: S. C. Griggs, 1878), 109–10.
36. Will Brooks, "A Fragment of China," *Californian,* July 1882, 7–8.
37. Brooks, "Fragment," 8.
38. "The Chinese in California," *New York Evangelist,* October 21, 1869, 2.
39. "My China Boy," *Harper's Bazaar,* December 1, 1877, 763.
40. "A California Housekeeper on Chinese Servants," *Harper's Bazaar,* May 8, 1880, 290.
41. Ira M. Condit, *English and Chinese Reader with a Dictionary* (New York: American Tract Society, 1882), 41.
42. William Speer, *An Humble Plea* (San Francisco: Office of the Oriental, 1856), 24.
43. Herman Francis Reinhart, *The Golden Frontier* (Austin: University of Texas Press, 1962), 104.
44. Mark Twain, *Roughing It* (New York: Harper, 1913), 110.
45. Charles Nordhoff, *California: for Health, Pleasure, and Residence* (New York: Harper, 1873), 190.

46. "California Culinary Experiences," *Overland Monthly*, June 1869, 558.

Chapter 5

1. Edwin H. Trafton, "A Chinese Dinner in New York," *Frank Leslie's Popular Monthly*, February 1884, 183.
2. Trafton, "Chinese Dinner," 183.
3. "Chinese in New-York," *New York Times*, December 26, 1873, 3.
4. "With the Opium Smokers," *New York Times*, March 22, 1880, 2.
5. "The Rush at Castle Garden," *New York Times*, May 15, 1880, 4.
6. "Mott-Street Chinamen Angry," *New York Times*, August 1, 1883, 8.
7. "Mott-Street Chinamen Angry."
8. Wong Ching Foo, "Chinese Cooking," *Brooklyn Eagle*, July 6, 1884, 4.
9. Wong, "Chinese Cooking," 4.
10. Ward McAllister, *Society as I Have Found It* (New York: Cassell, 1890), 305.
11. Allan Forman, "New York's China-Town," *Washington Post*, July 25, 1886, 5.
12. Forman, "New York's China-Town."
13. Wong Ching Foo, "The Chinese in New York," *Cosmopolitan*, June 1888, 297.
14. Wong Ching Foo, "Chinese Cooking," *Boston Globe*, July 19, 1885, 9.
15. Wong, "Chinese in New York," 305.
16. Allan Forman, "Celestial Gotham," *Arena*, April 1893, 623.
17. Li Shu-Fan, *Hong Kong Surgeon* (New York: Dutton, 1964), 211.
18. "The Viceroy Their Guest," *New York Times*, August 30, 1896, 2.
19. "Presents His Letter," *Washington Post*, August 30, 1896, 1.
20. "A Chinese Dinner," *Brooklyn Eagle*, September 22, 1896, 8.
21. "Queer Dishes Served at the Waldorf by Li Hung Chang's Chicken Cook," *New York Journal*, September 6, 1896, 29.
22. Margherita Arlina Hamm, "Some Celestial Dishes," *Good Housekeeping*, May 1895, 200.
23. "Chinatown Full of Visitors," *New York Tribune*, July 30, 1900, 3.
24. "Conversations with a Chorus Girl," *Washington Post*, November 2, 1902, 6.
25. "Chinese Restaurants," *New York Tribune*, February 2, 1901, B6.
26. "Chinese Restaurants."
27. "Chinese Cuisine a Christmas Dinner Oddity," *New York Herald*, December 14, 1902, E12.

28. "Quoe's Guests," *Boston Daily Globe*, March 1, 1891, 4.
29. "The Quest of Bohemia," *Washington Post*, October 23, 1898, 10.
30. "Where Chinamen Trade," *Chicago Tribune*, May 5, 1889, 26.
31. Theodore Dreiser, "The Chinese in St. Louis," *St. Louis Republic*, January 14, 1894, 15.
32. "Where Kansas City's Foreign Population Takes Its Meals," *Kansas City Star*, March 8, 1908, 1.
33. "The Most Original Hostess in San Francisco," *San Francisco Call*, May 10, 1903, 13.
34. "Who Is the Noodle Lady of Chinatown?" *Los Angeles Times*, September 18, 1904, A1.
35. "Credit Men's Year," *Los Angeles Times*, January 19, 1906, 16.
36. *San Francisco Call*, February 6, 1907, 2.
37. "Should Eliminate Chinese," *Washington Post*, June 28, 1909, 2.
38. "Chop Suey Injunction," *New York Times*, June 15, 1904, 7.
39. "Never Heard of Chop Suey in China," *Boston Daily Globe*, October 1, 1905, SM4.
40. Carl Crow, "Shark's Fins and Ancient Eggs," *Harper's*, September 1937, 422–9.
41. "Will the World Go on a Chop Suey Diet?" *Philadelphia Inquirer*, September 15, 1918, 5.
42. Jennifer Lee, *The Fortune Cookie Chronicles* (New York: Twelve, 2008), 49.

Chapter 6

1. William M. Clemens, "Sigel Girl Alive as Leon's Bride?" *Chicago Tribune*, August 15, 1909, 2.
2. Elizabeth Goodnow, *The Market for Souls* (New York: M. Kennerley, 1910), 151.
3. "Suey 'Joints' Dens of Vice," *Chicago Tribune*, March 28, 1910, 2.
4. *Lancet Clinic*, March 19, 1910, 305.
5. Marion Harland, "Chop Suey and Some Rice Dishes," *Los Angeles Times*, October 12, 1913, VIII6.
6. Sara Bossé, "Cooking and Serving a Chinese Dinner in America," *Harper's Bazaar*, January 1913, 27.
7. Sinclair Lewis, *Main Street*, in *Main Street & Babitt* (New York: Library of America, 1992), 87.
8. Lewis, *Main Street*, 88.
9. Lewis, *Main Street*, 107.
10. Lewis, *Main Street*, 231.
11. Fremont Rider, *Rider's New York City and Vicinity* (New York: Holt, 1916), 24.

12. George Ross, *Tips on Tables* (New York: Covici, Friede, 1934), 226–7.
13. "Chop Suey's New Role," *New York Times*, December 27, 1925, XX2.
14. "Chop Suey Sundae," *Lincoln (NE) Evening News*, July 18, 1904, 6.
15. "Chop Suey and How to Make It," *Alton (IL)Evening Telegraph*, August 26, 1910, 4.
16. Lin Yutang, *My Country and My People* (New York: Reynal and Hitchcock, 1935), 335.
17. Herman Wouk, *Marjorie Morningstar* (Garden City, N.Y.: Doubleday, 1955), 58.
18. Wouk, *Marjorie Morningstar*, 62.
19. Wouk, *Marjorie Morningstar*, 63.
20. Wouk, *Marjorie Morningstar*, 408.
21. Sam Liptzin, *In Spite of Tears* (New York: Amcho, 1946), 219.
22. Liptzin, *In Spite of Tears*, 220.
23. "Events in Society," December 20, 1901, *Hawaiian Gazette*, 6.
24. Albert W. Palmer, *Orientals in American Life* (New York: Friendship Press, 1934), 3.

Chapter 7

1. Frank C. Porter, "Area's 110 Chinese Restaurants Keep Going Despite Low Profits," *Washington Post*, April 27, 1958, C9.
2. Will Elder, "Restaurant!" *Mad* 1, October 1954, 1–6.
3. Craig Claiborne, "Food: Chinese Cuisine, Two New Restaurants That Specialize in Oriental Food Open on East Side," *New York Times*, July 22, 1958, 31.
4. Buwei Y. Chao, *How to Cook and Eat in Chinese* (New York: John Day, 1945), 15.
5. Chao, *How to Cook and Eat in Chinese*, 31.
6. "News of Food," *New York Times*, May 10, 1945.
7. Victor Nee and Brett de Bary Nee, *Longtime Californ'* (New York: Pantheon, 1972), 115.
8. Cecilia S. Y. Chiang, *The Mandarin Way* (Boston: Little, Brown, 1974), 265.
9. Craig Claiborne and Virginia Lee, *The Chinese Cookbook* (Philadelphia: Lippincott, 1972), xiii.
10. "Directory to Dining," *New York Times*, December 18, 1964, 38.
11. Richard H. Solomon, *A Revolution Is Not a Dinner Party*, New York, 1975, 53.

12. Memorandum of conversation, July 10, 1971, 12:10 P.M.–6 P.M., National Security Archive, electronic briefing book no. 66, doc. 35, 21.

13. John Holdridge, *Crossing the Divide* (Lanham, Md.: Rowman and Littlefield, 1997), 60.

14. Holdridge, *Crossing the Divide*, 60.

15. Henry Kissinger, *The White House Years* (Boston: Little, Brown, 1979), 783.

16. Holdridge, *Crossing the Divide*, 69.

17. Visit of Richard Nixon, President of the United States, to the People's Republic of China, notes for Mrs. Nixon, February 1972, box 43, Richard Nixon Presidential Library; briefing books, 1969–74, staff member and office files—Susan A. Porter, White House central files, National Archives, College Park, Maryland.

18. Howard Hillman, "Beware of Yankee Chow Mein," *Wall Street Journal*, June 22, 1972, 16.

19. Roy Andries de Groot, "One Great Dish," *Chicago Tribune*, September 11, 1978, D3.

20. B. H. Fussell, "An Oriental Touch in Cedar Grove," *New York Times*, December 17, 1978, NJ 35.

21. Fred Ferretti, "Chinese Dishes, American Style," *New York Times*, April 13, 1986, C1.

BIBLIOGRAPHY ·

Anderson, Eugene N. *The Food of China*. New Haven, Conn.: Yale University Press, 1988.

Arkush, R. David, and Leo O. Lee, eds. *Land without Ghosts*. Berkeley: University of California Press, 1989.

Arndt, Alice, ed. *Culinary Biographies*. Houston: Yes Press, 2006.

Avakian, Monique. *Atlas of Asian-American History*. New York: Facts on File, 2002.

Bancroft, Hubert Howe. *History of California*. Vol. 6. *1848–1859*. San Francisco: A. L. Bancroft, 1888.

———. "Mongolianism in America." In *The Works of Hubert Howe Bancroft*, vol. 38, *Essays and Miscellany*. San Francisco: A. L. Bancroft, 1890, 331.

Barbas, Samantha. " 'I'll Take Chop Suey': Restaurants as Agents of Culinary and Cultural Change." *Journal of Popular Culture* 36, no. 4 (spring 2003): 669–86.

Barth, Gunther. *Bitter Strength*. Cambridge: Harvard University Press, 1964.

Beck, Louis J. *New York's Chinatown*. New York: Bohemia, 1898.

Birrell, Anne. *Chinese Mythology: An Introduction*. Baltimore: Johns Hopkins University Press, 1993.

Bishop, William H. *Old Mexico and Her Lost Provinces*. New York: Harper, 1883.

Borthwick, J. D. *Three Years in California*. Edinburgh: W. Blackwood, 1857.

Bossé, Sara. "Cooking and Serving a Chinese Dinner in America." *Harper's Bazaar*, January 1913, 127.

———. "Giving a Chinese Luncheon Party." *Harper's Bazaar*, March 1913, 135.

———. "Giving a Chinese Tea in America." *Harper's Bazaar*, April 1913, 192.

Bowles, Samuel. *Across the Continent*. Springfield, Mass.: Samuel Bowles, 1865.

———. *Our New West*. Hartford, Conn.: Hartford, 1869.

Bridgman, Eliza J. Gillett. *The Pioneer of American Missions in China.*
New York: A. D. F. Randolph, 1864.

Brooks, Will. "A Fragment of China." *Californian*, July 1882, 6–14.

Brownstone, David M., and Irene M. Franck. *Facts about American Immigration.* New York: H. W. Wilson, 2001.

Capron, E. S. *History of California.* Boston: John Jewett, 1854.

Carpenter, Frank G. *China.* Garden City, N.Y.: Doubleday, Page, 1925.

Chan, Shiu Wong. *The Chinese Cook Book.* New York: Frederick A. Stokes, 1917.

Chan, Sou. *The House of Chan Cookbook.* Garden City, N.Y.: Doubleday, 1952.

Chan, Sucheng. *This Bittersweet Soil.* Berkeley: University of California Press, 1986.

———, ed. *Chinese American Transnationalism.* Philadelphia: Temple University Press, 2006.

Chang, Iris. *The Chinese in America.* New York: Viking, 2003.

Chang, K. C., ed. *Food in Chinese Culture.* New Haven, Conn.: Yale University Press, 1977.

Chao, Buwei Y. *How to Cook and Eat in Chinese.* New York: John Day, 1945.

Chapman, Mary. "Notes on the Chinese in Boston." *Journal of American Folklore* 5, no. 19 (October–December 1892): 321–4.

Chen, Yong. *Chinese San Francisco, 1850–1943.* Stanford, Calif.: Stanford University Press, 2000.

———. "The Internal Origins of Chinese Emigration to California Reconsidered." *Western Historical Quarterly* 28, no. 4 (winter 1997): 520–46.

Cheng, F. T. *Musings of a Chinese Gourmet.* London: Hutchison, 1954.

Chesterfield, Philip Dormer Stanhope. *Lord Chesterfield's Advice to His Son.* Philadelphia: Thomas Dobson, 1786.

Chiang, Cecilia S. Y. *The Mandarin Way.* Boston: Little, Brown, 1974.

Chinatown Handy Guide. San Francisco: Chinese, 1959.

Chinese Committee, International Institute, Y.W.C.A., Honolulu. *Chinese Home Cooking.* Honolulu: Paradise of the Pacific, 1945.

The Chinese Traveller. London: E. and C. Dilly, 1772.

Ching, Frank. "China: It's the Latest American Thing." *New York Times*, February 16, 1972, 1.

Chinn, Thomas W., ed. *A History of the Chinese in Calfornia: A Syllabus.* San Francisco: Chinese Historical Society of America, 1969.

Chu, Louis H. "The Chinese Restaurants in New York City." Master's thesis, New York University, 1939.

Chung, Henry W. S. *Henry Chung's Hunan Style Chinese Cookbook.* New York: Harmony, 1978.

Claiborne, Craig. *The New York Times Guide to Dining Out in New York*. New York: Atheneum, 1969.

Claiborne, Craig, and Virginia Lee. *The Chinese Cookbook*. Philadelphia: Lippincott, 1972.

Clark, Helen F. "The Chinese of New York, Contrasted with Their Foreign Neighbors." *Century*, November 1896, 104–13.

Clifford, Nicholas R. "A Revolution Is Not a Tea Party: The 'Shanghai Mind(s)' Reconsidered." *Pacific Historical Review* 59, no. 4 (November 1990): 501–26.

Cohen, Lucy M. *Chinese in the Post–Civil War South*. Baton Rouge: Louisiana State University Press, 1984.

Condit, Ira M. *The Chinaman as We See Him*. Chicago: F. H. Revell, 1900.

———. *English and Chinese Reader with a Dictionary*. New York: American Tract Society, 1882.

Conlin, Joseph R. *Bacon, Beans, and Galantines*. Reno: University of Nevada Press, 1986.

Conwell, Russell H. *Why and How: Why the Chinese Emigrate, and the Means They Adopt for the Purpose of Reaching America*. Boston: Lee and Shepard, 1871.

Crawford, Gary, and Chen Shen. "The Origins of Rice Agriculture." *Antiquity* 72, no. 278 (December 1998): 858–67.

Crawford, Gary, A. P. Underhill, J. Zhou, et al. "Late Neolithic Plant Remains from Northern China." *Current Anthropology* 46, no. 2 (April 2005): 309–18.

Crow, Carl. "Shark's Fins and Ancient Eggs." *Harper's*, September 1937, 422–9.

Culin, Stewart. "Customs of the Chinese in America." *Journal of American Folklore* 3, no. 10 (July–September 1890): 191–200.

Curti, Merle, and John Stalker. "'The Flowery Flag Devils'—The American Image in China 1840–1900." *Proceedings of the American Philosophical Society* 96, no. 6 (December 1952): 663–90.

Dall, Caroline. *My First Holiday*. Boston: Roberts, 1881.

Damon, Frank W. "The Chinese at the Sandwich Islands." *Missionary Herald*, December 1885, 518–9.

Danton, G. H. "Chinese Restaurants in America." *China Journal of Science and Arts*, May 1925, 286–9.

Davis, John Francis. *The Chinese*. New York: Harper, 1836.

De Casseres, Benjamin. "All-Night New York in the Dry Season of 1919." *New York Times*, August 17, 1919, 73.

De Groot, Roy Andries. "How to Get a Great Chinese Meal in an American Chinese Restaurant." *Esquire*, August 1972, 130.

Dean, William. *The China Mission*. New York: Sheldon, 1859.

Delfs, Robert A. *The Good Food of Szechwan*. Tokyo: Kodansha, 1974.

Denker, Joel. *The World on a Plate*. Boulder, Colo.: Westview Press, 2003.

Dennys, N. B., ed. *The Treaty Ports of China and Japan*. London: Trübner, 1867.

Densmore, G. B. *The Chinese in California*. San Francisco: Pettit and Russ, 1880.

"Diet of the Chinese." *Chinese Repository*, February 1835, 465.

Dirlik, Arif, ed. *Chinese on the American Frontier*. Lanham, Md.: Rowman and Littlefield, 2001.

Donovan, Holly Richardson, Peter Donovan, and Harvey Mole. *A Guide to the Chinese Food and Restaurants of Taiwan*. Taipei: By the authors, 1977.

Doolittle, Justus. *Social Life of the Chinese*. London: Sampson Low, Son, and Marston, 1868.

Downing, C. Toogood. *The Fan-Qui in China*. London: Henry Colburn, 1838.

Downs, Jacques M. *The Golden Ghetto*. Bethlehem, Penn.: Lehigh University Press, 1997.

Dreiser, Theodore. "The Chinese in St. Louis." *St. Louis Republic*, January 14, 1894, 15.

Du Halde, Jean-Baptiste. *The General History of China*. 4 vols. London: J. Watts, 1751.

Dufferin, Lady Helen. *Songs, Poems, and Verses*. London: John Murray, 1894.

Dunlop, Fuchsia. *Shark's Fin and Sichuan Pepper*. New York: Norton, 2008.

Dyce, Charles M. *Personal Reminiscences of Thirty Years' Residence in the Model Settlement Shanghai*. London: Chapman and Hall, 1906.

Ellis, George E. *Bacon's Dictionary of Boston*. Boston: Houghton Mifflin, 1886.

Elston, Robert G., X. Cheng, D. B. Madsen, et al. "New Dates for the North China Mesolithic." *Antiquity* 71, no. 274 (December 1997): 985–94.

Evans, Albert S. *Á La California*. San Francisco: A. L. Bancroft, 1873.

Fairbank, John King. *Trade and Diplomacy on the China Coast*. Cambridge, Mass.: Harvard University Press, 1953.

The "Fan Kwae" at Canton before Treaty Days. London: Kegan Paul, Trench, 1882.

Fanning, Edmund. *Voyages and Discoveries in the South Seas*. Salem, Mass.: Marine Research Society, 1924.

Ferretti, Fred. "Chinese Dishes, American Style." *New York Times*, April 13, 1983, C1.

Fisher, Vardis, and Opal Laurel Holmes. *Gold Rushes and Mining Camps of the Early American West*. Caldwell, N.J.: Caxton, 1968.

Forman, Allan. "Celestial Gotham." *Arena*, April 1893, 623.

———. "New York's China-Town." *Washington Post*, July 25, 1886, 5.

Fortune, Robert. *A Journey to the Tea Countries of China*. London: John Murray, 1852.

Franck, Harry A. *Roving through South China*. New York: Century, 1925.

Frost, John. *History of the State of California*. Auburn, N.Y.: Derby and Miller, 1851.

Fuess, Claude M. *The Life of Caleb Cushing*. 2 vols. Hamden, Conn.: Archon Books, 1965.

Fuller, Sheri G. *Chinese in Minnesota*. St. Paul: Minnesota Historical Society Press, 2004.

Fung Yu-Lan and Derek Bodde, eds. *A Short History of Chinese Philosophy*. New York: Macmillan, 1948.

Garner, W. E. *Reliable Recipes for Making Chinese Dishes*. Long Branch, N.J.: F. M. Taylor, 1914.

Gernet, Jacques. *Daily Life in China on the Eve of the Mongol Invasion 1250–1276*. London: Allen and Unwin, 1962.

Gibson, Otis. *The Chinese in America*. Cincinnati: Hitchcock and Walden, 1877.

Giles, Herbert A. *A History of Chinese Literature*. New York: F. Ungar, 1967.

Glick, Clarence E. *Sojourners and Settlers*. Honolulu: Hawaii Chinese History Center, 1980.

Goddard, Francis W. *Called to Cathay*. New York: Baptist Literature Bureau, 1948.

Gong, William K. *Insider's Guide to Gourmet Chinatown*. San Francisco: VCIM, 1970.

Goodnow, Elizabeth. *The Market for Souls*. New York: M. Kennerley, 1910.

Graham, Stephen. *New York Nights*. New York: George H. Doran, 1927.

Gray, John Henry. *China: A History of the Laws, Manners, and Customs of the People*. London: Macmillan, 1878.

Greene, Charles. "The Restaurants of San Francisco." *Overland Monthly*, December 1892, 561–72.

Greene, Gael. "A Scrutable Guide to New York's Chinese Restaurants." *New York*, April 2, 1979, 43–58.

Gutzlaff, Charles. *China Opened*. 2 vols. London: Smith, Elder, 1838.

Haig, Alexander M., Jr. *Inner Circles*. New York: Warner Books, 1992.

Haldeman, H. R. *The Haldeman Diaries*. New York: Putnam, 1994.

Haller, Henry. *The White House Family Cookbook*. New York: Random House, 1987.

Hamilton, Roy W., ed. *The Art of Rice*. Los Angeles: UCLA Fowler Museum of Cultural History, 2003.

Hamm, Margherita A. "The Anti-foreign Movement in China." *Independent*, July 26, 1900, 1785–8.

Hammond, Jonathan. "Ecological and Cultural Anatomy of Taishan Villages." *Modern Asian Studies* 23, no. 3 (1995): 555–72.

Hansen, Gladys, ed. *The Chinese in California: A Brief Bibliographic History*. Portland, Ore.: Richard Abel, 1970.

Harper, Donald. "Gastronomy in Ancient China." *Parabola* 9, no. 4 (1984): 38–47.

Harrison, Alice A. "Chinese Food and Restaurants." *Overland Monthly*, September 1917, 527–32.

Harte, Bret. *The Heathen Chinee*. Boston: James R. Osgood, 1871.

Hess, John L. "The Best American Food Is Chinese." *New York Times*, August 18, 1974, 206.

Hickey, William. *Memoirs of William Hickey*. 4 vols. New York: Knopf, 1921.

Higman, Charles, and Tracey L-D Lu. "The Origins and Dispersal of Rice Cultivation." *Antiquity* 72, no. 278 (December 1998): 867–78.

Hittel, John S. *The Resources of California*. San Francisco: A. Roman, 1863.

Hoizey, Dominique, and Marie-Joseph Hoizey. *A History of Chinese Medicine*. Edinburgh: Edinburgh University Press, 1993.

Holdridge, John. *Crossing the Divide*. Lanham, Md.: Rowman and Littlefield, 1997.

"Hot Hunan." *Sunset*, October 1976, 88–9.

"How about Sampling the Spicy Food of *She-chwan*?" *Sunset*, October 1974, 192–5.

Howells, William Dean. *A Hazard of New Fortunes*. New York: Harper, 1889.

The How Long Chinese Cook Book. New York: How Long, 1924.

Hu, Shiu-ying. *Food Plants of China*. Hong Kong: Chinese University Press, 2005.

Huang, H. T. *Fermentations and Food Science*. Vol. 6, pt. 5 of *Science and Civilization in China*, ed. Joseph Needham. Cambridge: Cambridge University Presss, 2000.

Hunter, William C. *Bits of Old China*. London: K. Paul, Trench, 1885.

Jenkins, Lawrence Waters. *Bryant Parrott Tilden of Salem, at a Chinese Dinner Party*. Princeton, N.J.: Princeton University Press, 1944.

Johnson, Bryan R. "Let's Eat Chinese Tonight." *American Heritage*, December 1987, 98–107.

Johnson, James Weldon. *Black Manhattan*. New York: Knopf, 1940.

Jones, Idwal. "Cathay on the Coast." *American Mercury*, August 1926, 453–60.

Keeler, Charles. *San Francisco and Thereabout*. San Francisco: California Promotion Committee, 1903.

Keeler, Ralph. "John Chinaman Picturesquely Considered." *Western Monthly*, May 1870, 348.

Kelly, William. *An Excursion to California*. London: Chapman and Hall, 1851.

Kilgannon, Corey. "In Search of Chow Mein." *New York Times*, November 23, 1997, CY1.

Kissinger, Henry. *The White House Years*. Boston: Little, Brown, 1979.

Klein, Jakob A. " 'For Eating, It's Guangzhou': Regional Culinary Traditions and Chinese Socialism." In Harry West and Parvathi Raman, eds., *Enduring Socialism: Explorations of Revolution and Transformation, Restoration and Continuation*. New York: Berghahn Books, 2008, 44–76.

Knechtges, David R. "Gradually Entering the Realm of Delight: Food and Drink in Early Medieval China." *Journal of the American Oriental Society* 117, no. 2 (April–June, 1997): 229–39.

——— "A Literary Feast: Food in Early Chinese Literature." *Journal of the American Oriental Society* 106, no. 1 (January–March 1986): 49–63.

Koutsky, Kathryn S., and Linda Koutsky. *Minnesota Eats Out*. St. Paul: Minnesota Historical Society Press, 2003.

Kwong, Peter. *The New Chinatown*. New York: Hill and Wang, 1988.

Kwong, Peter, and Dusanka Miscevic. *Chinese America*. New York: New Press, 2005.

Lapidus, Dorothy Farris. *The Scrutable Feast*. New York: Dodd, Mead, 1977.

Laudan, Rachel. *The Food of Paradise*. Honolulu: University of Hawai'i Press, 1996.

Lay, G. Tradescant. *The Chinese as They Are*. London: William Ball, 1841.

Lee, Calvin. *Calvin Lee's Chinese Cooking for American Kitchens*. New York: Putnam, 1958.

———. *Chinatown, U.S.A.* Garden City, N.Y.: Doubleday, 1965.

Lee, Jennifer. *The Fortune Cookie Chronicles*. New York: Twelve, 2008.

Lee, M. P. *Chinese Cookery*. London: Faber and Faber, 1943.

Lee, Ping Quan. *To a President's Taste*. Emmaus, Penn.: Rodale Press, 1939.

Lee, Robert G. *Orientals: Asian Americans in Popular Culture*. Philadelphia: Temple University Press, 1999.

Lee, Rose Hum. *The Chinese of the United States of America*. Hong Kong: Hong Kong University Press, 1960.

———. "The Decline of Chinatowns in the United States." *American Journal of Sociology* 54, no. 5 (March 1949): 422–32.

Leping Jiang and Li Liu. "New Evidence for the Origins of Sedentism and Rice Domestication in the Lower Yangzi River, China." *Antiquity* 80, no. 308 (June 2006): 355–61.

Lewis, Sinclair. *Main Street & Babbit*. New York: Library of America, 1992), 87.

Li Chi: Book of Rites. Trans. James Legge. 2 vols. New Hyde Park, N.Y.: University Books, 1967.

Li Shu-Fan. *Hong Kong Surgeon*. New York: Dutton, 1964.

Light, Ivan. "From Vice District to Tourist Attraction: The Moral Career of American Chinatowns, 1880–1940." *Pacific Historical Review* 43 (1974): 367–94.

Lim, Genny, ed. *The Chinese American Experience*. San Francisco: Chinese Historical Society of America, 1984.

Lin, Hsian Ju, and Tsuifeng Lin. *Chinese Gastronomy*. New York: Harcourt Brace Jovanovich, 1969.

Liptzin, Sam. *In Spite of Tears*. New York: Amcho, 1946.

Lloyd, B. E. *Lights and Shades of San Francisco*. San Francisco: A. L. Bancroft, 1876.

Lo, Kenneth. *Chinese Food*. London: Hippocrene Books, 1972.

Lobscheid, William. *The Chinese: What They Are, and What They Are Doing*. San Francisco: A. L. Bancroft, 1873.

Lui, Mary Ting Yi. *The Chinatown Trunk Mystery*. Princeton, N.J.: Princeton University Press, 2005.

Luo, Michael. "As All-American as Egg Foo Yong." *New York Times*, September 22, 2004, F1.

MacMillan, Margaret. *Nixon and Mao*. New York: Random House, 2007.

Malcolm, Elizabeth. "The *Chinese Repository* and Western Literature on China, 1800 to 1850." *Modern Asian Studies* 7, no. 2 (1973): 165–78.

McAdoo, William. *Guarding a Great City*. New York: Harper, 1906.

McAllister, Ward. *Society as I Have Found It*. New York: Cassell, 1890.

McCawley, James D. *The Eater's Guide to Chinese Characters*. Chicago: University of Chicago Press, 1984.

McGovern, Patrick E., J. Zhang, J. Tang, et al. "Fermented Beverages of Pre- and Proto-historic China." *Proceedings of the National Academy of Sciences* 101, no. 51 (December 21, 2004): 17593–8.

McLeod, Alexander. *Pigtails and Gold Dust.* Caldwell, N.J.: Caxton, 1947.

Mei, June. "Socioeconomic Origins of Emigration, Guangdong to California, 1850–1882." *Modern China* 4, no. 4 (October 1979): 463–501.

Meloney, William B. "Slumming in New York's Chinatown." *Munsey's Magazine*, September 1909, 818–30.

Miller, Hannah. "Identity Takeout: How American Jews Made Chinese Food Their Ethnic Cuisine." *Journal of Popular Culture* 39, no. 3 (June 2006): 430–66.

Miller, Stan, Arline Miller, Rita Rowan, et al. *New York's Chinese Restaurants.* New York: Atheneum, 1977.

Miller, Stuart Creighton. *The Unwelcome Immigrant.* Berkeley: University of California Press, 1969.

Minford, John, and Joseph Lau. *Classical Chinese Literature.* New York: Columbia University Press, 2000.

Morley, Charles, ed. *Portrait of America: Letters of Henry Sienkiewicz.* New York: Columbia University Press, 1959.

Moss, Frank. *The American Metropolis.* 3 vols. New York: Peter Fenelon Collier, 1897.

Nee, Victor, and Brett de Bary Nee. *Longtime Californ'.* New York: Pantheon, 1972.

Newman, Jacqueline M. *Food Culture in China.* Westport, Conn.: Greenwood Press, 2004.

Notes on California and the Placers. New York: H. Long, 1850.

Nordhoff, Charles. *California: For Health, Pleasure, and Residence.* New York: Harper, 1873.

O'Neill, Molly. "The Chop Suey Syndrome: Americanizing the Exotic." *New York Times*, July 26, 1989, C1.

Palmer, Albert W. *Orientals in American Life.* New York: Friendship Press, 1934.

Pan, Lynn. *The Encyclopedia of the Chinese Overseas.* Cambridge, Mass.: Harvard University Press, 1999.

———, ed. *Sons of the Yellow Emperor.* Boston: Little, Brown, 1990.

Peabody, A. P. "The Chinese in San Francisco." *American Naturalist*, January 1871, 660–4.

Peters, John R., Jr. *Miscellaneous Remarks upon the Government, History, Religions, Literature, Agriculture, Arts, Trades, Manners, and Customs of the Chinese.* Boston: John F. Trow, 1846.

"Philadelphia Is Getting the Chinese Restaurant Craze." *Philadelphia Inquirer*, November 12, 1899, 3.

Ping-Ti Ho. "The Introduction of American Food Plants to China." *American Anthropologist* 57, no. 2, pt. 1 (April 1955): 191–201.

Pitt, Leonard. "The Beginnings of Nativism in California." *Pacific Historical Review* 30, no. 1 (February 1961): 23–38.

Quincy, Josiah. *Memoir of the Life of John Quincy Adams*. Boston: Crosby, Nichols, Lee, 1860.

Rae, W. F. *Westward by Rail*. New York: D. Appleton, 1871.

Ransome, Arthur. *The Chinese Puzzle*. London: Allen and Unwin, 1927.

Rast, Raymond W. "The Cultural Politics of Tourism in San Francisco's Chinatown, 1882–1917." *Pacific Historical Review* 76, no. 1 (2007): 29–60.

Rawls, James J., and Walton Bean. *California: An Interpretative History*. New York: McGraw-Hill, 2002.

Rawski, Evelyn. *The Last Emperors*. Berkeley: University of California Press, 1998.

Reinhart, Herman Francis. *The Golden Frontier*. Austin: University of Texas Press, 1962.

Renqiu Yu. "Chop Suey: From Chinese Food to Chinese American Food." In *Chinese America: History and Perspectives, 1987*. San Francisco: Chinese Historical Society of America, 1987, 87–100.

Reynolds, I. P. "What Sam of Auburn Avenue Says." *Chicago Daily World*, March 18, 1932, 4.

Rhodes, F. S. "The Chinese in Honolulu." *Overland Monthly and Out West Magazine*, November 1898, 467–75.

Richardson, Albert D. *Beyond the Mississippi*. Hartford, Conn.: American, 1867.

Rider, Fremont. *Rider's New York City and Vicinity*. New York: Holt, 1916.

Roberts, Edmund. *Embassy to the Eastern Courts of Cochin-China, Siam, and Muscat*. New York: Harper, 1837.

Ross, George. *Tips on Tables*. New York: Covici, Friede, 1934.

Ruschenberger, W. S. W. *Narrative of a Voyage Round the World*. 2 vols. Folkestone, England: Dawsons, 1970.

Sakamoto, Nobuko. *The People's Republic of China Cookbook*. New York: Random House, 1977.

Scheffaner, Herman. "The Old Chinese Quarter." *Living Age*, August 10, 1907, 359–66.

"Seitz in Chinatown." *Frank Leslie's Popular Monthly*, May 1893, 612–8.

The Sentinel Jewish Cook Book. 4th ed. Chicago: Sentinel, 1936.

Serventi, Silvano, and Françoise Sabban. *Pasta: The Story of a Universal Food*. New York: Columbia University Press, 2002.

Shaw, Samuel, and Josiah Quincy. *The Journals of Major Samuel Shaw*. Boston: Wm. Crosby and H. Nichols, 1847.

Shaw, William. *Golden Dreams and Waking Realities*. London: Smith, Elder, 1851.

Sia, Mary Li. *Chinese Chopsticks: A Manual of Chinese Cookery and Guide to Peiping Restaurants*. Beijing: Peiping Chronicle, 1935.

Simoons, Frederick J. *Food in China: A Cultural and Historical Inquiry*. Boca Raton, Fla.: CRC Press, 1991.

Singleton, Esther, ed. *China, as Described by Great Writers*. New York: Dodd, Mead, 1912.

Smith, Richard J. *Chinese Maps*. Hong Kong: Oxford University Press, 1996.

Smyth, Albert H. *Bayard Taylor*. Boston: Houghton, Mifflin, 1896.

Solomon, Richard H. *A Revolution Is Not a Dinner Party*. New York: Anchor Press, 1975.

Soulé, Frank. *The Annals of San Francisco*. San Francisco: D. Appleton, 1855.

Spence, Jonathan D. *The Search for Modern China*. New York: Norton, 1990.

Spier, Robert F. G. "Food Habits of Nineteenth-century California Chinese." *California Historical Society Quarterly*, March 1958, 79–84.

———. "Food Habits of Nineteenth-century California Chinese (Concluded)." *California Historical Society Quarterly*, June 1958, 129–36.

Spiller, Harley. "Late Night in the Lion's Den: Chinese Restaurant-nightclubs in 1940s San Francisco." *Gastronomica*, 4, no. 4 (fall 2004): 94–101.

Starr, Kevin. *Americans and the California Dream, 1850–1915*. New York: Oxford University Press, 1973.

Strassberg, Richard E., ed. *A Chinese Bestiary*. Berkeley: University of California Press, 2002.

Sung, Betty Lee. *Mountain of Gold*. New York: Macmillan, 1967.

Swisher, Earl. *China's Management of the American Barbarians*. New Haven, Conn.: Far Eastern, 1953.

Takaki, Ronald. *Strangers from a Different Shore*. Boston: Little, Brown, 1989.

Taylor, Bayard. *Eldorado*. New York: Putnam: 1850.

———. *A Visit to India, China, and Japan, in the Year 1853*. New York: Putnam, 1855.

Taylor, Benjamin F. *Between the Gates*. Chicago: S. C. Griggs, 1878.

Taylor, Charles. *Five Years in China*. New York: Derby and Jackson, 1860.

Tchen, John Kuo Wei. *New York before Chinatown*. Baltimore: Johns Hopkins University Press, 1999.

Tiffany, Osmond, Jr. *The Canton Chinese*. Boston: James Munroe, 1849.

Tong, Michael. *The Shun Lee Cookbook*. New York: Morrow, 2007.

Trader Vic's Book of Food and Drink. Garden City, N.Y.: Doubleday, 1946.

Trewartha, Glenn T. "Field Observations on the Canton Delta of South China." *Economic Geography* 15, no. 1 (January 1939): 1–10.

"The Truth about Chow Mein." *New Yorker*, May 6, 1972, 32–3.

Tuthill, Franklin. *The History of California*. San Francisco: H. H. Bancroft, 1866.

Twain, Mark. *Roughing It*. New York: Harper, 1913.

Volkwein, Ann. *Chinatown New York*. New York: Collins Design, 2007.

Waley, Arthur. *Yuan Mei*. London: Allen and Unwin, 1956.

Walker, Anne C. *China Calls*. Lanham, Md.: Madison Books, 1992.

"Walks about the City of Canton." *Chinese Repository*, May 1835, 43.

Whymper, Frederick. *Travel and Adventure in the Territory of Alaska*. London: J. Murray, 1868.

Wilkinson, Endymion. *Chinese History: A Manual*. Cambridge, Mass.: Harvard University Press, 2000.

William Speer. *An Humble Plea*. San Francisco: Office of the Oriental, 1856.

Williams, Frederick Wells. *The Life and Letters of Samuel Wells Williams*. New York: Putnam, 1889.

Williams, Samuel Wells. *The Middle Kingdom*. 2 vols. New York: John Wiley, 1849.

Wilson, Richard, ed. *The President's Trip to China*. New York: Bantam Books, 1972.

Wimsatt, Genevieve. *A Griffin in China*. New York: Funk and Wagnalls, 1927.

Wines, E. C. *A Peep at China, in Mr. Dunn's Chinese Collection*. Philadelphia: Nathan Dunn, 1839.

Wong Ching Foo. "Chinese Cooking." *Boston Globe*, July 19, 1885, 9.

———. "Chinese Cooking." *Brooklyn Eagle*, July 6, 1884, 4.

———. "The Chinese in New York." *Cosmopolitan*, June 1888, 297.

Wood, W. W. *Sketches of China*. Philadelphia: Carey and Lee, 1830.

Wouk, Herman. *Marjorie Morningstar*. Garden City, N.Y.: Doubleday, 1955, 58.

Wright, G. N. *China, in a Series of Views*. London: Fisher, 1848.

Wu Tingfang. *America, through the Spectacles of an Oriental Diplomat*. New York: Frederick A. Stokes, 1914.

Yan-kit So. *Classic Food of China*. London: Macmillan, 1992.

The Yellow Emperor's Classic of Internal Medicine. Trans. Ilza Veith. Berkeley: University of California Press, 1972.

Yuan Jing and Rowen K. Flad. "Pig Domestication in Ancient China." *Antiquity* 76, no. 293 (September 2002): 724–33.

Yutang, Lin. *My Country and My People*. New York: Reynal and Hitchcock, 1935.

Zito, Angela. *Of Body and Brush*. Chicago: University of Chicago Press, 1997.

DATE DUE